AGRICULTURE AND INTELLECTUAL PROPERTY RIGHTS

Economic, Institutional and Implementation Issues in Biotechnology

Agriculture and Intellectual Property Rights

Economic, Institutional and Implementation Issues in Biotechnology

Edited by

V. Santaniello
Dipartimento di Economia ed Istituzioni,
Università degli Studi di Roma 'Tor Vergata', Rome, Italy

R.E. Evenson
Department of Economics, Yale University,
New Haven, Connecticut, USA

D. Zilberman
Department of Agricultural and Resource Economics,
University of California, Berkeley, USA

and

G.A. Carlson
Department of Agricultural and Resource Economics,
North Carolina State University, Raleigh, USA

CABI *Publishing*

CABI *Publishing* is a division of CAB *International*

CABI Publishing
CAB International
Wallingford
Oxon OX10 8DE
UK

Tel: +44 (0)1491 832111
Fax: +44 (0)1491 833508
Email: cabi@cabi.org
Web site: http://www.cabi.org

CABI Publishing
10 E 40th Street
Suite 3203
New York, NY 10016
USA

Tel: +1 212 481 7018
Fax: +1 212 686 7993
Email: cabi-nao@cabi.org

A catalogue record for this book is available from the British Library, London, UK.

Library of Congress Cataloging-in-Publication Data
Agriculture and intellectual property rights : economic, institutional, and implementation issues in biotechnology / edited by V. Santaniello ... [et al.].
    p. cm.
  Includes bibliographical references.
  ISBN 0-85199-457-1 (alk. paper)
  1. Germplasm resources, Plant. 2. Agricultural biotechnology.
3. Intellectual property. I. Santaniello, V.

  SB123.3 .A53 2000
  623.5'23–dc21
                                          99-054576

ISBN 0 85199 457 1

Typeset by Columns Design Ltd, Reading.
Printed and bound in the UK by Biddles Ltd, Guildford and King's Lynn.

Contents

Part II Economic Issues

Part III Biotechnology Inventions

Part IV Case Studies

Contributors

Susan H. Bragdon, IPGRI – International Plant Genetic Resources Institute, Via delle Sette Chiese 142, 00145 Rome, Italy

Gerald Carlson, Department of Agricultural and Resource Economics, North Carolina State University, Raleigh, NC 27695, USA

Donald D. Evenson, Evenson, McKeown, Edwards and Lenahan P.L.L.C., 120 G Street, NW, Suite 700, Washington DC 20005, USA

Robert E. Evenson, Economic Growth Center, Department of Economics, Yale University, P.O. Box 2108269, New Haven, CT 06520-8269, USA

Amir Heiman, Department of Agricultural Economics, Hebrew University, Rehovot, Israel

Daniel K.N. Johnson, Department of Economics, Wellesley College, Pendleton East, Room 310, 106 Central Street, Wellesley, MA 02181-8260, USA

Stéphane Lemarié, Université Pierre-Mendès, INRA-SERD, Grenoble, France; Present address: 603B Prospect Street, New Haven, CT 06511, USA

W. Lesser, Department of Agricultural, Resource and Managerial Economics, 405 Warren Hall, Cornell University, Ithaca, NY 14853, USA

Michele Marra, Department of Agricultural and Resource Economics, North Carolina State University, Raleigh, NC 27695, USA

Robert Mendelsohn, Yale School of Forestry and Environmental Studies, Yale University, 360 Prospect Street, New Haven, CT 06520, USA

Peter W.B. Phillips, University of Saskatchewan, Saskatoon, Canada

Vittorio Santaniello, Dipartimento di Economia ed Istituzioni, Università degli Studi di Roma 'Tor Vergata', Via di Tor Vergata snc, 00133 Rome, Italy

Brian D. Wright, Department of Agricultural and Resource Economics, University of California, Giannini Hall, Berkeley, CA 94720-3310, USA

Cherisa Yarkin, Department of Agricultural and Resource Economics, University of California, Giannini Hall, Berkeley, CA 94720-3310, USA

David Zilberman, Department of Agricultural and Resource Economics, University of California, Giannini Hall, Berkeley, CA 94720-3310, USA

A. Zohrabyan, Economic Growth Center, Department of Economics, Yale University, P.O. Box 2108269, New Haven, CT 06520-8269, USA

Acknowledgements

This book has arisen from the conference entitled 'The Shape of the Coming Agricultural Biotechnology Transformation: Strategic Investment and Policy Approaches from an Economic Perspective' convened by the International Consortium on Agricultural Biotechnology Research (ICABR), held at the University of Rome - Tor Vergata, Italy on June 17-19, 1999.

The editors would like to acknowledge the sponsorship by the following institutions:

- CEIS - University of Rome 'Tor Vergata'
- Center for Sustainable Resource Development, University of California at Berkeley
- Economic Growth Center, Yale University

The editors would also like to thank the Italian National Research Council for their financial support of the conference (grant no CNR - 9900136).

BF Title:

Introduction   N I A

V. Santaniello,[1] R.E. Evenson,[2] D. Zilberman[3] and G.A. Carlson[4]

[1]Dipartimento di Economia ed Istituzioni, Università degli Studi di Roma 'Tor Vergata', Rome, Italy; [2]Department of Economics, Yale University, New Haven, Connecticut, USA; [3]Department of Agricultural and Resource Economics, University of California, Berkeley, USA; [4]Department of Agricultural and Resource Economics, North Carolina State University, Raleigh, USA

In recent years, two important developments have altered the processes by which improved crop varieties and related technology are being discovered, commercialized and diffused to farmers. The first is the expansion and strengthening of intellectual property rights (IPR) that apply to processes (methods) and products (new cultivars). The second is the development of methods and techniques in genetic manipulation, generally described as biotechnology. Although both developments have been underway for more than 20 years their importance to government, non-government and private entities in the crop seed industry has increased in recent years. Analysis of these two developments should recognize that they are part of processes affecting other sectors outside of agriculture and may actually change the nature of agriculture.

Until these recent developments, the discovery and development of crop varieties was largely undertaken in public sector agricultural experiment stations. These public research centres were developed in response to the limited incentives provided by traditional IPR systems. With the exception of asexually reproduced crops, protected by the Plant Patent Act of 1930, crop breeders could not obtain rights over a new variety. This meant that a farmer (or other seed producer) could simply save seed from his crop at a low cost, thus making the seed sufficiently abundant to prevent a breeder from earning a premium for a superior variety. Hybrid crops, such as corn and sorghum, in which seed could not be saved because of the natural loss of heterosis, provided a natural incentive for private crop breeding. Private sector hybrid seed producers had dominated this part of the market even before recent developments.

Public sector national agricultural research systems (NARS) were well established in developed countries in the early 20th century. However, it was not until 1960 that most developing countries had NARS. The establishment of a system of International Agricultural Research Centers (IARCs) contributed to the expansion of NARS, beginning with the International Rice Research Institute (IRRI) in 1959 and shortly thereafter, the formation of IARCs for wheat, maize, sorghum, potatoes, cassava, beans and several other crops.

Both public and private crop-breeding programmes were, until recently, based on the search for more effective combinations of 'landraces' (farmer-selected plant types selected by farmers over previous centuries, known today as 'farmers' varieties') within the crop species. *Ex situ* collections of these landrace breeding materials, including mutants, weedy or wild relatives of the species, have been developed for all important crop species. Most IARCs maintain such collections. A long tradition of free exchange of these genetic resources, advanced breeding lines and finished varieties between public NARS and IARCs, has been maintained. This has been very important to the effectiveness of the NARS–IARC breeding programmes (Gollin and Evenson, 1996). These genetic resources have been unprotected by IPR and have been freely available to private sector seed companies as well as to public sector breeding programmes.

A new IPR, the 'Breeders' Rights', was established in the 1950s and 1960s. In the USA Breeders' Rights were provided with the passage of the Plant Varieties Protection Act of 1960. These rights provided a limited form of protection to breeders of seed-based, sexually reproduced crops (see Chapter 1 for more detail). They gave the breeder, or owner of the right, a 'right to exclude' others from reproducing seed from the variety subject to a 'farmer's exemption', allowing the buyer of the protected seed to save seed for his own use, and a 'research exemption', allowing the protected variety used as a parent in a breeding programme to produce another variety. Breeders' Rights have been adopted in a number of countries and are the subject of an international convention (UPOV, International Union for the Protection of New Varieties of Plants), which establishes procedures for the recognition of rights of foreigners in member countries. Breeders' rights have stimulated more private sector breeding activity in many crops, however, they have probably not altered the culture of public breeding programmes, nor the tradition of free exchange of genetic resources.

In contrast, the culture of public research programmes and the tradition of free exchange of genetic resources has been altered (threatened?) by the expansion of scope of the Patent Right, which now covers plant varieties in the USA, as well as specific plant parts, genome components and process methods in all countries with patent systems. The emergence of a new IPR, the Farmers' Right, which originated in the Convention on Biological Diversity (CBD), has also proven to be a threat to the public research culture, though in a different way. The expansion of both the Patent Right and the Farmer's Right has provided some form of 'right to exclude' others from using genetic resources.

The expanded patent right (see Chapter 1) evolved through case law (i.e. court decisions). This expansion was related to developments in both biological sciences and in techniques for genetic manipulation. Biotechnology methods have been developing rapidly during the last 25 years: transgenic techniques (i.e. the ability to insert an 'alien' gene from another species or, for that matter, from the same species) into a plant are now commonplace in most crops; stacking (multiple insertions) of genes is becoming commonplace; genome mapping has advanced in most crops; and maker-aided breeding is a reality in advanced programmes.

The first applications of transgenic technologies were in medicine, where intellectual rights for genetic manipulation techniques and gene sequencing were established. These new definitions of IPR gave rise to a dynamic biotechnology industry and induced ventures that emphasized investments in proprietary knowledge. The major pharmaceutical and agro-business multi-nationals established biotechnology activities by taking over some of these ventures and capitalizing on their IPR.

The expansion of IPR into biotechnology is part of the process of increased privatization of basic knowledge. For example, the Bayh-Dole Act of 1980 in the USA has enabled universities to patent results from major publicly supported research projects and sell the rights for use of these innovations. Since the introduction of this new legislation, universities have become very active in pursuing new forms of IPR and transferring the rights of knowledge. Biotechnology is the main field of this privatization and appropriator of knowledge.

The 'synergy' between IPR and new biotechnology is strong. Markets are being developed for specific genes where sellers offer a product in the form of a cloned, or ready-to-transfer segment of DNA, to buyers who collect licence revenues from customers from gene sellers. These markets would not exist without IPR. They are very important to crop-breeding systems because they enable genetic products that do not have a high degree of location-specificity to be easily incorporated into plants that do. The existence of many different breeding programmes such as the NARS programmes, through-out the world, produces location-specific plants into which these genetic products can be inserted.

At this point in time, there is a considerable amount of uncertainty as to the exact range of coverage IPR offer crop varieties. The process by which IPR take form, while based on specific laws, evolves with court cases and court decisions. IPR is a relatively young, evolutionary process, only recently extended to crop varieties in the USA, of less certainty in other countries, and bound by a highly tentative policy environment.

Biotechnology products are the subject of additional dispute and contentiousness. Opposition to genetically modified organisms (GMOs) is strong in many countries with bio-safety questions unsettled and ethical issues debated.

With a long tradition of IPR covering mechanical, chemical and electrical inventions, the dimension of expanded IPR systems in developed countries is relatively straightforward. Many new contractual licensing arrangements are required for biological IPR, as is commonplace for other IPR. Ethical issues associated with biotechnology products, along with other related concerns, are not as easy to resolve.

On the other hand, the policy environment in developing countries is burdened by both a lack of experience with IPR systems and with the emotional dimensions of biotechnology. Developing countries have generally been hostile to IPR. Most have accepted a number of commitments under the WTO-TRIPs (World Trade Organization trade-related aspects of international property rights) agreement, though grudgingly, and as a negotiated price to pay for other advantages; they have yet to deliver on their WTO-TRIPs commitments. These commitments consist of accepting some form of *sui generis* IPR systems for crop varieties. Also, Breeders' Rights systems are expected to be instituted. These systems actually have many positive elements for developing countries. Crop varieties are very location-sensitive and the extent of international exchange or marketing is small, therefore, the one-way exchange affecting patent IPR, where developed countries sell to developing countries but developing countries do not sell to developed countries, is not a serious issue. However, the WTO-TRIPs commitment does require the acceptance of patent rights for genetic products other than crop varieties. The actions of developing countries regarding patent IPR will not affect their prospects for participating in emerging gene markets.

Curiously, Farmers' Rights introduced at the CBD have been embraced by developing countries; they see themselves as net exporters of farmers' varieties to breeding programmes. Developed countries are generally opposed to these rights for the same reason. There is the possibility that disputes over these rights will for some time inhibit, and perhaps prevent, international and public–private exchange of genetic resources.

Economists have an important role to play in fashioning policy measures dealing with both IPR and with biotechnology product regulations. These policy measures may be particularly important for developing countries where experience has been limited. This volume is the second in a series of volumes addressing policy issues related to biotechnology. The first volume addresses IPR issues in the context of agricultural biotechnology.

This volume is organized in four parts. Part I includes five chapters addressing legal systems and their current state of implementation. Chapter 1 provides a legal perspective on the current state of case law (court rulings) affecting biotechnology. The chapter seeks to narrow the range of uncertainty over what is and what is not protected in an evolving legal system. Many policy-makers, especially in developing countries, express concern that private multinational companies may acquire IPR of inventions and achievements made in developing countries. A properly functioning IPR system, as noted in Chapter 1, not only provides rights to holders, but includes provisions allowing the holder to protect only the true invention increment achieved. The system should protect the rights of prior inventors as well the rights of new inventors.

Chapter 2 addresses the state of IPR affecting biotechnology in the European Union (EU). As noted in Chapter 1, the USA extended IPR to multicellular plant varieties and to animals in several important court cases in the 1980s and 1990s. The EU has not extended this protection to plants. Chapter 2 notes that a new right, the European 'Privative,' has developed. This is a form of Breeders' Rights. The European system of IPR for biological inventions continues to evolve. Whether it will evolve into the US form remains to be seen. Chapters 1 and 2 show that IPR systems are dynamic and respond to changes in technological methods and policies.

Chapter 3 addresses the IPR implications of the CBD (Rio 1992). These implications are complex and reflect the interests of groups that are quite different from the commercial or business interests supporting the expansion of conventional IPR. The CBD addresses rights in genetic resources in original landraces and farmers' varieties. It focuses on exchange and use, stressing the importance of 'equitable sharing of benefit' from 'traditional knowledge', as well as *in situ* conservation of genetic resources. Apparently, an 'equitable sharing of benefits' means payments to states who have sovereign rights over their natural resources.

In one sense, one could interpret the CBD as extending IPR beyond the boundaries of traditional IPR systems in order to encompass natural genetic resources. This extension can be seen as a bargain in which developing countries accept some provisions of traditional IPR in return for the CBD provisions. This has implications for incentives to conserve and to evaluate genetic resources.

Chapter 4 addresses the IPR implications of the GATT-TRIPs (GATT, General Agreement on Tariffs and Trades) agreement leading to the functions of the WTO. Signatory countries to this agreement commit to conventional patent IPR systems for a range of invention fields. For crops, signatories commit to a *sui generis* IPR system. This commitment actually allows for a considerable latitude in designing IPR systems. Unfortunately, most developing countries are poorly equipped to design IPR systems because they have generally maintained a position of hostility to IPR.

Chapter 5 discusses the ways in which IPR have affected the Consultative Group on International Agricultural Research (CGIAR) system of ICARs in developing countries. As with most public NARS, in both developed and developing countries, the CGIAR system did not take a pro-active role in IPR policy. Its role was largely reactive, attempting to proceed with its traditional system until events pressed it to respond. This is, by and large, the policy stance of most developing countries toward IPR change.

It is instructive to see the nature of the CGIAR response to the changing IPR systems because NARSs are undertaking similar responses. Chapter 5 describes several of these responses including its posture on disseminating advanced breeding lines from its gene-bank collections. The system has not yet really dealt with the implications of the IPR elements of the CBD. Also, since the CGIAR system has been slow to respond to research opportunities afforded by biotechnology methods, it has yet to develop a full response to IPR associated with biotechnology products.

Part II of this volume includes five chapters addressing economic issues. Chapter 6 provides a general economic treatment of IPR. It addresses both germplasm effects, and the stimulus effect on other inventions associated with bringing an invention out of secrecy. It addresses international recognition of IPR. It has long been recognized that international intellectual property exchange is asymmetric. Developing countries account for most of the world's research and development and produce almost all of the world's inventions. Developing countries are not in a position to compete for large invention markets in developed countries. Most of their invention is derivative or adaptive invention in which modifications to large, developed-country market inventions are made so as to adapt to their smaller markets.

Chapter 6 notes that, given this asymmetry (empirical evidence for the asymmetry is provided in the chapter), developing countries do not actually have a *quid pro quo* in international conventions calling for 'national treatment of foreigners'. Their inventors gain little from access to developed (or other developing) country markets. This provides an incentive to 'pirate' the IPR of developed countries. For a number of decades IPR piracy by developing countries was not considered to be a major international problem. However, in the past two decades it has emerged as a visible issue, causing the formation of sanctions and penalties that have rendered it an unviable strategy.

In regards to biotechnology, the chapter notes that there is a difference between biotechnology associated with 'quantitative' traits in plants and 'qualitative' traits. Quantitative traits, i.e. yield-enhancing, are created by on-site breeding programmes and require on-site capabilities in marker-aided breeding techniques. International exchange of varieties is relatively low and IPR do not play a major role in this exchange.

Qualitative traits for disease resistance, insect resistance, stress tolerance, etc. are more likely to be 'single gene' traits and hence, potentially supplied through gene markets. These gene markets are subject to IPR and the sanctions associated with them.

Chapter 7 addresses the potential market value of Farmers' Rights, i.e. landrace and related genetic resources. (Note that with biotechnology techniques genetic material from species, other than cultivated species, can be utilized for crop improvement.) The chapter notes that when multiple sellers are supplying genetic resources the market will not provide adequate incentives to conserve and evaluate these genetic resources. A monopoly IPR could be developed to provide these incentives, however, there are many problems with implementing this type of IPR. Chapter 7 provides an empirical and analytical extension to the CBD IPR discussed in Chapter 2.

Chapter 8 addresses economic and institutional issues of plant breeding in an international context. It addresses some of the issues facing the CGIAR system and discusses seed markets. The chapter describes current problems and reactions to IPR and offers a broader vision of the world of proprietary technology. There are many policy-makers in NARSs and IARCs who have relied on avoiding a world of proprietary technology for biotechnology. There are many interest groups, including most non-governmental organizations (NGOs) working in developing countries, and the majority of political farm groups in developing countries, who oppose the expansion of IPR in biotechnology and in developing countries. Many oppose the development of biotechnology itself. For most developing countries this opposition is not sufficiently politically dominant to preclude the *de facto* expansion of IPR in biotechnology, nor the use of biotechnology methods. (However, it is likely to affect regulation and labelling practices.)

Chapter 9 discusses the institutional and economic issues associated with biotechnology in the context of the generation and transfer of knowledge in the USA. The chapter draws on experience from medical biotechnology and technology transfer programmes. Some of the recent technical developments in the field are surveyed. One of these is the 'terminator' gene patented by Delta Pine, Land Company and the United States Department of Agriculture (USDA). This biotechnology product, which can be used to prevent seed reproduction from a crop, has become something of a symbolic representation of the 'threat' elements associated with biotechnology. Simple economic analysis applied to the product, however, shows that a termination product would have to bring a premium over a comparable product without the terminator gene, this is as a result of farm-produced seeds having economic value. Therefore, unless industrial monopoly or regulatory monopoly power can prevent the sale of non-terminator products, even inferior non-terminator products, the terminator product will not be sold.

A more general point in this context is that as long as public research programmes remain active, technological options available to farmers will increase with the use of agricultural biotechnology products, with terminator products increasing also. This is a critical point for policy-makers of developing countries. Chapter 10 provides further discussion of public–private complementariness in research and the ways in which this can be facilitated by IPR.

Chapter 10 addresses economic incentive problems for public research programmes. It analyses the spill-over problem between regions and demonstrates how IPR can lead to a more optimal solution (see Chapter 5 where optimal length and breadth of IPR is related to spillovers between countries). Duplication of research objectives is also considered and it is noted that competition produces duplication, however, it can be a productive duplication under conditions of uncertainty.

Agricultural biotechnology is a field where public and private sector activities are both important. Interestingly, it is probably correct to say that the original foundations for agricultural biotechnology were produced by more basic biological sciences, rather than the more applied agricultural sciences. This is true even though many public agricultural research systems conduct basic pre-invention science. There is little question that private firms have been better at commercializing, and bringing to the market, biotechnology products than have public research programmes. IPR incentives are important in allowing invention and commercialization to be conducted in different organizations. Therefore, public research programmes with little competence in commercializing inventions can have incentives to invent because they can licence rights to firms with commercialization capabilities.

Opposition in developing countries is unlikely to have very much effect on developed countries. It could delay or halt budding research programmes in biotechnology, delay reform of the CGIAR system and stronger NARS, and delay bringing more biotechnology into the developing world. The dilemma faced by developing countries is the ethical, economical, political and emotional issues associated with both IPR and biotechnology, though these are not the only important issues. In a globalized economy, developing countries will suffer economic losses if cost-reducing crop production technology evolves and is adopted in developed countries, yet denied to them.

Part III of the volume includes two chapters that exploit readily available data on patented inventions to draw conclusions about the state of biotechnology invention.

Chapter 11 compares patterns of biotechnology patents. It will compare these patents to patents in other fields of research, both in the USA and Europe. It has been found that in the field of biotechnology, more than in others areas, there exists a significantly larger lag time between the time of application and the process of granting. This larger amount of time allows firms to have a longer period of secrecy. The proposal to require publication of patents' contents, 18 months after application, may especially harm US biotechnology applicants. Most applications in biotechnology have been in the health field, while agricultural share has been very small, though it is increasing over time. Most of the applications are concentrated in only some parts of the USA and in Europe. Biotechnology patents use many more references, references that are relatively more recent than in other fields. There is much more authority to academic or scientific literature references in biotechnology, indicating that this is a more academic-oriented field and that the link between universities and industries is closer than in other areas. It is clear from the survey that application of biotechnology in agriculture and germplasm are much more recent, however, its rate of growth is higher than in other fields.

Chapter 12 extends the analysis of Chapter 11 in two dimensions. First, it fractionalizes the proportions of IPCs that are identified as biotechnology invention to produce an alternative means of identifying biotechnology invention. Second, it utilizes international data to draw inferences about the state of leadership in this new (young) field of invention. It concludes that US-based inventors have a dominant position in biotechnology invention, producing roughly half of the world inventions filed to date.

Part IV of the volume includes two chapters providing case studies of two important IPR-influenced agricultural biotechnology products.

Chapter 13 discusses the development of canola in Canada. This is a case where public sector research created an important agricultural industry. With regards to IPR, the private sector invested in research during the 1990s, becoming the leading producer of canola varieties. This is an especially interesting case because Breeders' Rights, trademarks and Patent Rights were important. Regulations and biotechnology methods were also important.

The chapter continues by describing the evaluation of production contracts with seed companies and the companies' enforcement mechanisms. Readers concerned with the complexity of new contracting arrangements will find the discussion of workable systems instructive.

Chapter 14 offers a historical discussion of transgenic crops experience in the USA. It discusses the response of regulatory agencies to transgenic products and biosafety (Refugia) regulations. The chapter clarifies the reality that transgenic crops are not only a 'growing concern' but that the pipeline is filled with many more transgenic products to be released in the future.

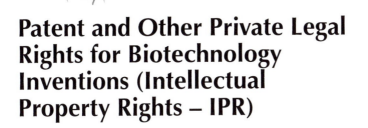

1

Patent and Other Private Legal Rights for Biotechnology Inventions (Intellectual Property Rights – IPR)

Donald D. Evenson

Evenson, McKeown, Edwards and Lenahan P.L.L.C., Washington DC, USA

This chapter describes the types of private legal rights, often denominated intellectual property rights or IPR, that are available for inventors and breeders for their contributions to agricultural technology. These IPR have become increasingly important in plant technologies. In view of the complexities of IPR generally, and the extra complexities due to the rapidly developing gene-splicing technologies involved in agricultural development, this chapter is necessarily only an overview. It is hoped that this overview will provide a general understanding of the workings of IPR systems and form a basis for assessing the IPR provisions that could or should be implemented to fairly balance the sometimes apparent competing interests of the public, public sector research institutions and private industry research entities.

The most significant legal rights to the results of agricultural breeding and research programmes can be categorized as follows: (i) trade secret rights; (ii) plant patent rights; (iii) plant variety protection certificate rights; and (iv) utility patent rights. These rights are similar in that they are intended to reward breeders and inventors for their technological contributions. They are all private property rights which can be sold and licensed to others. They all provide for obtaining money damages for past infringements and injunctive relief against further infringements. These rights are different in their scope, their duration and their practical impact in controlling the economic benefits of the contributions of breeders and inventors.

Although every country has some form of private legal rights protecting agricultural research discoveries, the US legal system is more expansive than most, especially with respect to the subject matter protectable under utility patents. This chapter refers to the US legal system in generally explaining these private legal rights. A brief comparison with selected other country

© CAB *International* 2000. *Agriculture and Intellectual Property Rights*
(eds V. Santaniello, R.E. Evenson, D. Zilberman and G.A. Carlson)

systems is also included in discussing similarities, as well as some fundamental differences between the various systems.

Reference is made to a hypothetical plant breeding and research company, AG Money Inc., to illustrate the various legal protective rights and their applicability to different contributions in the plant technology developments. Although I have addressed primarily plant technology, it should be understood that trade secret rights and utility patent rights would also apply to other agricultural biotechnology research results, such as animals, farming techniques and the like.

Hypothetical – AG Money Inc. Plant Breeding and Research Center

AG Money Inc. (AG Money) has spent millions of dollars over the past decade, *secretly* producing and/or discovering the following:

A. CORN A - A new variety of high-yielding hybrid corn (CORN A) was developed in a corn-breeding programme. AG Money controls the parents for CORN A and the crop from the seed corn (CORN A) is not usable as seed for a subsequent planting.

B. HEATHER B - A new variety of heather (HEATHER B) was discovered in a cultivated field of heather and was subsequently asexually reproduced by cutting.

C. SOYBEAN C - A new variety of soybeans (SOYBEAN C) was developed in a selective breeding programme.

D. MAIZE D - A new variety of maize (MAIZE D) was developed using gene technology. MAIZE D produces an oversupply of tryptophan.

E. GENE METHOD E - A new method of treating gene material (GENE METHOD E) was developed and used in producing MAIZE D. GENE METHOD E involves heat treatments at selected temperatures for selected periods of time.

F. MACHINE F - A new computer programmable machine (MACHINE F) was developed for automatically carrying out GENE METHOD E.

In the following discussion of the respective categories of available legal rights, reference will be made to these hypothetical research and breeding results.

Trade Secret Rights

Eligible Subject Matter

In the USA, trade secrets are governed by respective individual US state laws. The Uniform Trade Secrets Act is a model statute governing trade secret rights which has been adopted in large part by respective states of the USA and will be referred to in the following discussion.

The Uniform Trade Secrets Act defines a trade secret as follows:

> 'Trade secret' means information, including a formula, pattern, compilation, program, device, method, technique, or process, that:
> (i) derives independent economic value, actual or potential, from not being generally known to, and not being readily ascertainable by proper means by, other persons who can obtain economic value from its disclosure or use, and
> (ii) is the subject of efforts that are reasonable under the circumstances to maintain its secrecy.
>
> (Uniform Trade Secrets Act, §1)

This definition of a protectable 'trade secret' is very expansive and includes any information, whether patentable or not, which is the subject of reasonable efforts to maintain secrecy and has independent economic value. Referring to our hypothetical example, where AG Money has operated in secret, information regarding each of the developments would qualify as eligible subject matter for trade secret protection. As a practical matter, once the AG Money developments are commercially exploited, the trade secret may be lost by no longer being a trade secret. However, the CORN A seed could be sold while maintaining a trade secret in the parent stock. Also the MAIZE D could be sold while maintaining a trade secret in the GENE METHOD E used to produce it.

Duration and Scope of Protection

The duration of a trade secret right is theoretically as long as the owner maintains the secrecy thereof, or at least takes reasonable steps to maintain the secrecy. An oft-cited example of a valuable and long-duration trade secret is the formula and process for making Coca Cola.

The scope of the trade secret right is commensurate with the scope of the trade secret itself. The trade secret right is enforceable against persons who use 'improper means' to 'misappropriate' the trade secret.

Typically, the trade secret rights are enforceable against competitors who knew, or reasonably should have known, that they were improperly misappropriating trade secrets.

As a practical matter, one of the most important trade secret rights in plant technologies involves the control of parents by hybrid seed corn development breeding companies. Prior to the plant variety protection act and, more recently, the expansion of utility patents to cover plants, this trade secret protection was the basic protective right used by seed corn companies to protect their investments in corn-breeding programmes. The normal situation is that an ex-employee, or someone else having access to the parent hybrid corn stock, transfers information (genetic plant material) to a competing hybrid corn-breeding company, as is explained more fully below.

Limitations on the scope of protection under trade secrets are that it is uncertain protection for many types of inventions and developments because (i) it does not protect against independent development of the same information; and (ii) it does not form a cause of action against 'innocent' recipients of the trade secret. If someone independently discovers GENE METHOD E, they are free to use and publicize it. With the internet publication possibilities, certain information such as GENE METHOD E could be published by a disgruntled employee/ex-employee. Although a trade secret cause of action for damages caused could be maintained against the employee, the resources of the employee would likely not be any real adequate compensation.

Remedies for Infringement or Misappropriation of Trade Secret Rights

The owner of the trade secret rights can collect damages and, if still possible to do so, gain injunctive relief against further use or misappropriation of the trade secret (Uniform Trade Secrets Act, §2).

Example – Control of Parent Corn Stock for Hybrid Corn

The case of Pioneer v. Holden (Pioneer Hi-Bred Intern. v. Holden Foundation Seeds, Inc., 35 F.3d 1226, 31 USPQ2d 1385 (8th Cir. Iowa, 12 July, 1994) is an instructive example of trade secret right protection for the seed corn-breeding industry. Pioneer was able to recover a substantial judgement in the amount of $47.6 *million* for misappropriation of genetic messages of parent stock which was owned by and reasonably controlled to be secret by Pioneer. In this case, Pioneer did not have to, and did not, prove that a Holden employee had 'stolen' specific secretly controlled Pioneer parent corn stock. Rather, the circumstantial evidence, including the evidence of actual trade secret controls implemented by Pioneer, and the fact that the Holden corn must have emanated from this parent stock as a scientific fact was sufficient for Pioneer to establish violation of its trade secret rights. Thus, the AG Money CORN A would be a proper subject for trade secret protection.

Plant Patents (Asexually Reproduced)

Eligible Subject Matter

In 1930, the USA adopted a plant patent statute, the current version of the statute, as amended 26 January, 1998, providing:

Whoever *invents or discovers and asexually reproduces any distinct and new variety of plant*, including cultivated spores, mutants, hybrids, and newly found seedlings, other than a tuber propagated plant or a plant found in an uncultivated state, may obtain a patent therefor, subject to the conditions and requirements of this title. The provisions of this title relating to patent for invention shall apply to patents for plants, except as otherwise provided.

(35 USC §161)

As a practical matter, this 'plant patent' provision, because it requires that the variety be 'asexually reproduced', covers primarily ornamental plants and fruit trees.

The HEATHER B that was discovered in AG Money's cultivated field and asexually reproduced by cutting would be eligible for plant patent protection. Note that the statute protects mutant plants found in a cultivated field or state, but precludes plants found in an 'uncultivated state', such as in a wilderness area.

Duration and Scope of Protection

The term of protection is for 20 years from the date of application for plant patent. The scope of protection for a plant patent is defined in the US statute as follows:

In the case of a plant patent, the grant shall include the right to exclude others from asexually reproducing the plant, and from using, offering for sale, or selling the plants so reproduced, or any of its parts, throughout the United States, or from importing the plants so reproduced, or any parts thereof into the United States.

(35 USC §163)

The US statute requires that the plant be described as completely as is reasonably possible and the patent claim is to be in formal terms to the plant shown and described. This means that there is but a *single claim, to a single plant* (35 USC §162).

US Courts have construed the plant patent statute to cover only *the progeny of the single plant variety described and claimed* (Imazio Nursery, Inc. v. Dania Greenhouses, 69 F.3d 1560, 36 USPQ2d 1673 (Fed. Cir. (Cal.), 3 November, 1995). In Imazio, US Plant Patent No. 5,336 (incorporated herein by reference) covering a plant similar to the hypothetical HEATHER B was asserted in a US District Court infringement action. The Court found infringement and awarded substantial damages of over $400,000.00 against the 'infringer'. The Circuit Court reversed this District Court decision, refusing to broaden the scope of protection to cover heather with similar distinguishing flowering characteristics as described in the plant patent. The court interpreted the plant patent provision of the patent act as limiting protection to *only the progeny of the single plant described* in the patent. Accordingly, unlike utility patents, the plant patent section does not permit claiming of the invention or discovery in functional or characteristic terms.

Remedies for Infringement

The remedies for infringement are the same as for other utility patents and include injunctions against future infringement and damages for past infringements, including lost profits caused by the infringement (35 USC §§281, 283, 284, 285).

Plant Variety Protection Certificates

Eligible Subject Matter

A plant variety protection (Breeder's Right) statute was introduced in the USA in 1970. The US statute provides in pertinent part:

> The breeder of any novel variety of a *sexually reproduced plant* (other than fungi, bacteria, or first generation hybrids) who has so reproduced the variety, or his successor in interest, shall be entitled to plant variety protection therefor, subject to the conditions and requirements of this subchapter unless one of the following bars exists: ... [Italics added for emphasis]
>
> (7 USC §2402(a))

Plant variety protection is not patent protection as there are no patent 'claims' and the statute is administered by the US Department of Agriculture (USDA), not the US Patent and Trademark Office (USPTO).

The plant variety protection system is basically a breeder's rights system, protecting new varieties developed by selective breeding.

Duration and Scope of Protection

The term of a plant variety protection certificate is 20 years from the date the certificate is issued (7 USC §2483(b)). The statute defines infringement of a plant variety:

> Except as otherwise provided in this subchapter, it shall be an infringement of the rights of the owner of a novel variety to perform without authority, any of the following acts in the United States, or in commerce which can be regulated by Congress or affecting such commerce, prior to expiration of the right to plant variety protection but after either the issue of the certificate or the distribution of a novel plant variety with the notice under section 2567 of this title:
>
> (1) sell the novel variety, or offer it or expose it for sale, deliver it, ship it, consign it, exchange it, or solicit an offer to buy it, or any other transfer of title or possession of it;
>
> (2) import the novel variety into, or export it from, the United States;
>
> (3) sexually multiply the novel variety as a step in marketing (for growing purposes) the variety; or
>
> (4) use the novel variety in producing (as distinguished from developing) a hybrid or different variety therefrom; or

(5) use seed which had been marked 'Unauthorized Propagation Prohibited' or 'Unauthorized Seed Multiplication Prohibited' or progeny thereof to propagate the novel variety; or

(6) dispense the novel variety to another, in a form which can be propagated, without notice as to being a protected variety under which it was received; or

(7) perform any of the foregoing acts even in instances in which the novel variety is multiplied other than sexually, except in pursuance of a valid United States plant patent; or

(8) instigate or actively induce performance of any of the foregoing acts.

(7 USC §2541)

There are significant infringement *exemptions* that differentiate the plant variety protection from patent protection, namely:

1. there is a *research exemption* permitting use and reproduction of a protected variety for plant breeding or other bonafide research (7 USC §2544);

2. there is a *saved crop exemption* permitting farmers to save sufficient seed for replanting (7 USC §2543); and

3. there is a general *public policy saving provision* that authorizes the Secretary of Agriculture to force the certificate owner to permit others to supply seeds sufficient for public needs, subject to remuneration (7 USC §2404).

The saved crop exemption only allows replanting of the same amount of saved seeds as were purchased from the certificate owner. The US Supreme Court Asgrow decision (Asgrow Seed Co. v. Winterboer 513 US 179, 33 USPQ2d 1430 (US Iowa, 18 January, 1995)) is instructive in explaining the plant variety protection act, and specifically limits the scope of the saved crop exemption. The Imazio case discussed above is also instructive in explaining the difference between the plant variety and plant patent protection rights.

Remedies for Infringement

The owner of the plant variety certificate can obtain a court injunction against future infringements as well as damages, with the court authorized to increase damages up to three times the actual amount of damages determined. There is a limitation on damages which requires clear labelling of the protected variety (7 USC §§2564, 2567).

Utility Patents

Eligible Subject Matter

The US patent statute provides in pertinent part that:

> Whoever invents or discovers any new and useful process, machine, manufacture, or composition of matter, or any new and useful improvement

thereof, may obtain a patent therefor, subject to the conditions and
requirements of this title ...

(35 USC §101)

The invention must also represent an inventive step or non-obviousness
as compared to the prior art (35 USC §§102, 103).

US Courts and the USPTO have very broadly construed the scope of
eligible subject matter for patenting to include any 'non naturally occurring
manufacture or composition of matter', including plants and animals that are
the result of human intervention.

This expansive view of patentable subject matter is premised on the
famous 1980 US Supreme Court Chakrabarty decision (Diamond v.
Chakrabarty, 447 US 303, 206 USPQ 193 (US, 16 June, 1980) where
bacteria capable of breaking down multiple components of crude oil were
determined to be an appropriate subject matter for a US utility patent.
Based on Chakrabarty, the USPTO has adopted guidelines to patent
Examiners concerning the patentability of living subject matter, which basically allows the patenting of living subject matter, except for claims to a
human being (MPEP §2105). In the decision of *Ex parte* Hibberd *et al.* (*Ex
parte* Hibberd *et al.*, 227 USPQ 443 (Bd. Pat. App. & Interferences 1985)),
the USPTO Board of Patent Appeals and Interferences (the highest tribunal
within the USPTO) specifically ruled that plants are appropriate subject matter for utility patent protection. Hibberd is currently being questioned in a
pending case (Pioneer Hi-Bred Intern. v. J.E.M. AG Supply, Inc., 49
USPQ2d 1813 (N.D. Iowa, 1998)) before the Federal Circuit. This pending
appeal is of special interest since it is limited to the very specific issue of
whether plants *per se* can be patentable under the utility patent statute. The
argument against utility patents for plants is that this conflicts with
Congress' intention in providing specific protection for asexually reproduced
plants by way of the Plant Patent provision and for sexually reproduced
plants by way of the Plant Variety Protection Act as discussed in the previous two sections.

Duration and Scope of Protection

Utility patents for plants (however reproduced) are enforceable for 20 years
after the application filing date.

The scope of protection for utility patents is fundamentally different and
more expansive than the 'patent' protection under the Utility Patent Statute
sections covering asexually produced plants and under the Plant Variety
Protection Act. *This fundamental difference is that the scope of exclusionary protection is
defined by the patent claims.* Any interpretation of the scope of the utility patent
claims must be done in conjunction with the patent application specification
description, the pertinent governing statutory section reading in pertinent
part:

The specification shall contain a written description of the invention, and of the manner and process of making and using it, *in such full, clear, concise, and exact terms as to enable in a person skilled in the art to which it pertains, or with which it is most nearly connected, to make and use the same, and shall set forth the best mode contemplated by the inventor of carrying out his invention* ...

(35 USC §112, ¶1)

As you can well imagine, inventor(s), applicants (owners) and their patent attorneys assert every effort to describe and claim their inventions in the broadest form permitted by the statute, while accused infringers and their attorneys do everything they can to convince the courts that the claim interpretation proposed is unduly broad and invalid as not supported by the patent description as required by this very important first paragraph of 35 USC §112.

The patent that ultimately issued from the application considered in the Hibberd *et al.* decision of the USPTO which held that plants were patentable subject matter is US Patent No. 4,581,847, titled 'Tryptophan Over Producer Mutants of Cereal Crops'. This Hibberd '847 patent is instructive as to the scope of utility patent claims that are possible, as exemplified by the following independent claim: '16. A maize plant having an average endogenous free tryptophan content of at least about 0.04 milligrams per gram fresh weight'. Assuming that the USPTO properly performed its duties in requiring a written description commensurate with the scope of the claims allowed in the Hibberd '847 patent, this claim 16 would be literally enforceable against any maize plants having tryptophan content above the 0.04 milligrams per gram of fresh weight. If this Hibberd '847 patent is ever litigated, this claim 16 would presumably be attacked as too broad in violation of the requirements of the first paragraph of 35 USC §112.

The US courts have strictly interpreted the written description and enabling requirement of the first paragraph of 35 USC §112 in 'unpredictable technologies' to require a limitation of claims to only the examples for which an enabling disclosure is provided in the specification and permitting only claims as broad as the written description enables and describes. The Federal Circuit court decision in Amgen (Amgen, Inc. v. Chugai Pharmaceutical Co., Ltd, 927 F.2d 1200, 18 USPQ2d 1016 (Fed. Cir. Mass., 5 March, 1991), App. 4) is instructive as to the analysis that US courts apply in interpreting the requirements of 35 USC §112, first paragraph in conjunction with biotechnology inventions. In Amgen, the Federal Circuit discussed the requirements of the first paragraph at 35 USC §112 in affirming invalidity of broadly formulated claims, including the following statements:

[7] Whether a claimed invention is enabled under 35 U.S.C. §112 is a question of law, which we review *de novo*. *Moleculon Research Corp. v. CBS, Inc.*, 793 F.2d 1261, 1268, 229 USPQ 805, 811 (Fed. Cir. 1986) *cert. denied*, 479 U.S. 1030 (1987). 'To be enabling under §112, a patent must contain a description that enables one skilled in the art to make and use the claimed invention.'

Atlas Powder Co. v. E.I. duPont De Nemours & Co., 750 F.2d 1569, 1576, 224 USPQ 409, 413 (Fed. Cir. 1984).

That some experimentation is necessary does not constitute a lack of enablement; the amount of experimentation, however, must not be unduly extensive. *Id.* The essential question here is whether the scope of enablement of claim 7 is as broad as the scope of the claim. *See generally In re Fisher*, 427 F.2d 833, 166 USPQ 18 (CCPA 1970); 2D. Chisum, Patents §7.03[7][b] (1990).

The specification of the '008 patent provides that:

one may readily design and manufacture genes coding for microbial expression of polypeptides having primary conformations which differ from that herein specified for mature EPO in terms of the identity or location of one or more residues (e.g., substitutions, terminal and intermediate additions and deletions).

DNA sequences provided by the present invention are thus seen to comprehend all DNA sequences suitable for use in securing expression in a procaryotic or eucaryotic host cell of a polypeptide product having at least a part of the primary structural conformation and one or more of the biological properties of erythropoietin, and selected from among: (a) the DNA sequences set out in Figs. 5 and 6; (b) DNA sequences which hybridize to the DNA sequences defined in (a) or fragments thereof; and (c) DNA sequences which, but for the degeneracy of the genetic code, would hybridize to the DNA sequences defined in (a) and (b).

The district court found that over 3,600 different EPO analogs can be made by substituting at only a single amino acid position, and over a million different analogs can be made by substituting three amino acids. The patent indicates that it embraces means for preparation of 'numerous' polypeptide analogs of EPO. Thus, the number of claimed DNA encoding sequences that can produce an EPO-like product is potentially enormous ...

... [8] It is well established that a patent applicant is entitled to claim his invention generically, when he describes it sufficiently to meet the requirements of Section 112. See *Utter v. Hiraga*, 845 F.2d 993, 998, 6 USPQ 2d 1709, 1714 (Fed. Cir. 1988) ('A specification may, within the meaning of 35 U.S.C. §112¶1, contain a written description of a broadly claimed invention without describing all species that claim encompasses.'); *In re Robins*, 429 F.2d 452, 456–57, 166 USPQ 552, 555 (CCPA 1970) ('[R]epresentative samples are not required by the statute and are not an end in themselves.') *Here, however, despite extensive statements in the specification concerning all the analogs of the EPO gene that can be made, there is little enabling disclosure of particular analogs and how to make them. Details for preparing only a few EPO analog genes are disclosed. Amgen argues that this is sufficient to support its claims; we disagree.* This 'disclosure' might well justify a generic claim encompassing these and similar analogs, but it represents inadequate support for Amgen's desire to claim all EPO gene analogs. There may be many other genetic sequences that code for EPO-type products. *Amgen has told how to make and use only a few of them and is therefore not entitled to claim all of them* [emphasis added] ...

As one can see from this Amgen decision, interpretations of patent claims under 35 USC §112, first paragraph, are very fact-sensitive and depend upon the 'predictability' and the level of skill in the technology at the time of the application for patent. For example, in the early stages of the gene-splicing technology, deposit of actual specimens was required to meet the 'enabling disclosure requirements'. Actual specimens are no longer always required for many gene technology inventions, as also reflected in the court's discussion in the Amgen case. The test for satisfying the 'enabling description' requirement depends on what those skilled in the art at the time of the application would be able to ascertain from the patent application specification. As a practical matter today, many, if not most, applications for gene-splicing technology, describe the invention by reference to existing public libraries of information and existing public depositories, without the submission of an actual specimen.

Important to note is that the US courts can and should invalidate claims that are broader than the patent specification description. Thus, proper implementation of the requirements of the first paragraph of 35 USC §112 should avoid blocking patent claims to subject matter that is not adequately described in the patent specification.

Remedies for Infringement

The remedies for infringement of utility patents include injunctions against future infringement and damages for past infringement, including lost profits damages (35 USC §271). The issue of damages in the USA is resolved expansively in favour of the patent owner against an infringer. Essentially, any provable consequential damage is recoverable, including loss of profits due to suppression of prices by infringing competitive products, loss of profits by loss of infringing sales and any other provable consequential economic damage. This is in contrast with most countries where, at most, usually a small percentage royalty corresponding generally to industry-established royalty rates are the measure of infringement damages. The potential high damages in the USA have a very substantial 'chilling effect' on would-be infringers. Further, if the infringers do not have a reasonable basis for infringing after notice of the patent, they can be adjudged to be 'wilful infringers' subject to multiplication of up to three times actual damages (35 USC §284).

IPR for AG Money Developments

Table 1.1 depicts the available IPR categories for each of the hypothetical AG Money developments. Note that US Utility Patent protection is available for all developments. In most cases, the Utility Patent protection is the most comprehensive. However, trade secret protection may be recommended for the GENE METHOD E, assuming this method could not be easily independently developed or reverse engineered from public distribution of the resultant products.

Table 1.1. Available IPR for AG Money developments.

Contribution	Trade secret	Plant patent (asexually produced)	Plant variety protection (sexually produced)	Utility patent
CORN A	Yes (control parent)	No	Yes	Yes
HEATHER B	No	Yes	No	Yes
SOYBEAN C	No	No	Yes	Yes
MAIZE D	No	No	Yes	Yes
GENE METHOD E	Yes	No	No	Yes
MACHINE F	No (unless never public)	No	No	Yes

International Legal Framework

The previous sections have described the US legal system for protecting inventors' and breeders' contributions. Other countries have generally similar legal frameworks and there are international conventions with respect to administrative aspects of utility patents and plant variety protection certificates.

The Paris convention provides for granting of patent application filing dates based upon applications filed in one country, as long as they are filed in another convention country claiming priority within one year of the first filing. There is also a Patent Cooperation Treaty which permits preservation of first filing rights, while allowing a delay of most filing costs in other countries for up to 30 months.

There is also a plant variety protection act convention which grants priority filing rights between countries.

Most countries have a 'first to file' system which does not take into account inventive acts prior to the filing of the first patent application. This contrasts with the USA wherein the 'first to invent' principle allows proof of pre-application inventive acts to establish a first date of invention to avoid prior art published within one year preceding the US application and to establish priority of invention when multiple applications for patent are pending in the USPTO which claim the same invention.

Some countries require 'working' or commercialization of inventions to maintain the patent rights. Also, different maintenance fee schemes for maintaining patents in force are provided by various countries.

A very significant and controversial difference between various country systems are the provisions regarding the eligible subject matter, especially when it comes to living subject matter such as plants and animals. For example, the European Patent Act includes a provision:

European patents shall not be granted in respect to: ...
(b) plant or animal varieties or essentially biological processes for the production of plants or animals; this provision does not apply to microbiological processes or the products thereof.

Also, many individual country patent systems preclude utility patent protection for plant and animal varieties, food and processes for producing food products, treatments for human or animal bodies, etc. See the *Manual for the Handling of Applications for Patents, Designs and Trademarks Throughout the World* (1998) for a comprehensive comparison of different IPR provisions for most of the countries of the world.

Special Situation – Patenting of Process/Product Using Publicly Available Gene Material

Plant breeding and gene-splicing technology research is based on use of existing gene materials. This gene material includes samples of plant varieties that have been categorized and controlled and made freely available for further plant breeding and research.

Concern has been expressed that a comprehensive utility patent system covering plants could lead to private companies using their patents to block certain uses of this gene material and thereby retard plant research efforts based on these publicly available gene material sources. This concern is understandable, but somewhat misplaced because of the (i) *novelty*, (ii) *inventive step*, and (iii) *enabling disclosure* requirements of a properly administered patent system.

The *novelty requirement* assures that no patent system permits monopolizing what is old. The existing gene material itself will always be available.

The *inventive step requirement* of all patent systems requires not only that the claimed invention be new, it must also be a significant (non-obvious) advance in the technology.

The *enabling and written description requirements* provide that the scope of patent claims is (or should be) limited to only cover what was added to the technology and clearly disclosed in the patent specification. Open-ended claims in unpredictable technologies like gene splicing should not be permitted.

Special Situation – Downstream Control of Patented Plants – 'Terminator' Technology

Included herein by reference is US Patent No. 5,723,765 to Oliver *et al.* covering what has been termed 'terminator' technology. This technology basically provides that the plants are so predisposed they will not produce a seed crop for subsequent generations. This would obviate the difficulties in downstream control of plant varieties once the seed is sold. It is understood that, for example, Monsanto requires purchasers of its patented seed to sign contracts limiting use of the seed for only one planting, without allowing subsequent sale or use of the crop produced as seed. This approach is problematical since it requires policing customers and their farmer neighbours. Thus, although the DNA-tracing technology is developed so that it can be determined whether crop seeds have been replanted on a widespread basis due to purchasers reselling their crop as seed, the investigative and litigation efforts involved are costly and not very customer-friendly. It is for this reason that the 'terminator' technology reflected in this patent may be of interest to large-scale private plant breeders that have patented plant varieties with monopoly competitive advantages in the marketplace with respect to competing varieties.

Conclusion – Policy Considerations for Crafting an IPR System to Protect Rights of Breeders and Inventors

Under the GATT-TRIPs provisions, member countries, especially developing countries, have flexibility in designing their own laws. For example, utility patent protections for living organisms need not be provided (GATT, Annex 1C, Agreement on Trade-related Aspects of Intellectual Property Rights, Section 5, Article 27). The following is a checklist of features that could be considered in establishing IPR for plant technology innovations:

1. Plant breeders' rights, such as Plant Variety Protection Certificates, could be adopted which include appropriate exemptions to balance private and public interests.
2. The utility patent laws could be modified to include the exemptions now included under the US Plant Variety Protection Act, namely (i) a crop replanting exemption for farmers; (ii) a research exemption; and (iii) a public policy exemption allowing the government to require availability of sufficient seed stock to provide food needs.
3. The duration of the patent right protection could be modified or controlled by requiring 'working' or commercialization so as to prevent the holding of blocking patents that are not exploited.
4. The term of the patent rights could be structured to include rapidly escalating maintenance fees to maintain patents in force, especially in the downstream years of the patent life when the blocking effects may be the most adverse, and the patent rights will presumably be the most valuable and be able to support the higher fees.
5. The scope of the patent claims allowed could be carefully limited to preclude coverage of open-ended ranges that were never enabled in the original patent application specification.

This chapter should provide a basis for understanding, analysing and implementing legal systems that can properly balance the public and private interests in agricultural biotechnology inventive contributions.

References

Manual of Patent Examining Procedure (MPEP), 7th edn (1998) US Department of Commerce, Patent and Trademark Office, Woolcott & Company.

Manual for the Handling of Applications for Patents, Designs and Trademarks Throughout the World (1998) Manual Industrial Property BV, Octrooibureau Los En Stigter, Amsterdam.

Plant Variety Protection Act, 7 USC §§2321, 2401, 2402, 2403, 2404, 2422, 2541, 2543, 2544, 2563, 2564, 2567.

US Plant Patent No. 5,336 for 'Heather Named Erica Sunset' invented by Bruno L. Imazio.

US Plant Patent No. 10,832 for 'Apple Tree Named "Cumberland Spur"' invented by Deutscher *et al.*

US Patent No. 4,581,847 for 'Tryptophan Over Producer Mutants of Cereal Crops' invented by Hibberd *et al.*

US Patent No. 5,872,304 for 'Soybean Cultivator 94348595302' invented by William K. Rhodes.

US Patent No. 5,723,765 for 'Control of Plant Gene Expression' invented by Oliver *et al.*

Uniform Trade Secrets Act, §§1–6 (1985).

Utility Patents: 35 USC §§100, 101, 102, 103, 112, 154, 161, 162, 163, 271, 281, 283, 284, 285 (specific to asexually reproduced plants: §§161, 162, 163).

Intellectual Property Rights of Plant Varieties and of Biotechnology in the European Union

Vittorio Santaniello

Dipartimento di Economia ed Istituzioni, Università degli Studi di Roma 'Tor Vergata', Rome, Italy

Preparatory work to harmonize European patent legislation started as early as 1959, when a first comparative study was conducted on the regulatory norms in force in the six countries forming the original nucleus of the European Union (EU). The Haertel Study recommended that the future European legislation should not include all of the exclusionary provisions that were present in the national laws. Two exemptions, however, were foreseen namely the invention that violated public order and morality and those that related to plant varieties.[1]

Although the Coordinating Committee of the Secretary of States stated that the only exclusion present in the future legislation should be for inventions contrary to order and public morals, subsequent formulation by the working groups reintroduced exclusionary provisions for plant varieties and essentially biological processes for the production of plants and animals.

Until now the principles that have informed the legislation on patents of the countries of the EU were those agreed upon and included in the European Patent Convention (EPC) of 1973.

Article 52 of the EPC stated that 'European patents shall be granted for any inventions which are susceptible of industrial application, which are new and which involve an inventive step'. At the same time, and unlike the US legislation where exceptions to the rule of patentability are set by case law, Articles 52 and 53 of the same Convention identify those cases in which European patents could not be granted. In those two Articles, in fact, it was stated that 'methods for treatment of the human body by surgery or therapy and diagnostic methods practised on the human and animal body shall not be regarded as inventions which are susceptible of industrial application'. Moreover, the other two exceptions to the rule of patentability of innovations were:

(a) inventions, the publication and the exploitation of which would be contrary to the *ordre public* or morality, provided that the exploitation shall not be deemed to be so contrary merely because it is prohibited by law or regulation in some or all Contracting States, (b) plant or animal varieties or essentially biological processes for the production of plants or animals; this provision does not apply to microbiological processes or the product thereof.

According to the interpretation of the Convention, innovations that relate to plants and animals could be patentable if it could be proved that they did not relate to a specific variety. Hybrids, for example, are patentable because they are not considered a plant variety nor do they comply with the stability requirement.[2] On the contrary, transgenic plants, although considered as not obtained through an essentially biological process, were deemed not to be patentable because they presented distinctive features and therefore were to be considered varieties.

Concerning microorganisms and microbiological processes, the Technical Board of the European Patent Office (EPO) has constantly interpreted this provision as relating to all cellular organisms with dimensions beneath the limit of vision and which can be manipulated and propagated in a laboratory (Jaenichen, 1997).

Until 1991 one of the justifications for not allowing patents for plant varieties to be granted was the need to avoid any conflict between decisions made under the EPO and the Plant Varieties Protection Acts. Based on Article 2 of the UPOV (International Union for the Protection of New Varieties of Plants) Convention, in fact double protection was explicitly forbidden. In 1991, however, the revised version of the UPOV Convention did not any longer prevent the possibility of protecting plant varieties using both systems.

The Protection of Plant Varieties

Since 1994, the protection of crop varieties in the EU has been defined by Regulation 2100/94, concerning the creation of a European privative on vegetable innovation. This Regulation follows and accepts all the indications included in the 1991 revision of the UPOV.

After 1994, the EU granted a European privative on any new variety if it can be claimed that the variety is distinctive, homogeneous, stable and it represents a novelty. The nature of this privative is such that it can be classified as a Breeders' Rights type. This privative is not compatible with any other type of protection and can be obtained for whatever organism belonging to any genus and species of the vegetable world.

The Regulation introduced a new criterion to evaluate the distinctive requirement. The test to be used to determine if a variety is distinguishably different from all other existing ones could not be based on one or more relevant characters alone. It had to consider, instead, the complete set of characters which resulted from a specific genotype or combinations of genotypes.

To be considered new, a variety needs not to have been made available, with the breeder's consent, to anyone and for whatever reason, for more than 1 year. For trees and vines this period is lifted up to 4 years. This length of time is raised to 6 years if the variety has been made available in a country outside the EU.

The Regulation defines stability and homogeneity requirements in the traditional way. As is usually the case in fact, the proposed variety is considered stable if the characters – which are used to describe it and/or for which it is claimed to be distinct – remain unchanged after several reproduction periods. At the same time a variety is considered to be homogeneous if the variance of those same characters remains within the usual boundary.

In the case of herbaceous crops, the duration of the privative is 25 years from the date in which it is granted. For vines and trees, instead, the privative lasts for 30 years.

Any production, reproduction, sale, import in the EU, export from the EU or storage – for those uses – of the protected variety has to be authorized by the owner of the European privative. If a variety is used without the consent of the proprietor of the privative, those limitations apply also to the product obtained from it. In other words, for example, the grain or the seed produced from a pirated variety cannot be traded within the EU, nor imported in or exported from it.

The Breeders' Right extends also to the 'essentially derived variety'. This is the case of protected genotypes used in the production of other varieties or of varieties obtained from other genotypes by a simple minor or cosmetic change.

The Regulation specifies forage, cereal, potatoes and fibre species for which farmers have the privilege of using *farm saved seed* on their own farms. This privilege does not apply to horticultural and tree varieties. Farmers' privilege, however, is subject to a quantitative restriction which sets a limit to the quantity of seed that each farmer can produce. Farmers of medium- and large-sized farms are required to pay royalties to the owner of the Breeders' Right. The amount of this payment is set based on area-specific criteria. Farmers of small farms are exempt from the payment of any royalties.

Upon a request of a Member State and in the pursuing of a public interest the Commission can issue a compulsory licence.

The New European Directive on the Protection of Biological Invention

On 11 May 1998, the European Parliament approved a new Common Position (CP) on the legal protection of biotechnological inventions. This CP aims to eliminate the differences that still exist among the legislation and administrative practices in force in the Member States. The persistence of those differences, in fact, could be a barrier to trade and impede the proper functioning of the internal market. A previous version of this document was rejected by the European Parliament in 1995.

The CP sets the principles on which Member States will have to base their legislation, namely they should: (i) make a difference between a discovery and an invention and state that a simple discovery cannot be patented; (ii) define the scope of a biotechnological invention; (iii) include the right to use a deposit mechanism in addition to the written description; and (iv) offer the option of obtaining a non-exclusive compulsory licence.

One of the most controversial points of this CP has been the possibility of patenting human genes.

The CP states that patent must be applied so as to safeguard the dignity and integrity of the human body at any stage of development including the germinal cells. However,

> an invention based on an element isolated from the human body or otherwise produced by means of a technical process, which is susceptible of industrial application, is not excluded from patentability, even where the structure of that element is identical to that of the natural element, given that the rights conferred by the patent do not extend to the human body and its elements in their natural environment.

Moreover the CP states that a

> mere DNA sequence without the indication of a function does not contain any technical information and is therefore not a patentable invention.

The implication of this is that the simple discovery of the partial or complete sequence of a human gene or of one of its products cannot be patented. However, in view of the significant progress made in the treatment of diseases, thanks to elements isolated from the human body, this exclusionary provision does not apply to the genetic information included in the human genes, nor in the genes of any other living organism. Although a single gene or a single protein, or part of a protein, cannot be patented, the industrial use of the information they contain can be. The inventor, however, has to know and make public 'which protein, or part of protein, is produced and what function it performs'.

As we have already seen in the countries of the EU, plant varieties are presently protected under a Breeders' Right regime. This new Directive does not change the previous exclusion for granting patents to plant and animal varieties. Only those inventions whose application is not confined to a single plant or animal variety are patentable.

Transgenic plants and animals *per se* are not patentable, due to the exclusion from this type of protection of varieties. However, as we have just mentioned, the Directive states that, under given conditions, a partial or a complete gene sequence is patentable and the protection covers also the products in which this gene is present. From this it derives that the protection offered to a patented gene, present in a transgenic plant or animal, extends also to the plant or to the animal.

The Release of Genetically Modified Organisms in the EU

In December 1996, the Commission issued a Review Report of Directive 90/220 that regulates the deliberate release into the environment of genetically modified organisms (GMO), identifying a number of areas in which improvements are needed. A new Directive is presently under preparation and should be out in a couple of years.

Although the new Commission Directive will propose few changes, it will not – most likely – modify in any substantive way the Regulation now in force. The new text in fact, most likely, will propose some simplification in the present rules and procedures and will introduce additional monitoring requirements, like the proposed one at the end of a 7-year period after the GMO has been released into the environment.

The EU requires that GMO can be deliberately released in the environment only after an assessment of any potential risk for human health and/or the environment in conformity of the rules and techniques specified in the Directive 90/220. According to this Directive, the release of GMO can be classified in two categories. In the first category are classified those GMO for which the taxonomy, the biology and the safety for human health and environment of the recipient organism is well known and, moreover, the pathogenicity, the allergenicity and the toxigenicity of the GMO is claimed not to represent an additional risk to the corresponding non-modified organism. All the other cases are included in the second category.

The procedure followed to authorize the deliberate release into the environment is obviously different depending upon the category in which the organism is classified and if the release takes place for R&D purposes or for placing on the market products containing the GMO. Any person intending to deliberately release a GMO of the first category has to submit a notification to the competent authority of the Member State within whose territory the release is going to take place. Within 30 days from receiving the request the Member State has to tell the notifier whether it judges that all the requisites set in the Directive are met or not. The procedure is obviously more complex in the case of an organism that belongs to the second category. In this case, the notifier's request is communicated to the competent authorities of the other Member States, whose observations will have to be considered in granting or not, within 90 days, the permit for the deliberate release. The notifier can decide to apply for a deliberate release in more than one location within the EU. In this case, the notifier can apply directly to the Commission or to each of the concerned Member States. In either case, the procedure is similar to the one previously mentioned. During the experimental phase, the release of the GMO is monitored by the competent authorities.

If based on the data produced in the experimental phase, plus any other additional information available, the notifier can prove that the release of the GMO is safe, the notifier can apply for a permit to sell the new product on the markets within the EU. The Commission, at the end of a rather complicated procedure, can grant this permit and indicate the labelling procedures that the seller has to follow. The new Directive will most likely simplify to some extent this procedure.

The Future Development of a European Gene Market

After the approval of the Directive on the Protection of Biological Inventions, the creation of a wide and complete gene market in the EU is only a matter of time, and most likely not a very long time. Recent technological developments are contributing to making this event closer.

As we have seen, the patenting of a partial or complete gene sequence is possible only when the biological function of this DNA fragment is known. Up to now, the determination of the biological role of even a single gene has been a rather complex and time-consuming exercise. Recent development, however, through the use of DNA array and massive plant observation technologies, are making all this more speedy and efficient.

The application of DNA array technology can provide an image of the complete set of the active genes in a cell. This has been applied to a simple eukaryote like *Saccharomyces cerevisiae* but the door is now open for the application to more complex organisms. The technique consists of synthesizing a high-density matrix of oligonucleotides on a glass wafer support.[3] Those nucleotides are arranged on the support in the same order in which they appear in the chromosome. The entire mRNA population is produced, marked and hybridized to the nucleotide array. The complete set of active genes is then detected by identifying and measuring the fluorescent spots.

Mutagenesis processes can be determined by using transposons that can randomly cause the inactivation of a single gene. The use of DNA array technology allows a rapid identification of which gene has been made silent, while a protocol of massive plant observations – developed by the Max Planck Institute – permits identification of the phenotypic expression of the genomic change and consequently the biological function of the gene that has been made silent.[4]

The other question that is frequently posed is: will the new Directive effectively and decisively stimulate the development of the biotechnology industry in the EU? The answer is that the Directive is most likely a necessary but not a sufficient condition. A more active industrial policy needs to be implemented to create the other complementary conditions. Among them are the availability of risk capital, an appropriate tax policy, a greater uniformity in the regulation of R&D among the different Member States, a greater transparency in the application of the European Directives and a simplification of the approval procedures for the GMO.

In the USA, venture capital has played an effective role in providing the financial resources for this risky industry. In the EU, with the notable exemption of the UK, this form of financing is not yet well developed. Although this financial sector has grown recently, most of the resources have gone to finance takeover of firms and only a minor fraction has been used to finance knowledge-intensive firms.

Small start-up companies could play an important role in the development of a biotechnology industry in Europe. This would require an appropriate tax policy on capital gains to stimulate the flow of financial resources towards those enterprises, to take account of the high level of risk. Those aspects that relate to industry structure and to needed policy measures require, however, further study. It is not clear, for example, if the development of the biotechnology industry in Europe will follow the US pathway or not. Available partial evidence tends to show the existence of main differences. In the UK, for instance, the attempt to create new biotechnology start-up companies has led to failure (Thackray, 1998). Biotechnology developed, instead, in pre-existing pharmaceutical companies while only more recently are there signs of a reversal of this trend.

Notes

1. During the preparatory phase of the working groups, the same principle was extended to animal races on the analogy of what had been proposed for plants.
2. 'Hybrid seed and plants from such seed, lacking stability in some trait of the whole generation population, cannot be classified as plant varieties within the meaning of Article 53(b), T 320/87 Hybrid plants/Lubrizol, OJ EPO, 1990, p. 71.
3. In the case of *Saccharomyces cerevisiae* the array contained 260,000 DNA sequences each containing 25 nucleotides (Wodicka *et al.*, 1997).
4. F. Salamini, personal communication.

References

Jaenichen, H.R. (1997) *The European Patent Office's Case Law on Patentability of Biotechnology Inventions*. C. Heymanns Verlag KG, Bonn.

Thackray, A. (ed.) (1998) *Private Science: Biotechnology and the Rise of the Molecular Sciences*. University of Pennsylvania Press, Philadelphia.

Wodicka, H., Dong, M., Mittmann, M., Ho, H. and Lockart, D.J. (1997) Genome wide expression monitoring in *Saccharomyces cerevisiae*. *Nature Biotechnology* 15(13).

Intellectual Property Rights under the Convention on Biological Diversity

3

W. Lesser

Department of Agricultural, Resource and Managerial Economics, Cornell University, Ithaca, New York, USA

The Convention on Biological Diversity (CBD) set into motion a number of complex forces as regards technology transfer, access and benefit-sharing for genetic resources and their products in the forms of genetically modified and traditionally derived organisms. The Convention recently completed its fourth Conference of the Parties with little apparent progress in these areas.[1,2] Thus it may be helpful from outside the Convention process to summarize the current state of knowledge in each of these areas, identify gaps in our command of the factors and suggest possible ways forward.

Each component is quite complex in its own right, but time and space limitations dictate some need for economy in presentation. Thus what is presented here is a synopsis of each topic, hopefully one which does not violate the subtleties of the subject too seriously. The interested reader is directed to supplemental readings.

When reference is made herein to intellectual property rights (IPR), it is as systems establishing the five major classes of protection: patents, Plant Breeders' Rights (PBR), copyright, trademark and trade secrets. By inference, newer more specialized forms like maskworks (semiconductors) would be included as well, but are not specifically mentioned as being unrelated to the subject matter considered here. Indeed, the three most relevant forms of protection associated with the CBD are patents, PBR and trade secrets, singly or in combination. The functional definition of IPR is of importance because sometimes in the CBD-related literature, IPR is referred to broadly as a multitude of means of maintaining control over knowledge-based products. But as the functioning of the various systems can lead to very different outcomes, the term IPR is used herein to refer only to the five systems identified above.

This chapter is organized as follows. First, the institutional and theoretical bases of IPR under the CBD are considered. Next considered are the scope and applicability of IPR to genetic resources, followed by a discussion of the use of access legislation as a means of controlling the use of genetic resources. As part of the discussion, the status of Farmers' Rights is introduced. Finally, I end with an identification of areas where economists can contribute to the implementation of the Biodiversity Convention.

Institutional and Theoretical Bases

IPR and the CBD

The Biodiversity Convention, contrary to some perceptions, is as much focused on technology transfer and use with equitable sharing as on conservation. The components are most apparent in Articles 8(j), 15 and 16 which read:

A. Article 8(j): *In Situ* Conservation
Subject to its national legislation, respect, preserve and maintain knowledge, innovations and practices of indigenous and local communities embodying traditional lifestyles relevant for the conservation and sustainable use of biological diversity and promote their wider application with the approval and involvement of the holders of such knowledge, innovations and practices and encourage the equitable sharing of the benefits arising from the utilization of such knowledge, innovations and practices.

B. Article 15: Access to Genetic Resources
1. Recognizing the sovereign rights of States over their natural resources, the authority to determine access to genetic resources rests with the national governments and is subject to national legislation.
2. Each Contracting Party shall endeavor to create conditions to facilitate access to genetic resources for environmentally sound uses by other Contracting Parties and not to impose restrictions that run counter to the objectives of this Convention.
3. For the purpose of this Convention, the genetic resources being provided by a Contracting Party, as referred to in this Article and Articles 16 and 19, are only those that are provided by Contracting Parties that are countries of origin of such resources or by the Parties that have acquired the genetic resources in accordance with this Convention.
4. Access, where granted, shall be on mutually agreed terms and subject to the provisions of this Article.
5. Access to genetic resources shall be subject to prior informed consent of the Contracting Party providing such resources, unless otherwise determined by that Party.
6. Each Contracting Party shall endeavor to develop and carry out scientific research based on genetic resources provided by other Contracting Parties with the full participation of, and where possible in, such Contracting Parties.

7. Each Contracting Party shall take legislative, administrative or policy measures, as appropriate, and in accordance with Articles 16 and 19 and, where necessary, through the financial mechanism established by Articles 20 and 21 with the aim of sharing in a fair and equitable way the results of research and development and the benefits arising from the commercial and other utilization of genetic resources with the Contracting Party providing such resources. Such sharing shall be upon mutually agreed terms.

C. Article 16: Access to and Transfer of Technology
1. Each Contracting Party, recognizing that technology includes biotechnology, and that both access to and transfer of technology among Contracting Parties are essential elements for the attainment of the objectives of this Convention, undertakes subject to the provisions of this Article to provide and/or facilitate access for and transfer to other Contracting Parties of technologies that are relevant to the conservation and sustainable use of biological diversity or make use of genetic resources and do not cause significant damage to the environment.
2. Access to and transfer of technology referred to in paragraph 1 above to developing countries shall be provided and/or facilitated under fair and most favorable terms, including on concessionary and preferential terms where mutually agreed, and, where necessary, in accordance with the financial mechanism established by Articles 20 and 21. In the case of technology subject to patents and other intellectual property rights, such access and transfer shall be provided on terms which recognize and are consistent with the adequate and effective protection of intellectual property rights. The application of this paragraph shall be consistent with paragraphs 3, 4 and 5 below.
3. Each Contracting Party shall take legislative, administrative or policy measures, as appropriate, with the aim that Contracting Parties, in particular those that are developing countries, which provide genetic resources are provided access to and transfer of technology which makes use of those resources, on mutually agreed terms, including technology protected by patents and other intellectual property rights, where necessary, through the provisions of Articles 20 and 21 and in accordance with international law and consistent with paragraphs 4 and 5 below.
4. Each Contracting Party shall take legislative, administrative or policy measures, as appropriate, with the aim that the private sector facilitates access to, joint development and transfer of technology referred to in paragraph 1 above for the benefit of both governmental institutions and the private sector of developing countries and in this regard shall abide by the obligations included in paragraphs 1, 2 and 3 above.
5. The Contracting Parties, recognizing that patents and other intellectual property rights may have an influence on the implementation of this Convention, shall cooperate in this regard subject to national legislation and international law in order to ensure that such rights are supportive of and do not run counter to its objectives.

Articles 18 and 19 make related references to technology and sharing, but do not change the basic requirements or interpretation of the articles reproduced above.

While doing some injustice to the complexity of the matters, the present situation can be approximated as one where the developing, predominately tropical, countries provide the raw inputs, the genetic resources, which are transformed in the industrialized countries through biotechnology and other technical operations. Article 16 can then be seen as applying principally to the protection of commercializable products and technologies of the developed nations, and Article 15 to the resources from the developing countries. The juxtaposition of these articles, along with the reality of the needs, implies an interdependence between the two major groups; the developing nations provide the genetic resources and require enhanced technologies while the developed countries need the genetic resources along with the potential markets for their commercializable products. Thus the Convention provides for the necessary incentives for both sides to support it. This, however, does not imply any kind of direct swap, but rather a mutual protection of individual rights.

Where the situation differs is in the form of those rights. Article 16 refers three times to respect for IPR, which has been developed to protect just such finished products and processes. Genetic resources, however, have no such established protection systems (see below). Hence, there are in Article 15 requirements for mutually agreed terms, prior informed consent and equitable sharing of benefits, all aspects of a negotiation over the licensing of a technology. What IPR permits in addition is a clear basis for the identification of a violation (an infringement) and legal means of redress.

Article 8(j) suggests that local and indigenous peoples require special consideration under the Convention. They have much to contribute towards conservation and use, but their contributions are often in very intangible forms of traditional knowledge. Compensating this group for its contributions, and providing incentives for continued conservation of biodiversity, will require additional consideration, possibly a new form of formalized rights.

IPR and Economic Theory and Empirical Studies

IPR has been justified as either a personal right, according to the philosophy of the enlightenment, or as an incentive. From the economist's perspective, IPR serves as a mechanism to transform non-exclusionary knowledge into private property by defining it in a fixed form. The theoretical treatment has been presented previously (see, e.g., Maclup, 1958; Helpman, 1993) and will not be repeated here. IPR also serves to enhance technology transfer, which has direct relevance under the CBD, but this aspect of the literature is less well developed as a theoretical concept.

The promotion of the concept of the *absence* of IPR as a non-tariff barrier is of fairly recent origin, dating to the negotiations for the Uruguay Round of the GATT. The US position was that, 'Foreign violations of U.S. intellectual property rights ... severely distort international trade and deprive innovators, creators and inventors of rewards and opportunities that are right-fully theirs' (Office of the US Trade Representative, 1986). Adequate protection is credited with three benefits: (i) encourage investment and creativity; which in turn (ii) enhances technological progress, a critical aspect of US competi-tiveness; and (iii) attract(s) needed foreign know-how and investment to developing countries. The US position was drawn largely from examples of counterfeiting, and trademark violation in general (see Stern, 1987).

The association between investments and IPR is well established theoretic-ally. Available empirical evidence generally supports the theory. Studies of PBR, a patent-like system for plants of commercial application, for example, generally indicate an increase in private-sector investment following imple-mentation of the agreement (see literature review in Lesser, 1997a). For example, at this time, the majority of US soybean variety releases and the bulk of acreage planted is to privately bred varieties. Several provisos must be added, as follows:

1. Studies are available for only a few countries, and but one developing one, Argentina.
2. US PBR legislation has been weak compared with other national systems and thus attracts limited investment.
3. Investment varies widely across crops according to the value of the crop, response to breeding efforts and needs for localized adaptation.
4. Legislation is ineffective unless and until enforcement is accessible.

Empirical verification for the investment–incentive effect of patents is somewhat more difficult to establish because they are of longer standing, reducing the opportunity for before and after analysis. Nonetheless, Deolalikar and Evenson (1990) showed that investment in pharmaceutical research in India fell by 40% which they attributed to a weakening in patent protection in 1970. Surveys have indicated that pharmaceuticals and biotechnology are two of the areas where IPR protection is considered most critical due to the cost of development and relative ease of copying (Nogues, 1990, pp. 11–14).

IPR plays a particularly significant role for regulated products. Where, as with pharmaceuticals and agricultural chemicals, registration can cost hundreds of millions of dollars, no firm will invest without the assurity that a com-petitor cannot achieve the same approvals at one-quarter the cost. Agbiotech also has costly regulatory requirements, but more in the millions range. For these technologies, exclusive licensing is often required.

To these generally supportive findings, others have noted that many countries are not at the technological stage to make world-class contributions. Critics, referring to the position of developing countries, sometimes note that the ratio of patents granted to nationals compared to foreigners is often in the single digits, which is taken as evidence that developing countries are not benefiting by the R&D incentives of IPR (Primo Braga *et al.*, 1998). Certainly the data are correct, but two comments can be made regarding the inter-pretation. First, Evenson (1988) found that IPR-protected inventions often

stimulated in-country adaptive activities. Second, the same ratios identified by
Primo Braga *et al.* also characterize most smaller (in terms of population and
GDP) developed countries as well, countries like Canada and Norway.
Indeed, only the USA and Japan among the large technological countries
have a ratio below 50%.[3] What this says is that many inventions have world-
wide applications.

From the patent data, the patenting of an invention in multiple
countries, it can be inferred that IPR is a component of technology
transfer. Direct evidence for that position is however limited. Mansfield
(1995) found that the strength of a country's IPR regime was directly
associated with the amount of US foreign direct investment. Primo Braga
(1995), in a literature review, concluded that enhanced IPR in a country
typically expanded both imports of protected products and direct investment
(see also Henderson *et al.*, 1996). These cross-sectional studies use aggregated
trade and investment data, along with rather crude measures of IPR effectiveness. This means that it has not been possible to be very specific about
the effects of particular changes in IPR systems on product categories. In
particular, little is known about the strategic decisions made by firms when
introducing easily copied products into national markets. Will seed and
biotechnology firms, for example, demand very secure IPR prior to introducing their products, or will they acknowledge the relative ease with which
they can be appropriated and transfer under less secure conditions? Our
absence of insights into these strategic positions of agribusiness firms is a
serious gap in predicting the effects of IPR on agricultural technology
transfer in particular.

We turn next to a detailing of the current and future status of IPR
protection world-wide.

Scope and Extent of IPR Protection

As of 1988, the most recent data available, 49 countries with patent legislation excluded patents for pharmaceutical products and 45 for plant and
animal varieties (WIPO, 1990, Annex II). Additionally, an unspecified
number of countries permit the exclusion from patentability for products
deemed to offend *ordre public* and morality; the EU in the past has used that
wording as the basis on which to reject a patent application for a higher
animal. The treatment of the term plant variety has been quite complex in
the EU over a period of more than a decade. A recent Directive (No. 9,
February 1998) establishes a variety as a fixed form and non-patentable;
conversely, an improvement which can be applied to multiple varieties is
patentable.

As of late 1998, 38 countries were members of UPOV, the international
association for PBR. Of those, but eight are developing nations.[4] Membership
is anticipated to reach 50–80 by 2000.

Trade-related Aspects of IPR

As a consequence of this limited protection, defined both geographically and in terms of patent scope, the Uruguay Round of the GATT characterized limited IPR as a trade barrier. Signatory nations were committed to adopt specified minimum levels of IPR protection by 2000, or 5 additional years for the least developed nations. An additional 5 years is permitted for the extension of protection to areas of technology not previously protected (Article 65). As applied to agriculture, the relevant aspects of TRIPs are as follows (MTN/FA II-A1C):

- Subject to the exclusions identified below, patents shall be available for any invention, in all fields of technology (Section 5, Article 27(1)).
- Contracting parties shall provide for the protection of plant varieties by patents and/or by an effective *sui generis* system (Section 5, Article 27(3b)).
- Patents may be prohibited to protect *ordre public* or morality, provided there is a justification exceeding the mere prohibition in domestic law (Section 5, Article 27(2)).
- Plants and animals other than microorganisms and 'essentially biological processes for the production of plants and animals' may be excluded from protection (Section 5, Article 27(3b)).
- Compulsory licences may be issued in limited cases of due diligence to make a licensing agreement, adequate remuneration and subject to judicial review (Section 5, Articles 30 and 31).
- For process patents, the burden of proof of infringement may in some specified circumstances be shifted to the defendant to prove that the patented process was not used (Section 5, Article 34).
- Persons shall have the option of preventing others from using without permission information of commercial value so long as reasonable efforts have been made to keep it secret (Section 7, Article 39).

Countries generally have been selecting the *sui generis* option over patents for plants. While *sui generis* (literally, unique) is nowhere defined in TRIPs, it has generally been interpreted to include three major options (Leskien and Flitner, 1997; Seiler, 1998):

1. Join UPOV, the international convention of PBR.
2. Adopt UPOV-like terminology but as national law.
3. Develop a new national law.

To date, most countries have been electing to join UPOV. Membership allows for reciprocal rights in other Member States.

The final point (Article 39) is a commitment for national trade secret protection, for which there is no international convention. Trade secrets provide a legal basis for recovering damages for information improperly acquired.

Perhaps though, the complex requirements of TRIPs are in regards to maintaining competition and judicial reform. Maintaining competition can be partitioned into the granting of compulsory licences and the prohibition of unfair competition. Unfair competition (Articles 17, 22-24 and 39) is, however, addressed principally through the endorsement of trade secret legislation. Compulsory licences (Articles 30 and 31) are more complex in treatment and dependent on and to be interpreted in conjunction with the relevant parts of the Paris Convention (Articles 5 and 10; see Heinemann, 1996; Reichman, 1993; Straus, 1996). 'Members may provide limited exceptions to the exclusive rights conferred, subject to conditions of individual merits of requests, substantial efforts to achieve agreement with the owner, non-exclusivity and subject to judicial review. When the request applies to dependent patents, the request must be for, an important technical advance of considerable economic significance.'

Countries, particularly the number lacking antitrust legislation, have justifiable concerns over the undue extension of IPR monopoly power, yet the functioning of remedial steps, particularly the use of compulsory licences, is poorly documented in recent years. Significant prior work dates to UNCTAD in the 1970s (see Roffe, 1974; UNCTAD, 1975). Yet other recent examples exist; the recent Community Directive on the protection of biotechnological inventions provides for the grant of a compulsory cross-licence conditional on the showing of due effort to secure a licence voluntarily and the stature of the invention as constituting significant technical progress of considerable economic interest. Under TRIPs, these specifications are voluntary on the part of the adopting country (Article 30, TRIPs reads, in part, 'Countries may provide').

Judicial reform provides perhaps the most substantive task for countries. The study of the history of PBR in Argentina documented well, if there was any question, that enforceability and remedies were essential to a functioning system (see Jaffé and van Wijk, 1995). Many countries would not appear to have such a judicial system in place, whether it be due to insufficient capacity with resulting backlogs, lack of technical competence in these complex matters, or a system where decisions are not based on merit. Some observers have proposed a specialized court for addressing IPR matters (e.g. Sherwood, 1990), a model which has worked well in the USA. But that does not resolve the fundamental issue in some countries of a corrupt legal system.

A TRIPs-based IPR system retains other limitations regarding the protection of biotechnology-based plant improvements. PBR is insufficient to protect plants with genetically engineered genes for the focus is on the protection of the propagating material, extended to the entire plant and parts of plants when obtained through unauthorized use (UPOV 1991 Act, Article 14). Individual genes, however, can be removed and inserted in other varieties without violating PBR and without falling within the scope of the original grant. Unless plant patents are mandated in the scheduled 1999 TRIPs review, agricultural biotechnology is left without effective protection. Alternatively, patents on gene constructs combined with PBR protection will provide extensive protection for the inventor (see Lesser, 1998). However, most national laws are silent on the patentability of genes so that their eligibility is indeterminate until a grant has been made. Under many national systems, that can be a protracted process.

Protection of Genetic Resources

Use of IPR

The CBD with its designation of genetic resources lying within the 'sovereign rights of States' has raised a number of questions regarding the mechanism by which that 'right' may be implemented. Some have suggested that the mere reference in the Convention prohibits the removal of genetic resources without prior informed consent. That interpretation has, however, been judged to be incorrect, and positive steps are required for securing control and compensation (FAO, 1995, App. 3). Indeed, the CBD refers in each of the articles pertinent to the discussion here the need for action by 'each Contracting Party'.

An obvious approach is the use of current IPR systems for genetic resources. That, however, would seem to be applicable only in special instances. The argument needs to be traced separately for PBR and patents, as follows.

Use of PBR
UPOV-style PBR, which dominate in terms of systems currently in place, are intended for commercialized plants only. This is most evident from the Preamble of the 1961 Act, which justifies the Convention as 'the protection of new varieties of plants … for the development of agriculture'. Thus uncultivated materials, as well as other forms of living materials would seem not to be applicable. Even under the most recent Act of 1991 which does not contain the Preamble, rights are granted to a breeder as the person who bred, or discovered and developed, a variety (Article 1(iv)). Varieties must exhibit uniformity and stability (Article 9), which uncultivated plants and even many landraces do not do in this technical sense. Hence, PBR at the extreme would seem to apply to only a small portion of genetic resources.

Lest the requirement of stability and uniformity seem incidental to the PBR system, and thus possibly subject to modification, it should be recognized that a system is unenforceable if it is not possible to identify and distinguish the protected materials. Stability and uniformity contribute to that identification process by helping assure the materials retain their identity across multiple generations. Moreover, stability and uniformity are a commercial requirement for many cultivated products, and hence an appropriate requirement for materials intended for commercial cultivation.

Use of Patents

The applicability of patents is more complex to identify, for (with the exception of the limitation identified above) all subject areas are potentially patentable once the TRIPs requirements are fully implemented. Yet to be patentable, inventions must exhibit novelty, non-obviousness (inventive step) and industrial application (utility). The final, pertinent requirement here is not to be interpreted literally to mean industry as opposed to agriculture. Nor does it imply usefulness in the sense of being economically efficient compared with available substitutes. What it does imply is that some application, some use, has been identified; mere existence is insufficient for the award of a patent. This means in simple terms that a product identified from the wild but lacking an identified use is not eligible for a patent.

At a more pragmatic level is the issue of cost. Biotechnology patent applications in the USA cost in the range of $12,000–25,000, the majority for attorney fees, and $100,000+ for all industrialized countries. Then there is the issue of identifying what has been protected. Genetic fingerprinting is technically possible, but costs on the order of $170 per accession, and 10–20 times that for non-heterogeneous species (Lesser, 1997b). On several levels then, patents are inapplicable for large quantities of genetic resources of no known use and value.

Access Legislation

For extending control over the bulk of a country's genetic resources, nations will require some form of access legislation. Legislation may take several forms, either generic to all resources or composites of multiple laws each with specific authority, and be enacted as law or promulgated as an executive order. The general form in all cases is through the prohibition of removing materials from a country without prior informed consent, incorporating benefit sharing when required (UNEP/CBD/COP/4/23, February 1998).

Any legislation needs to take into account several factors, including: (i) scope – what materials are to be included; (ii) designation of a responsible authority serving as a contact point for inquiries, acceptance of required information, and (critically) with the authority to grant a permit; (iii) consideration of indigenous/traditional rights; and (iv) operationalization of prior informed consent.

Here I shall proceed as if a range of materials are to be protected, while recognizing that the identification of each class of materials is a complex task. One contentious component is the ownership of derivative materials, as is claimed under the Andean Pact legislation, among others (see below). Property rights regimes typically recognize some scope beyond direct copying, but the limits are typically identified through case law as opposed to definition. The claiming of rights to all derivatives, including those for which there was considerable additional input, could provide a significant disincentive to developing genetic resources.

Secondary to the scope matter is the possible designation of two classes of permits, those intended for research and those for commercial purposes. The Philippines regulations (see below) contain such a distinction, but only Philippine institutions qualify for research permits. Research permits generally are subject to less-demanding application and disclosure requirements. The prior informed consent mandates can be quite different.

Elsewhere (Lesser, 1998, chap. 5) I argue that the scientist seeking a research permit has a different level of responsibility to the country and community than would be the case for a commercial permit. The granting of a commercial permit places the two parties in the traditional adversarial position so that the licensor must be responsible for substantiating its own negotiating position by amassing information on possible value. The notion that the would-be licensor must be required to provide detailed information on value, information which may weaken the bargaining position, runs counter to commercial practice and is unrealistic. For research permits, however, the supplier may receive no material benefits, and may possibly incur some costs, so the licensor has elevated responsibilities for disclosure. Research permits, of course, should contain a clause requiring a commercialization side agreement be established should a commercial product inadvertently be discovered. Lesser and Krattiger (1994) have proposed the establishment of a voluntary, fee-based facilitator which could assist countries/communities with information on standard contract terms, and, on request, with negotiations.

The designation of an entity with the authority to issue a permit is of critical importance to the operationalization of legislation. Without it, an acquiring firm or institution, no matter how diligent, is vulnerable to charges that it operated improperly. Yet much legislation grants broad authority to contest an agreement, but sometimes none to declare all requirements satisfactorily completed.

An aspect of the permit-granting process is the determination of the parties from whom consent is required. This is particularly true when local communities are involved. The Philippines regulations stipulate consent of local communities in accordance with traditional law when materials are collected from ancestral lands (see below). This can be a complex issue for foreign entities in particular to satisfy, so that some national guidance is required in identifying and securing the necessary consent. One approach which can be used for non-literate communities, particularly for research agreements, is to ask the responsible officials to repeat in their own words the consequences as explained to them (see Lesser, 1998, chap. 5). Some impartial body may be required to designate the satisfaction of informed consent requirements.

Indigenous and traditional rights interact with while retaining some distinction from access issues. A principal distinction is the community rights over the genetic materials themselves; some countries appear to grant ownership of the materials with property rights while others (including the Andean Pact nations) reserve ownership rights for the state. Similar national differences are seen with mineral and energy resources. Yet few dispute that the local/indigenous community owns the rights to its knowledge, which can have value in, for example, identifying promising specimens, allowing a more focused search process. Yet knowledge unembodied in a designated form is particularly difficult to protect and reward. It is especially so when the source of the information is unclear.

I (Lesser, 1998, chap. 7) have previously proposed that an indigenous rights system be based on information revealed in a volume, with source and contact information. That information would serve to 'reserve' the community claim; compendiums could incorporate multiple countries but some priority of rights – say the first to reveal gains the rights – would be needed to prevent overlapping claims. Parties interested in access under legislation could then be required to satisfy groups identified in the volume as part of the informed consent requirement of the access legislation. The CBD recognizes a related distinction between the ownership of the genetic materials proper and the informational value (UNEP/CBD/COP/4/23, February 1998, para 38).

Current Status of Access Legislation

At the time of writing, only six countries had adopted broad access legislation, as follows (UNEP/CBD/COP/4/23, February 1998): Philippines; Andean Pact nations, including Colombia, Peru, Ecuador, Venezuela and Bolivia of which to date only Ecuador and Bolivia have adopted the requisite legislation into national law; Costa Rica; Brazil; and India. The USA provides an interesting counterpoint for while it lacks comprehensive legislation it does permit a national park (Yellowstone) to benefit from any products derived from materials found there. Legislation covering that and other non-encompassing claims to genetic resources are reviewed in Lesser (1998, chap. 3). Box 3.1 contains an overview of existing legislation.

Additionally, there must be some mechanism in recipient countries for prosecuting those who flaunt the law and acquire materials illegally. The CBD (UNEP/CBD/COP/4/23, para 64) recommends special legislation, possibly along the lines of the Basel Convention on the Control of Transboundary Movements of Hazardous Wastes which prohibits importation from non-member states. That position, however, is possibly in contradistinction to the WTO and its non-discrimination requirements. Perhaps a simpler approach is the requirement of an export permit; recipient countries can prevent entry of materials lacking the necessary documentation. Once inside a country, it can be difficult to prove ownership of materials improperly acquired.

Box 3.1. Synopsis of current access legislation for genetic resources.

Philippines (May 1995)
Scope: genetic resources and parts thereof, extracts taken from or modified from a product *in* and *ex situ.*
Forms: academic (Philippine entities only), commercial.
Agreement: Philippine government and concerned communities.
PIC: within ancestral lands requires prior informed consent of communities, in accordance with customary laws (government agencies to enforce).
Benefit Sharing: deposit samples, access to Philippine citizens, for endemic species royalty-free use allowed.
Focal Point: Inter-Agency Committee on Biological and Genetic Resources.

Costa Rica (December 1992)
Scope: wild plants and animals collected in Conservation Areas.
Forms: single permit.
Agreement: permit from the Ministry of Natural Resources.
PIC: permit.
Benefit Sharing: based on agreement with INBio and its licensing arrangements.
Focal Point: Ministry of Natural Resources.

Andean Pact (July 1996)
Scope: any biological material with genetic information plus derivatives and intangible components, *in* and *ex situ.*
Forms: no distinction as to type.
Agreement: two-tiered government, and private/commercial.
PIC: to be detailed in national legislation.
Benefit Sharing: two-tiered permit required, one from national government and one from local community. National government first mandates certain benefits; local communities negotiate over residual.
Focal Point: identified nationally.

PIC, prior informed consent.

Farmers' Rights and Materials Held ex situ

The term 'Farmers' Rights' arose from the FAO's Revised Undertaking for Genetic Resources (Resolution 5/89) where they were defined as 'rights arising from the past, present and future contributions of farmers in conserving, improving, and making available plant genetic resources'. In 1991, an international fund was established for implementing Farmers' Rights, but has yet to receive any substantive contributions (Resolution 3/91, Annex 3).

At present, the major debate is in regards to materials held *ex situ* and collected prior to December 1993 when the Convention came into force. Under Article 15(3), those materials are not subject to the Convention, but are a focus of the Nairobi Final Act which in Resolution 3(4) calls for a solution to access to *ex situ* materials not collected in accordance with the Convention, and the question of Farmers' Rights. The Nairobi Final Act can be considered as a kind of preface to the CBD which contains some moral if not legal commitments which could not be resolved within the time-frame for negotiating the Convention. FAO Resolution 4/89 recognized PBR, which Barton and Siebeck (1994) interpreted as the *quid pro quo* for the recognition of Farmers' Rights. Resolution 3/91 dropped the concept of plant genetic resources as being a world resource in favour of national sovereignty over their disposition. Farmers' Rights have been discussed at every Conference of the Parties of the CBD to date, but with no consensus on how to proceed.

Complicating the discussions is the multiple interpretations of Farmers' Rights; Collins and Petit (1998, p. 8) define it variously as 'a farmer's rights to replant, save, exchange and/or sell protected seeds, as well as the potential availability of legal mechanisms to protect farmers' traditional varieties'. The initial portion is in partial conflict with UPOV which grants farmers rights to save and replant seeds (optionally under the 1991 Act) but not to sell or exchange them. To prevent confusion, those rights are sometimes referred to as farmers' privilege. The US Plant Variety Protection Act of 1980 did allow farmers the rights to sell protected seed on a limited basis and not by variety name, but the process was subject to frequent abuses and the privilege was not extended in the revised Act of 1993 (which adopted the text of the 1991 UPOV Act). It seems highly unlikely any seed sale privilege will be permitted in the future.

Certainly there is the potential of legal mechanisms for protecting Farmers' Rights to traditional varieties, but something more than PBR will be required. In a parallel fashion to the discussion of the general inapplicability of PBR to wild materials, traditional varieties also typically lack the stability and uniformity to qualify for PBR. Hence, some new system would seem to be required. But even that would not resolve the situation for the bulk of materials collected prior to December 1993.

From my personal perspective, Farmers' Rights are miscast when described as even quasi-IPR. IPR provide specific market success-based incentives for commercialization of products and processes. Farmers' Rights is more of a moral commitment – a compensation for 'past and present' conservation and development not directly associated with the market value for each contribution. The Rights do recognize 'future' contributions as well, but again not in terms of individual, market rewards. This is not to say the contributions made by traditional farmers past and present are not real and the concept of compensation is misdirected, but rather that what is implied is quite different from traditional IPR.

India in drafts of a national PBR system (see Damania, 1996) recognizes Farmers' Rights internally with a proposed tax on seed sales, with proceeds to be directed to source communities when identified, otherwise to conservation. While commendable, this is in effect a national tax and a far cry from the initial concept of the 'North' compensating the 'South' for the use of genetic resources. At this stage it is difficult to imagine a voluntary system for compensation for materials used in the past. Conversely, the use value of most accessions (the average accession) is estimated to be small and the transaction costs high so that raising significant sums through sale is also unlikely (see Perrings, 1995; Lesser, 1997b). Moreover, the vast bulk of requests for materials comes from national programmes in developing countries. Available data indicate the private sector requests few accessions so there is not much of a paying base from which to generate funds even if a system could be implemented.

My own recommendation is to emphasize value-added activities through the characterization of materials held in public collections. Much of such materials have little more than passport (e.g. location and date of collection) data attached meaning it has little immediate use in breeding programmes. A broad evaluation programme would add value, which could be sold separately from the genetic materials themselves, and generate more use for the current collections. Selling characterization information raises some issues in its own right, which I explore more thoroughly in Lesser (1998, chap. 6).

Where to Go from Here

The Biodiversity Convention has in the 7 years since its introduction raised a number of complex questions, as well as expectations of a range of stakeholders from indigenous peoples to conservation NGOs. Central to many of them are matters of value, access and compensation. Overlapping are issues of intellectual property rights, both as currently operationalized and as exist in the imaginations of observers. Four Conferences of the Parties of the CBD appear to have made little progress in reaching consensus on these matters, and frustration seems to be increasing.

As economists, our role in the often-political matters is limited, but there are contributions which only we can make. By my accounts, the five major ones are as follows:

1. Develop a theoretical explanation for the roles of IPR in technology transfer.
2. Extend empirical studies of the roles of IPR in technology transfer.
3. Develop studies, including case studies, of the effects of strengthening IPR in accordance with TRIPs, and the strategic IPR requirements of firms for the transfer of sensitive products and technologies.
4. Evaluate the uses and effects of compulsory licences.
5. Continue to estimate the use value of genetic resources.

Notes

1. A biosafety protocol was scheduled for adoption by the Parties in February 1999 – see UNEP/CBD/COP/4/9 and Decision IV/3. Actual adoption did not occur until 2000.

2. Daily reports on the meeting are provided by the Earth Negotiations Bulletin at www.biodiv.org.
3. Examples of foreign to domestic patent grants for 1995: Algeria, 100%; Argentina, 79%; Brazil, 80%; Canada, 92%; Cuba, 19%; Denmark, 97%; Japan, 13%; USA, 45%. *Source:* WIPO, Ind. Property Statistics, Part A.
4. The seven are: Argentina, Chile, Colombia, Ecuador, Paraguay, South Africa, Trinidad and Tobago, and Uruguay.

References

Barton, J.H. and Siebeck, W.E. (1994) *Material Transfer Agreements in Genetic Resource Exchange – the Case of the International Agricultural Research Centers. Issues in Genetic Resources No. 1.* IPGRI, Rome.

Collins, W. and Petit, M. (1998) *Strategic Issues for National Policy Decisions in Managing Genetic Resources.* ESDAR Special Report No. 4. World Bank, Washington, DC.

Damania, A.B. (1996) Swaminathan Foundation holds technical consultation to develop framework for Farmers Rights in India. *Diversity* 12, 6–8.

Deolalikar, A.B. and Evenson, R.E. (1990) Private inventive activity in Indian manufacturing: its extent and determinants. In: Evenson, R.E. and Rains, G. (eds), *Science and Technology: Lessons for Development Policy.* Westview Press, Boulder, Colorado, chapter 10.

Evenson, R.E. (1988) Technological opportunities and international technology transfer in agriculture. In: Antonelli, G. and Quadrio-Curzio, A. (eds), *The Agro-Technological System Towards 2000.* Elsevier Science Publishers, New York, chapter 7.

FAO, Commission on Plant Genetic Resources (1995) *Revision of the International Undertaking on Plant Genetic Resources – Analysis of Some Technical, Economic and Legal Aspects for Consideration in Stage II: Access to Plant Genetic Resources and Farmers Rights.* CPGR-6/95/8 Supplement, June.

Heinemann, A. (1996) Antitrust law of intellectual property in the TRIPs agreement of the World Trade Organization. In: Beier, F.-K. and Schricker, G. (eds), *From GATT to TRIPs – An Agreement on Trade-related Aspects of Intellectual Property Rights.* VCH, Weinheim, Vol. 18, pp. 239–247.

Helpman, E. (1993) Innovation, imitation and intellectual property rights. *Econometrica* 61, 1247–1280.

Henderson, D.R., Voros, P.R. and Hirschberg, J. (1996) Industrial determinants of international trade and foreign direct investments by food and beverage manufacturing firms. In: Sheldon, I.M. and Abbott, P.C. (eds), *Industrial Organization and Trade in Food Industries.* Westview Press, Boulder, Colorado, pp. 197–215.

Jaffé, W. and van Wijk, J. (1995) *The Impact of Plant Breeders' Rights in Developing Countries.* University of Amsterdam, Amsterdam.

Leskien, D. and Flitner, M. (1997) *Intellectual Property Rights and Plant Genetic Resources: Options for a Sui Generis System. Issues in Genetic Resources No. 6.* IPGRI, Rome.

Lesser, W. (1998) *Sustainable Use of Genetic Resources Under the Convention on Biological Diversity: Exploring Access and Benefit Sharing Issues.* CAB International, Wallingford.

Lesser, W. (1997a) Assessing the implications of IPR on plant and animal agriculture. *AJAE* 79, 1584–1591.

Lesser, W. (1997b) Estimating cost components for distributing genetic materials held *ex situ*. *Ass. Systematics Collections Newsletter* 25, 35–40.

Lesser, W.H. and Krattiger, A.F. (1994) Marketing genetic technologies in South–North and South–South exchanges: the proposed role of a new facilitating organization. In: Krattiger, A.F., McNeely, J.A., Lesser, W.H., Miller, K.R., St Hill, Y. and Senanayake, R. (eds), *Widening Perspectives in Biodiversity*. International Academy of the Environment and World Conservation Union, Geneva.

Maclup, F. (1958) An economic review of the patent system. Study of the Subcommittee on Patents, Trademarks and Copyright, Committee on the Judiciary, US Senate, Study No. 15.

Mansfield, E. (1995) *Intellectual Property Protection, Direct Investment, and Technology Transfer: Germany, Japan and the United States*. Discussion Paper No. 27, September. International Finance Corporation, Washington DC.

Nogues, J. (1990) *Patents and Pharmaceutical Drugs: Understanding the Pressures on Developing Countries*. WPS 502, September. World Bank, Washington DC.

Office of the United States Trade Representative (1986) Administration statement on the protection of U.S. intellectual property rights abroad. 3 April. Washington DC.

Perrings, C. (1995) Economic values of biodiversity. In: Heywood, V.H. (ed.), *Global Diversity Assessment*. Cambridge University Press, Cambridge, Chap. 12.

Primo Braga, C.A. (1995) Trade-related intellectual property issues: the Uruguay Round agreement and its economic implications. In: Martin, W. and Winters, L.A. (eds), *The Uruguay Round and the Developing Economies*. Discussion Paper No. 307. World Bank, Washington DC.

Primo Braga, C.A., Fink, C. and Sepulveda, C.P. (1998) *Intellectual Property Rights and Economic Development*. Background paper to the World Development Report. World Bank, Washington DC.

Reichman, J.H. (1993) The TRIPs component of the GATT's Uruguay Round: competitive prospects for intellectual property owners in an integrated world market. *Fordham Intellectual Property, Media and Entertainment Law Journal* 4, 171–266.

Roffe, P. (1974) Abuses of patent monopoly: a legal appraisal. *World Development* 2, 15–26.

Seiler, A. (1998) *Sui generis* systems: obligations and options for developing countries. *Biotechnology and Development Monitor* 34, 3–5.

Sherwood, R.M. (1990) *Intellectual Property and Economic Development*. Westview Press, Boulder, Colorado.

Stern, R. (1987) Intellectual property. In: Finger, J.M. and Olechowski, A. (eds), *The Uruguay Round: A Handbook on the Multilateral Trade Negotiations*. World Bank, Washington DC, Chap. 25.

Straus, J. (1996) Implications of the TRIPs agreement in the field of patent law. In: Beier, F.-K. and Schricker, G. (eds), *From GATT to TRIPs – An Agreement on Trade-related Aspects of Intellectual Property Rights*. VCH, Weinheim, Vol. 18, pp. 160–215.

UNCTAD (United Nations Conference on Trade and Development) (1975) The role of the patent system in the transfer of technology to developing countries. TD/B/AC.11/19/Rev. 1.

UNEP (United Nations Environment Programme) Convention on Biological Diversity, 'Review of National, Regional and Sectoral Measures and Guidelines for the Implementation of Article 15'. UNEP/CBD/COP/4/23, 19 Feb. 1998.

WIPO (World Intellectual Property Organization) (1990) Exclusions from patent protection. WIPO, HL/CM/INF/1 Rev., May.

An Economic Approach to Identifying an 'Effective *sui generis* System' for Plant Variety Protection Under TRIPs[*]

W. Lesser

Department of Agricultural, Resource & Managerial Economics, 405 Warren Hall, Cornell University, Ithaca, New York, USA

The US Patent Act of 1790 is often thought of as the first of the 'modern' patent systems. It, along with the slightly later acts of France (1791) and subsequently Germany's unified law (1877) among others, have over the ensuing 200 plus years shaped an intellectual property rights (IPR) system which is carefully crafted to strike a balance between public costs and benefits (see, e.g., Dam, 1994). For sure, there remains much to do to make the balance optimal for little is known about the detailed functions of IP law and its consequences both domestic and international. The systems will continue to evolve to accommodate new needs and technologies, such as in recent years, biotechnology; and there has been acknowledgement of major errors, as in the USA, the issuing of the 1895 Selden patents for the engine, transmission and differential configuration for motor cars (see Allen, 1990) and possibly the granting of rights for all transgenic cotton. Another example is the conundrum of the European Patent Convention's (EPC) Article 53(b) wording, 'plant and animal varieties and essentially biological processes for the production of plants and animals' – whatever that may mean.

With a number of issues, well-argued matters have been raised about system operation. Deardorff (1992), for example, raises questions about the benefits of patent systems to developing countries with limited technological competence. Others have been less analytical and more vociferous in their critiques, particularly as applies to developing countries (see, e.g., Nijar and Ling, 1994); but overall the system is a carefully crafted one with numer-

[*]An earlier version of this paper was presented at the UPOV-WIPO-WTO Joint Symposium, 'The Protection of Plant Varieties under Article 27.3(b) of the TRIPS Agreement'. Geneva, 15 February 1999.

ous checks and balances. For that reason it provides an appropriate model for developing countries which by the end of 1999 are committed under the trade-related aspects of intellectual property rights (TRIPs) appendix to the World Trade Organization (WTO) agreement to adopt a form of IP protection for plants.[1] A choice may be made among patents or Plant Breeders' Rights (PBR), or both (Article 27.3(b)), but most countries are selecting the PBR option. However, the complete direction accorded to countries is the option of 'an effective *sui generis* system' for the protection of plant varieties.

Now, the meaning of *sui generis* is evident – it refers to a special purpose system; hence, my shorthand use of PBR. Regrettably though, just what is meant by 'effective' and 'plant variety' is anything but clear. Here, I do not attempt the definition of plant variety[2] but do attempt to construct an 'effective', in an economic context, PBR system which parallels patent systems, making due adjustments for biological and institutional differences between the classes of products. I focus particularly on the kinds of checks and balances in patent legislation to understand their possible roles in PBR systems. A PBR system which parallels the checks and balances of major patent systems is for the purposes of this paper considered to be 'effective' within the TRIPs context. From an economic perspective, the next step is identifying what makes a system efficient as well as effective in terms of achieving its objectives.

The next section presents in a general way the components of the checks and balances of patent systems, while the following section 'constructs' a PBR system structured on the patent system while making adjustments for the technical and institutional differences between the two. This section also examines the requirements of the International Convention for the Protection of New Varieties of Plants (UPOV), the only existing international *sui generis* system for the protection of plant materials, for its concurrence with the identified 'effective' system. The final section also considers what is known about the 'effectiveness' of that constructed system and makes proposals for a system which is both effective and efficient.

Checks and Balances of Patent Systems

The purpose of patent systems is to provide an incentive for investment in inventive activities and to enhance technology transfer.[3] Hence, patent systems provide the inventor or successor-in-title a limited period to exploit the invention free from direct copying. That is the benefit to the inventor – a negative one for sure, as it allows only the right to prevent others from practising the invention without permission. In exchange, society receives additional investment in inventive activities plus the revealing of the practice of the invention through the disclosure requirement. The outcome, however, is economically inefficient, for placing a charge on new inventions slows their dissemination compared to the economically efficient zero marginal cost solution (see Carlton and Perloff, 1994, chap. 17).

In order to limit the monopoly grant offered, patent law and practice restrict the scope and breadth of the grant in multiple ways. These may be grouped into (i) patentability requirements and (ii) rights and limitations of the patent holder. Here these components will be reviewed in brief, then compared to a possible *sui generis* system for plant varieties.

Patentability Requirements

Essentially all patent law requires that patentability inventions satisfy the novelty, inventive step (non-obviousness under US law), utility and disclosure requirements. General requirements are specified below, with the reader directed to national law for specific mandates.

Novelty
An invention must be new so that society is not providing privileges for materials already in the public domain. Some systems specify absolute novelty (no prior disclosure, e.g. EPC) while others allow up to one year following initial public announcement (e.g. USA). Detailed stipulations specify the exact terms and conditions under which a patent is judged to be revealed for novelty purposes.

Inventive Step
An invention must encompass more than an obvious extension of what was previously known. Combined with novelty, inventive step (non-obviousness under the US system) determines the scope of a patent grant. Scope defines the degree of differentness which is required for a related non-infringing invention – the 'doctrine of equivalents' in patent terminology.

Utility
Utility requirements specify that a use for the invention must be identified. The use need not be economically viable in any way – a worse mouse trap is just as patentable as a better one – but it must function as described. Depending on the type of patent granted – *per se* use; product-by-process; process – as defined by the patent claims, additional uses may or may not be covered under the patent grant.

Disclosure
A patentable invention must be disclosed fully and completely, whereas with life forms if a written disclosure is judged inadequate by the patent examiner, a deposit of the material may be required (see Straus and Moufang, 1990). The decision criterion is if the disclosure is 'enabling', that is, if it allows for a relatively direct re-creation of the invention. If the description is overly

general, or the re-creation requires a protracted trial and error process – undue experimentation in patent terminology – then the deposit is mandated (unless the material is presently and openly available from other sources). Under US law, the 'best method' of practising the invention must be disclosed. Other systems allow the disclosure of a less efficient but still workable method.

Patent disclosures serve multiple functions, the revealing of the invention, the provision of information which allows the invention to be duplicated on patent expiration, and a contribution to the 'storehouse' of technical information which the patent system provides. Indeed, full disclosure to a large degree separates patents from trade secrets, which are perpetual as long as the information remains secret.

Duration
All patent laws provide a point when rights expire. Under the TRIPs agreements (Article 33), that period is being standardized as 20 years from date of first filing.

Rights and Limitations of the Patent Holder

Many of the factors which determine the effective scope of protection lie outside the formal patentability requirements. The more significant of those, summarized here, include the research exemption, exhaustion of rights, and compulsory licences and related antitrust applications, as well as general factors involved with determining patent scope and reciprocal rights in other countries.

Research Exemption
The research exemption delineates the ways and forms of research which can be done on patented products and processes. As the exemption is based on the case law in most systems, it is often difficult to characterize in detail. Within the US system, reference is often made to Roche Products v. Bolar Pharmaceutical Co. which established the principle that only 'idle curiosity' is protected by the exemption. From that decision, a narrow exemption is often inferred. However, Roche was not dicta as regards the broader interpretation of the experimental use exemption (i.e. was not part of the case so the decision does not set precedent) as regards research use, so that the actual latitude is likely greater (see Bent, 1989). Goldstein (1985), for example, distinguishes between research *with* a patented product (generally disallowed) and research *on* one (often permitted).

A broad research exemption expedites the process of incremental improvements whereas a narrow exemption effectively extends the scope of protection around an invention. Despite the allegedly narrow US research exemption, studies have shown that many inventions have been 'invented around' (see, e.g., Harabi, 1995).

Exhaustion of Rights

The exhaustion of rights refers to the point at which the rights of the patent holder are terminated. In general, this occurs at point-of-first-sale, for with the exchange goes an implied right to use the invention as intended. It makes little sense to purchase, say, a cream separator if the sale does not confer the right to actually use the device for the separation of cream.

Several caveats need to be added to this general principle. First, additional rights or grants of permission may be required for use, particularly of more complex process inventions. Second is the issue of the resale rights of the purchaser, particularly as regards the right to export to a third country. Most laws are silent on such 'grey market' exports, while TRIPs Article 6 also allows full national discretion on this matter. In general, permitting international exhaustion of rights allows arbitrage to keep prices in line transnationally. Conversely, not permitting patent owners to maximize revenues through any price discrimination encourages a uniform price policy world-wide, which as a general matter could raise prices or reduce availability for developing countries.

Compulsory Licences and Antitrust Applications

All patent systems have a means of granting a patent licence without the consent of the patent owner, a system known as compulsory licensing. Terms and requirements for these licences vary considerably across countries. The USA, for example, grants licences only to the government and only for matters of national security (Patent Act, Sections 181 and 183). In Canada, grounds are broader, including non-national use on a commercial scale after 3 years with no adequate justification given, or if demand in Canada is not being met to an adequate extent. Under these circumstances, a compulsory licence may be granted (Sections 65 and 66). (In Canada, special conditions apply to food and pharmaceuticals.) Most developing countries have requirements closer to those of Canada than to those of the USA, with maximum permitted terms based on the Paris Convention of 1883 (Article 5).

TRIPs allows specific rights to limit the extent of a patent grant, including the option to provide 'limited exceptions' to the rights conferred by patents (Article 30) and including the granting of compulsory cross licences (Article 31). The grounds for granting compulsory licences are quite broad. They are limited primarily in procedural terms by the requirement to negotiate first in good faith with the patent owner, to be evaluated on individual merits, to be non-exclusive and non-assignable, and to provide for equitable remuneration for the patent owner. In the case of a cross licence for the dependent patent, which cannot be exploited without infringing the rights of the first, a patent may be granted when: '(i) the invention claimed in the second patent shall involve an important technical advance...' (Article 31(l)). Patent revocation must be subject to judicial review (Article 32).

The effects of compulsory licences are very uncertain. The most recent thorough review of applications dates to the 1970s during a period of quite different attitudes toward technology transfer (UNCTAD, 1975). The review indicated very limited grants of compulsory licences, which some have taken as an indication of their ineffectiveness. Just as plausibly, the mere threat of the granting of licences could be curbing much opportunistic behaviour, voiding much of the need for actual licence grants.

Compulsory licensing provisions tend to be broader in developing countries than in industrialized countries. This appears to be the case, in part, because smaller economies are understandably concerned about the economic power of multinational firms, yet many such countries lack the legislation and legal processes for administering antitrust law. Thus, they rely on compulsory licences to curb some possible applications of excessive market power. The USA is again towards the extreme with a broad body of antitrust legislation, so that it is instructive to know if any relief from delays would be forthcoming from that source.

Antitrust issues related to patents can, and have been, brought under both the Sherman and Clayton Acts (especially Section 3). In general, what has been found illegal is the use of patents as a mechanism for price fixing, or the treatment of a patented product as a tying good. Receiving particular scrutiny is the patent pool – if it can be construed that the pool was structured primarily to limit horizontal competition. Similarly, patents may not be used to mandate retail price maintenance or otherwise impede vertical competition if the intent of the actions was to limit competition. While the underlying decisions were reached in the context of cases involving patents, the offence is the conduct of limiting competition, not the existence of patents *per se*. Thus, the same decisions could apply to the use of Material Transfer Agreements (MTAs) and other contractual arrangements. Indeed, the only decisions which specifically require patents in their case development are those which forbid the continuation of royalty payments following a patent's expiration.

The position of the Department of Justice as regards licensing of IP was codified in 1995 in the Antitrust Division's *Antitrust Guidelines for the Licensing of Intellectual Property*. Those Guidelines recognize 'the principle that "antitrust concerns may arise when a licensing arrangement harms competition among entities that would have been actual or likely potential competitors in a relevant market in the absence of the licence"'. As research and development (R&D) is a scarce factor, the Guidelines recognize the potential for harm from licence-based restraints which could reduce competition from related inventive activity and the integration of complementary research. Nonetheless, recognizing that antitrust applications in that area are according to the Rule of Reason, a 'safety zone' has been established, under which, excluding extraordinary cases, action will not be taken for non-exclusive licences if:

1. licence restraints are not of the type typically found to be *per se* violations of antitrust laws; and
2. the aggregate market share of the licensor and licensee does not exceed 20% of each relevant market affected by the restraint.

As a general matter, non-exclusive licences will rarely result in antitrust action.

What of exclusive licences if utilized within a concentrated market? The Antitrust Division defines exclusivity according to its character. There is no presumption of exclusivity 'merely because a party chooses to deal with a single licensee or licensor, or confines his activities to a single field of use or location, or because only a single licensee has been chosen to take a licence'.

Thus the Guidelines reflect the prevailing view at the Justice Department that vertical licences, such as the type considered here, seldom have the capacity to harm competition. Even when there is evidence of vertical restraints, such as the practice of tying, the terms will be challenged under the Guidelines only if:

1. the seller has market power in the tying good;
2. the arrangement has an adverse effect on competition in the market for the tied good; and
3. the anticompetitive effects are not outweighed by the efficiency justifications.

Overall, it is as difficult to prevail with an antitrust action which *mandates* licensing. For sure, some antitrust cases have been resolved by requiring licensing,[4] but in general if the argument is for enhancing the public good, the vehicle is compulsory licences, not antitrust law.

Patent Scope
Formally, scope is determined by the patent claims in combination with novelty. In practice, patent scope is an outcome of patent office practice and negotiations between the applicant and examiner. Perhaps the most relevant practice for purposes here is that of placing the burden of proof for the exclusion of a claim on the patent office – an examiner must show within the allowed novelty sources or based on prior grants why a claim should be denied. As a result of this practice, early, path-breaking applications for a new technology tend to be quite broad and narrow naturally as the technology matures. Certainly this has occurred with agricultural biotechnology patents in such cases as the grant in the USA of the rights to methods to transform all soybeans, since rescinded. More generally though, optimal scope choices, made on an application-by-application basis, effectively determine the social balance which defines the patent system.

Merges and Nelson (1990), using a case study method, show that broad grants tend to limit subsequent innovation. That, however, begs the issue of whether the initial breadth of grants was necessary to attract the needed investment. Studies have tended to show that the lottery-like atmosphere of R&D tends to require the potential of large payoffs, however small the probability of success might be, as Schumpeter (1950) observed 50 years ago. An important caveat was noting (not surprisingly) that open, non-exclusive licences led to more rapid technological advancement than restrictive practices. Often the openness of licensing practices was a response to governmental pressure, as is demonstrated in the case of airplane design during the Second World War. More economic theoretical approaches lead to less intuitive results, but are of sufficient abstraction to limit their application.

Klemperer (1990), for example, considers both patent width (scope) and length factors under the assumption that consumers prefer variety but differ in their demands and costs of substituting among products (treated as transport costs). Welfare losses are attributable to two sources: (i) switching to less preferred products sold at competitive prices, and (ii) foregoing consumption of a class of products altogether. Klemperer shows that when all consumers have the same costs of substitution, patents should be 'narrow' but of infinite duration. Conversely, when preferences are strong so that the value of consuming the preferred variety is greater than not consuming that product class altogether, then patents should be 'wide' but of short duration. More formally, as the elasticity for the cost of substituting among goods increases, welfare losses from substitution intensify. In cases where valuation of preferred varieties becomes more elastic, the significance of this second form of welfare loss becomes more important.

Reciprocal Rights

Patent laws are strictly national, meaning owners have rights only in countries where patents have been secured. Even regional systems like the EPC operate based on the awarding of a 'bundle' of national patents compared to a single multinational one. Hence it is critical for inventors to be able to secure roughly similar types of protection in multiple countries, as indicated by the market potential of each invention.

National laws typically do not make reference to reciprocal rights as those rights are a key component of the Paris Convention of 1883. Article 2.1 guarantees that nationals of any country in the Union 'enjoy in all the other countries of the Union the advantages that their respective laws now grant, or may hereafter grant, to nationals; all without prejudice...'. In the absence of national rights, patent systems break down into a series of bilateral agreements, creating uncertainty and different standards for inventors.

Subsection Conclusions

This section has summarized the multiple checks and balances of patent systems to emphasize the careful balance which has emerged over centuries of use. No attempt is made to demonstrate that the balance is optimal, but rather the intent is to use it as a basis for constructing an 'effective' PBR system.

Constructing an Effective *sui generis* System for Plant Varieties from Patent Systems

This section considers first the transition of patent system efficacy requirements to an effective system for PBR, and then evaluates the current acts of UPOV for compatibility with that constructed system.

Comparable Requirements for an Effective sui generis System

In this subsection, the minimal effective patent requirements identified above are applied to construct an 'effective' PBR system.

National Treatment
The national treatment issue under PBR is identical to that for patents – the thwarting of the home country incentive to restrict protection to nationals, which in the longer term undermines the system. To be fully effective, PBR must grant full and equal rights to non-residents and residents alike.

Identification of Protectable Subject Matter
The minimal TRIPs statutes require the definition of protectable subject matter be broad within the context of plant varieties, with only a few restrictions allowed. In this context, the definition of 'plant variety' and 'plant' are central, but such definitions lie outside the scope of this chapter. Yet some limiter may be needed to distinguish what within the plant kingdom is protectable by PBR, particularly as PBR have been applied to varieties of use in agriculture and horticulture, although cultural terms are not used. One approach is the patent law distinction often made between inventions and discoveries, where inventions require some human effort beyond identification. Another aspect is the utility/industrial application requirement, limiting protection to those varieties with some identified application beyond mere existence (see below). However, many important plant improvements result from discoveries, and it is important that useful discoveries, such as mutants, are reproduced and made available to growers. In particular, it is notable that the US Plant Patent Act makes provision for the protection of 'cultivated sports, mutants, hybrids and newly found seedlings' (Section 161 of the Patent Act of 1952).

Protection Requirements
The patentability requirements identified earlier are novelty, inventive step (non-obviousness) and capability of industrial application (utility), plus disclosure. The novelty requirement has direct correspondence with PBR, but the inventive step/non-obviousness requires somewhat different considerations (see UPOV, 1989). At one level, a traditional process of developing a new variety – cross and select – is a formulated one, with ingenuity applied in identifying the crosses for further development. Conceptually, there is no distinction from the production of traditional varieties in farmers' fields except the process is less systemized, but astute selection remains the key aspect for success (see, e.g., Eyzaguirre and Iwanaga, 1996). This non-obviousness standard would be low compared to path-breaking industrial inventions, but not all that different from many mature industrial technologies such as pipe fittings. The inventive step requirement for PBR could be specified by requiring a showing of some unique contribution, some distinctness. That

would be sufficient for genera and species for which a reference variety is known, but not in the case of, say, a previously unknown wild relative. In that case, an input measure – human effort – would have to be submitted for the standard output measure – distinctness.

Industrial application/utility at a minimum requires some use for the invention to be identified in the application, but the use need not be efficient in the sense of being commercially viable compared to competing products. For plant varieties capable of being used in agriculture and horticulture, even indirectly as pure lines for subsequent breeding, the utility is self-evident. This is not necessarily so for wild-discovered materials, although wild relatives, for example, could contain useful resistance or other beneficial traits. In such cases, the identified distinctness characteristics of applicant varieties would presumably specify the useful attributes. Thus, effective PBR requires some specification of utility to prevent the potential protection of a large mass of discovered materials of no known use.

Disclosure likewise serves a somewhat more limited role for PBR compared to patents. The storehouse of technical knowledge and access components for patents does not strictly apply, for the general techniques are widely known and materials can be generated from those purchased on the market. Disclosure also occurs as soon as varieties are placed on the market, although this does not occur in the case of the inbred parent lines of hybrids which do not become publicly available. Thus, PBR disclosure is largely for the purpose of identifying the protected variety, a critical element in an operational system. However, new technologies, like genetic markers, may have reduced the need to use a visual description for identification purposes.

Rights Granted

Producers of plant varieties as a general matter must have the same rights to exclude unauthorized use for making, using, offering for sale, and selling or importing for those purposes as do other inventors; and because plant varieties combine attributes of products and technologies, it is essential the exclusionary rights extend at least to products directly produced, such as flowers. Here, though, the biological attributes of plants and the practical considerations of agriculture necessitate additional considerations.

It is the practice with many open pollinated crops for farmers to retain part of the harvest as a seed source for subsequent plantings, something which would generally be an infringement under patents. For commercial-scale row crop farmers, new seeds are purchased about every third generation, while at the more subsistence level the periods would be far longer. Such reuse of seed is very efficient for farmers as it avoids the handling costs associated with producing and selling seed annually, and its allowance does avoid the costly task of attempting to enforce rights among dispersed customers. But farmer-saved seed does limit breeders' revenue. The amount of the loss is debated; industry sources claim large amounts, but studies in the USA indicate the price of seed to be used for more than one crop season is higher. Stated more formally, seed producers can appropriate part of the value for the stream of benefits from seeds (Hansen and Knudson, 1996). Thus, the incentive effect of farmer-saved seed is an empirical issue by crop, location and type of farmer so that operationally it seems appropriate to optionally allow farmers the legal right to such use, known as the farmers' privilege. Sale of saved seed, originally allowed in the USA (Plant Variety Protection Act of 1970, Section 113), is inappropriate however and an unnecessary loss for rights holders.

More significant overall is the sequential nature of plant breeding where current generations of seed stock are used as a basis for subsequent generations. To maintain the process of improvements, such a process requires free access to protected materials as the basis for initial variation. This right, known as the breeders' exemption, combines aspects of the (non-statutory) research exemption in patent law with compulsory licensing privileges.

Inclusion of the breeders' exemption removes much of the role for compulsory licences. Once a variety is marketed it can be improved and marketed independently, bypassing the control of the original rights holder. However, access to a new variety of great public importance could still be inhibited (i) if it were never marketed and (ii) for the period required to improve and market a substitute variety. Given these considerations, compulsory licensing provisions for public needs are still appropriate.

A Constructed 'Effective sui generis System for Plant Varieties'

Based on the preceding discussion, it is possible to construct a *sui generis* system for plant varieties mimicking the TRIPs requirements, as follows.

NATIONAL AND MOST-FAVOURED-NATION TREATMENT. National treatment is central, at minimum for the WTO member states: most-favoured-nation treatment is a less essential component.

PROTECTABLE SUBJECT MATTER AND EXCLUSIONS. One approach, not attempted here, is the use of the definition of 'plant variety' to distinguish between protectable and non-protectable types of plants. Another approach, more in line with an economics-based system, is to separate discovered materials from those to which human effort and ingenuity have been applied – the discover versus invent issue under patent law (see Reed, 1993). Patent laws, however, do not define the term 'invent', raising some interpretation issues, particularly if a word like 'breeding' is substituted in a *sui generis* system. Perhaps a comparable approach is to use an operable definition such as 'any form of plant which has been subject to a systematic effort to enhance one group of traits relative to another' or plants which have been 'bred or discovered and developed'. This restricts protection to the class of plants which has been subject to human efforts, but not artificially to any specified species.

PROTECTION REQUIREMENTS. **Novelty** – not previously known for some specified period. However, unlike inventions which can be accessed by a written description, plant varieties exist physically and only become available when physical material is accessed. Accordingly, novelty should only be lost when physical material of the variety is freely available. This will usually occur when a variety is commercialized.

Inventive step/non-obviousness – as is discussed above, the threshold needs to be changed compared to patents to an operational one of some observable distinction when a reference variety is available and human developmental effort otherwise.

Industrial application/utility – in most instances the utility will be obvious – a new soybean variety or rose. But if there is a doubt, a line of commerce could be identified for the applicant variety. Otherwise, the specified distinctness characteristics can identify the useful attributes.

Disclosure – at minimum, the description should clearly identify the protected variety and its parts for enforcement purposes. The matter of providing for replication is largely resolved through the allowance of a breeders' exemption (see below).

Rights granted and limitations – rights granted can be the same as under patents, including unauthorized use, offering for sale, and selling or importing with the intent of using for those purposes the product directly obtained, such as seeds or flowers. Limitations can include the limited restrictions and compulsory licensing provisions as in TRIPs (Articles 30 and 31). Additionally, the characteristics of plant varieties and their use necessitates the provision of an optional additional limitation of farmers' privilege and a breeders' exemption.

Is UPOV 'Effective'?

In Table 4.1 a comparison is made between the derived effective PBR system and the UPOV Acts of 1978 and 1991. The UPOV Acts are selected as a basis of comparison for they are the only existent international form of PBR protection, adhered to by 43 countries.[5] Areas where there is a substantial difference between the constructed system and UPOV are discussed further below.

National Treatment
The UPOV Acts are considerably more restrictive in their minimum requirements as regards national treatment than the Paris Convention requirements, raising the issue of whether UPOV is TRIPs-effective. However, all UPOV Member States are free to grant national treatment to States which are not UPOV members and some do so, e.g., the UK.

Protectable Subject Matter
UPOV 1978 with its minimal requirement of 24 species and genera falls far short of the TRIPs mandate for a very broad treatment of protectable subject

matter, and appears TRIPs incompatible. The 1991 Act eases that requirement by requiring all species and genera be protected, but over a 10-year period.

Inventive Step

The 1978 Act (Article 6.1) requires a variety be distinguishable in 'one or more important characteristics from any other variety of common knowledge'. If the scope of protectable subject matter is extended to include plant genera and species varieties not in commercial use, then, at least initially, examiners will have no reference variety with which to compare. This may present some practical considerations, but no fundamental ones. However, for non-cultivated materials where the dimensions of the population might not even be known, this means of measuring the inventive step is not applicable.

Uniformity and Stability

These requirements have no parallel under patent systems due in part to the different subject matter. There are at least two justifications for their inclusion in the UPOV Acts, (i) description and identification, and (ii) practicality – uniform and stable varieties are generally more useful in commercial agriculture. As to (ii), practicality is a consideration, but there is no requirement in patent law that a patented invention be competitive with other products on the market. Indeed, survey reports that only some 15% of patents achieve commercial success underscore that point (Nogues, 1989). Presumably an inventor would wish to make the product commercially viable, but it is not the task of the patent examination process to require it be so. Thus justification (ii) can be rejected.

Regarding (i), uniformity and stability are important aspects of the distinguishing characteristics for without them a variety is not distinguishable over time, making a protection system inoperative. However, those requirements have attracted comment particularly from those who link the requirements with the uniformity and vulnerability of major crops. Recent work by Olufowote *et al.* (1997) among others has shown that non-inbred materials display a wide variation in heterogeneity at randomly selected alleles, but any material which has been selected, even using less formal techniques (such as might be applied by local farmers in selecting landraces), to be useful would presumably be stable in its target characteristics, say yield. It is presently possible to specify that level of stability in a probabilistic sense, but only following considerable investment. In the more distant future, it is conceivable that marker technology – microsatellite markers give evidence of particular promise – can assist in the process.

The UPOV terminology of 'sufficiently uniform in its relevant characteristics' and 'relevant characteristics remain unchanged after repeated propagation' (UPOV 1991, Articles 7 and 8) is sufficiently flexible to allow for changing interpretations. Thus it is possible to protect at least some landraces under the current systems, but the practical effect will be minimal as the costs of specifying the variety will be high.

Table 4.1. Comparisons between the 'constructed' sui generis system and the UPOV 1978 and 1991 Acts.

Component	Constructed TRIPs	UPOV 1978	UPOV 1991
Component			
National and most favoured nation treatment	Equal rights for WTO members	Nationals of Member States (3.1) Nationals of non-Member States on condition of varietal examination (3.2) Above applicable on a reciprocal basis with states protecting a genus or species (3.3)	Nationals of contracting parties (4.1)
Protectable subject matter			
Protection	All plants subject to systematic effort	May be applied to all genera and species, but minimum requirement is 24 genera and species within 8 years (4)	Existing members: all genera and species within 5 years (3.1) New members: all genera and species with 10 years (3.2) None – following phase-in period
Exclusions	Ordre public, morality and protect environment	None – except as above	
Protection requirements			
Novelty	Must be new	Novelty: for protected genera and species not sold in territory of member for more than 1 year and elsewhere more than 4 years (6 for vines and trees) (6.1(b))	Same (6.1)
Inventive step	Observable differences	Distinguishable by one or more important characteristics from any other variety of common knowledge (6.1)	Clearly distinguishable from any other variety of common knowledge (7)
Utility	Must serve industrial application	—	—
Disclosure	Describe for identification purposes	Distinguishing characteristic capable of precise recognition and description (6.1); other description requirements in application	

Uniformity	—	Sufficiently homogeneous (6.1(c))	Sufficiently uniform in its relevant characteristics (8)
Stability	—	Stable in essential characteristics (6.1(d))	Relevant characteristics remain unchanged after repeated propagation (9)
Rights granted and limitations			
Granted	Permission to make, sell, etc. including products produced directly	Permission for production of reproductive materials for marketing or offering or marketing such material – including ornamental plants or parts (5.1)	Permission required for: Propagating material: production, sale, importing, exporting (141(a)) Harvested material: including plants and plant parts – as above (14.2) Certain products: made directly as above (14.3)
Limitations	Compulsory licences	Restrictions of rights allowed only for public interest with equitable remuneration (9)	Same (17)
Breeders' exemption	Change – add	Permission not required for use as source of variation for creating new varieties or marketing such varieties (5.3)	Permission not required for acts for experimental purposes or for breeding other varieties (15.1)
Farmers' privilege	Change – add provisionally	Implicit in not being covered under rights granted	(optional) Permit farmers to use for propagating purposes on own holdings (15.2)
Duration	Twenty years from filing date	Min. 15 years from grant, 18 years for vines and trees (8)	Min. 20 years from grant, 25 years for vines and trees (19.2)

Farmers' Privilege

The use of the crop as a seed source for a subsequent season would be an infringement under patent systems. The farmers' privilege is allowed (indirectly, by not being identified as an infringing use) under UPOV 1978, and made optional under UPOV 1991. Countries have responded differently; the USA, for example, adopted a blanket authorization for the privilege, while the EU grants the privilege only for small farms. Larger operations are required to pay royalties.

International Exhaustion of Rights

PBR systems are silent as regards international exhaustion of rights, but the matter has limited practical importance due to the general need to adapt seeds to local growing conditions and market requirements.

Subsector Conclusions

Existing PBR systems as exemplified by the UPOV Acts of 1978 and 1991 parallel closely the functioning of patent systems. This is not surprising, for the two systems have similar objectives, and the framers of PBR would of course be conscious of the operation of patent systems. Nonetheless, there are important differences in the additional exemptions allowed under PBR in national treatment and protectable subject matter and in application of the systems. Thus it is to those matters we turn for a final judgement on efficacy, and its economic definition.

But is the Constructed System Effective?

In order to make a judgement on whether the constructed system is indeed effective, it is necessary to examine its operation in addition to the legal text. That is undertaken here, first by examining what is known of the breeding investment response to PBR, and then considering the administrative application of the law in detail.

Investment Responses to PBR Legislation

Being comparatively recent and restricted in geographic scope provides both benefits and limits for the analysis of the economic effects of legislation. The limitation is that to date few studies have been conducted, but for those available there is a better accounting of cause and effect.

A detailed early study was commissioned by the US Department of Agriculture to investigate expressed concerns about the possible negative effects of PBR (Butler and Marion, 1985). Regarding the effect on private

R&D investments, significant increases in the number of plant breeding programmes were recorded while investments increased most rapidly in the 1967–1970 period, provisionally in anticipation of the passage of the Act in 1970. Expenditures were (and remain) unevenly distributed across crops with major investments directed to soybeans. That allocation has been explained as an economic response to relative profit opportunities (Foster and Perrin, 1991). The observed investment response is somewhat surprising because the scope of protection granted in the USA is narrow compared with that in Europe (Lesser, 1986).

There has been no systematic effort to evaluate the effects of PBR in Europe or Canada. But the development of one key Canadian crop, canola, has been documented in detail. Following 1985 there was a sharp increase in private-sector canola development attributable to several factors of which 'perhaps the most critical factor was the introduction of intellectual property rights for biological inventions' (Phillips, this volume, Chapter 14).

For developing countries in Latin America, Jaffé and van Wijk (1995) found only Argentina combined several years of experience under PBR with effective enforcement. There, PBR appears to have restrained 'companies from reducing or even eliminating their breeding programs and enabled the reactivation of soybean breeding'; but those effects occurred only after rights could be effectively enforced. To date, no systematic efforts have been made to document the effects of PBR on access to materials developed elsewhere, but both Canada and Chile justified enacting the legislation in part to enhance that access.

Application of PBR Systems

Scope Issues

The application of any legal economic system allows for a myriad of approaches. For the purposes of this chapter it is primarily important to distinguish between two, referred to here as the European (examination) and US (registration) systems. In Europe, for major crops, commodity committees are empanelled with the responsibility to identify relevant attributes for protection, and in some cases to establish a minimum statistical standard for meeting that requirement compared with the reference variety. Thus, for example, storability of onions could be set as a distinctness criterion with a protectable variety required to show 1% less sprouting than the reference. Growout trials are then undertaken to measure performance in field conditions.

The EU operates with a legally separate registration system for row crops known as Value in Cultivation and Use (VCU). Under that system, varieties must demonstrate superiority in economically important traits to be placed in the Common Catalog and be eligible for sale. That is, VCU acts as a form of quality certification. Operationally, the VCU testing is done concurrently with distinctiveness, uniformity and stability (DUS) testing (see Lesser, 1987).

The US system is quite different in that essentially no variety testing is undertaken, and further distinctness can be established in any dimension, even far from something of practical value. As a result, many competing varieties are available on the market, which previously led me to refer to the US system as one of registration which protects the variety name, not the germplasm *per se* (Lesser, 1986). Canada and Australia operate hybrids with European-type growouts conducted by the applicant under government supervision.

From this perspective, it is likely the scope of coverage in the USA is too limited, potentially not 'effective'. Stated more formally, farmers' substitution functions among closely related varieties can be expected to be highly elastic as they share similar objective functions for varieties, and information is good. Under those conditions, owners of rights will price competitively to minimize lost sales so that protection must be long to allow the recovery of the R&D investment. Correspondingly, protection may be narrow with no loss to the breeder. Klemperer's (1990) analysis also indicates that balance of scope and duration minimizes social loss. However, variety life is typically more limited by natural factors such as increasing susceptibility to insects and diseases co-evolving with the varieties than by statutory limits. Indeed, the commercial life of a variety in the USA has been placed at 7 years, but is declining due to competition. Thus we can anticipate US protection is too limited to be effective. Partial corroborative information comes from complaints of breeders, efforts to find alternative protection mechanisms, including utility patents for varieties, and projections of low estimated values for certificates of plant variety protection (PVP).

The latter reference applies particularly to my own efforts to use hedonic pricing techniques to value returns to PVP (Lesser, 1994). For soybeans sold in New York state – certainly no major producing area – the estimated return was 2.3% of the seed value (as contrasted with the large portion of the seed price which reflects the crop value). While the percentage may seem large, the value per bag of seed amounted to only $0.32. That analysis needs to be replicated in other areas and times, but is suggestive of the low value of PVP in the USA.

In Europe, the wider protection offered allows higher prices, encouraging switching among varieties. However, Klemperer (1990) shows that activity increases social loss so it is inefficient socially. A third alternative exists, that of delaying the introduction of new (replacement) varieties. It can be shown easily that such an approach allows charging higher prices:

Let r_j = price of seed variety j
$\quad\quad Q_j$ = sales of seed variety j

$$TR = r_j Q_j \tag{1}$$

$$MR = R_j + \frac{\mathrm{d}r_j}{\mathrm{d}Q_j} \cdot Q_j = r_j \left(1 - \frac{1}{|\eta|} \right) \tag{2}$$

where η is the market demand elasticity for varietal improvement.

While η is akin to the monopolist-quarterly restriction, it is interpreted here in terms of restrictions of forthcoming varieties. That interpretation can be seen by decomposing η into two components, as follows:

$$\text{Supply elasticity of innovation } (I): \varepsilon = \frac{dQ_j}{dI} \cdot \frac{I}{Q_j}. \tag{3}$$

This is the relative percentage change in sales of new seed varieties to a change in innovation effort (I), $\varepsilon > 0$.

$$\text{Own-price effort elasticity: } \delta = \frac{dI}{dr_j} \cdot \frac{r_j}{I}. \tag{4}$$

This is a cost efficiency characteristic – the change in innovative effect by a firm given a change in varietal prices. As an increase in innovation leading to the production of variety k, $k > j$, k will compete with and reduce the revenue from j so that the higher r_j, the less will be the investment in innovation I; that is, $\delta < 0$.

Substitution into the first order conditions where k_j is the productivity enhancement of variety J and C_j all non-seed production costs:

$$r_j = \frac{Pf'(Q_j) - (1+k)Z_j - \dfrac{\partial C_j}{\partial Q_j}}{1 - \dfrac{1}{\varepsilon |\delta|}}. \tag{5}$$

So that reducing the investment in breeding – increasing the period between releases of improved varieties – under PBR raises the price of varieties.

However, this approach also raises social costs by delaying the introduction of more efficient technology. As an alternative, it is possible selectively to increase the scope of protection for more significant contributions. That goal was effectively accomplished with the distinction between 'initial' and 'derived' varieties in the 1991 UPOV Act, although for different reasons. Article 14(5) allows for the permission of the breeder to be required for a variety which is 'essentially derived from [a] protected variety, where the protected variety is not itself an essentially derived variety'. A variety is essentially derived when 'it is predominately derived from an initial variety, or from a variety that is itself predominately derived from the initial variety, while retaining the expression of the essential characteristics'. Essentially derived varieties may be obtained in a number of identified ways, including 'transformation by genetic engineering'. That is, of course, a principal objective of the new approach – preventing agricultural biotechnology companies from usurping a variety by inserting genes into it, while having no responsibility to the breeder.

Operationally, 'essentially derived' behaves as a limit to the breeders' exemption, itself a form of research exemption. Article 15.1(iii) allows the use

of a protected variety for the 'purpose of breeding another variety'; but when
the resultant new variety is derived, permission of the owner of the initial
variety is required for commercialization. Rights are non-pyramiding; that is,
if A is an initial variety and B is derived from it and C from B, owners of
both B and C varieties must have the permission of variety A's owner before
commercialization.

Clearly, this process will prevent biotechnology firms from appropriating
protected varieties, as is intended. The effects of this approach are not
known; I am unaware of any cases having been brought to date. In most
countries, the owner of an initial variety must assert his/her rights by suing
the derived variety's owner for infringement. This is how patent rights are
enforced. It means that until court challenges have been made, the scope of
protection granted to initial varieties will be unclear.

Initial variety legislation can, however, have additional effects. Consider,
for example, a case in which annual varietal improvement is at the rate of
1% annually, while a 3% improvement is needed to qualify as an initial
variety. All benefits go to the owner of initial varieties. Producers of essentially derived varieties act as royalty collectors for the owner of the initial
variety. The initial owners (under competitive conditions) receive only the
value of their contribution, and then only until it is superseded by an
improved one. What to do? Why not delay the release of a new variety until
it qualifies as an initial one, in our example withholding release for three
generations? That approach would have the social cost of delaying access to
improved technologies (see equation 5).

Farmers' Exemption

Another aspect of PBR legislation which makes it weaker than comparable
patent protection is the allowance of the right to hold back harvested
material for use as a seed source, that is, the farmers' privilege. Here
reference is made only to open-pollinated materials, for the use of asexually
propagating materials like tree cuttings would clearly obviate any profit
potential for breeders, while first generation hybrids (which do not reproduce
true to form) cannot be economically used as a seed source. The 1978
UPOV Act allows a universal farmers' privilege – indirectly by not classifying
such use as an infringement.[6] The 1991 Act (Article 15.2), however, makes
the farmers' exemption optional at the national level. The USA has decided
to allow a full farmers' exemption, while the EU requires large farms to pay
a royalty.

Breeders have long and understandably complained that the exemption
significantly reduces their sales and profits. The latter point is valid; row crop
seeds in the USA are replaced only every third year as saved seed becomes
contaminated while new seed has the benefit of additional breeding work.
Small seeds like alfalfa and vegetables are typically purchased annually due to
handling difficulties. But are breeders' *profits* reduced as a result of the use
of the privilege? Hansen and Knudson (1996) argue, not by much. They use

a field-level model for US soybean production to show that seed companies can indirectly appropriate rents by charging a sufficiently high price for the parent seed.

High seed prices, however, have an indirect societal effect. Knudson and Hansen (1991) show that US farmers sometimes under-invest in new seed, suffering a yield loss as a consequence. Considering seed sources in a regional production model for wheat, the authors show that lower quantities of purchased seed led on average to an 11% yield loss. As the proportion of purchased seed varied according to the crop price, it seems likely that farmers were responding to cash flow rather than profitability factors. Raising seed prices would exacerbate this matter, particularly under current low crop prices, while disallowing farmer seed-saving could enhance production efficiency. If indeed seed companies are appropriating most of the net new seed value anyway, then costs to farmers would rise only in respect to the costs of new seed distribution compared to on-farm handling and conditioning costs. Data on the net cost difference are not available at this time.

The EU practice of requiring owners of large farms to pay royalties on saved seed is an intriguing alternative position, but one which begs more economic analysis. Presumably, the underlying concept is that large farms are more profitable and can afford to pay the royalties. This may be broadly true, as scale economies in production do exist. In general, however, US experiences with basing policy on farm size considerations have been problematic, for ownership-of-record can be and is adjusted for cost purposes. Moreover, the prior version of US PBR legislation allowed limited farm seed sales, not to exceed 50% of farm sales (Plant Variety Protection Act of 1980, Section 113). That limitation proved unworkable as the practical definition of what constituted 'farm sales' for this purpose could not be specified effectively, and it was dropped in 1995 when the USA adopted the 1991 Act of UPOV. Conversely, the policy may focus on the higher efficiency of collecting royalties from large versus small farms. In either case, and depending on what royalty is charged, the practice of under-investing in new seed would be reduced.

Subsection Conclusions

Clearly, the European approach provides broader protection than is extended in the USA, but both are socially inefficient. The one provides a socially non-optimal broad protection, but the degree of protection likely necessary to attract investment, while the other provides narrow and short-term protection, probably too little overall for the optimal level of breeding investment.

The 1991 UPOV system provisions allowing for varietal dependency deal effectively with an objective – preventing biotechnology firms from appropriating varieties through genetic engineering. Under the dependency approach, those firms must seek the permission of the variety owner for commercialization.

However, excluding the consideration of biotechnology, if the non-dependency threshold is set too low, firms will have the incentive to avoid dependent status by withholding multiple generations from sale. This would be a social loss. Better then that the bar be set relatively high.

Evidence indicates that farmers' privilege does not substantially reduce breeders' profits for open-pollinated seed, and thus no restrictions are needed. However, requiring annual royalty payments for large farms, as is being practised in the EU, will reduce the inefficient custom of replacing seeds infrequently. Placing the requirement on all farm sizes reduces the wasteful incentive to accommodate the legal stipulation of a farm size to avoid the payment.

Conclusions

It is relatively easy to derive a PBR system based on centuries of experience with patent systems. The public/private benefit balance, which characterizes IP, is well served by the long history of such a derived system. Indeed, it appears that UPOV, the international PBR convention, has accommodated institutional and biological differences between products. Reference is made in particular to the breeders' exemption (the right to use protected seed in breeding programmes) and farmers' privilege (the right to use the harvest material as a seed source).

In the past, PBR systems have functioned well in increasing investment in plant breeding activities, particularly from the private sector. That is a highly important consequence in an era of worldwide reductions in public investment in agricultural research. It also is a necessary component of the TRIPs requirement for an 'effective *sui generis* system'. But the system should be efficient in terms of the public/private trade-off as well. Globally, an IP trade-off is inefficient due to welfare losses of delayed distribution of new varieties with a non-zero price. Locally, there are some possible improved efficiency trade-offs. That is, PBR systems can be and are applied in multiple ways, with distinct efficacy and efficiency effects.

What can be said about ways to enhance the efficiency of PBR?

Situation: The US registration approach leads to quite weak protection, potentially too weak to be effective, to judge from firm efforts to find alternative mechanisms. Conversely, the European model allows far stronger protection, but is costly in administration and delays.

Enhancement: Perhaps an efficient hybrid would be the US registration process with higher distinctness standards, but not limited to few varietal dimensions as is the case under the EU varietal committee systems.

Situation: The UPOV dependency provisions (depending on how implemented) provide incentives for delaying the release of new varieties, which is inefficient.

Enhancement: Setting high criteria for initial varieties would minimize that effect, for firms could not reasonably expect to withhold market release for several generations with the expectation of qualifying as an initial variety (and with the potential to earn rather than pay royalties).

Situation: The limited available research on the breeders' cost of farmers' privilege is convincing in that there is little need to restrict the privilege to provide greater royalty payments for breeders. Conversely, research shows that farmers sometimes under-invest in new seed purchases, leading to lost production potential. The two aspects are linked, for pricing varieties in a way which appropriates the royalty value for multiple years provides producers with an incentive to delay seed replacement.

Enhancement: Restricting the farmers' privilege under those circumstances – that is, requiring annual seed replacement – could actually improve agricultural productivity with little cost effect.

Notes

1. The least-developed countries are allowed an additional 6 years (until 1 January 2006) to comply with this requirement.
2. But see, e.g., UPOV 1991, Article 1.
3. See, e.g., Machlup, 1958. TRIPs specifies its objectives to be a contribution 'to the promotion of technological innovation and to the transfer and dissemination of technology' (Article 7).
4. At the time of writing, a non-exclusive compulsory licensing agreement was being considered as a possible remedy for the Microsoft antitrust case, should there be a finding against the company.
5. Membership information is available from the UPOV web page, www.upov.int.
6. Article 5.1 mandates the breeder's authorization only for 'production for the *purpose of commercial marketing*' [emphasis added]. As saved seed does not involve commercial marketing, it does not violate the breeder's rights.

References

Allen, O.E. (1990) The power of patents. *American Heritage* Sept./Oct., 46–59.

Bent, S. (1989) Issues and prospects in the USA. In: Lesser, W. (ed.), *Animal Patents: The Legal, Economic and Social Issues.* Stockton Press, New York, pp. 5–15.

Butler, L.J. and Marion, B.W. (1985) *The Impacts of Patent Protection on the Seed Industry and Public Plant Breeding.* University of Wisconsin, N.C. Project 117, Monograph 16, September.

Carlton, D.W. and Perloff, J.M. (1994) *Modern Industrial Organization*, 2nd Edn. Harper Collins, New York.

Dam, K.W. (1994) The economic underpinnings of patent law. *Journal of Legal Studies* XXIII, 247–271.

Deardorff, A.V. (1992) Welfare effects of global patent protection. *Economica* 59, 35–51.

Eyzaguirre, P. and Iwanaga, M. (eds) (1996) *Participatory Plant Breeding.* IPGRI, Rome.

Foster, W.E. and Perrin, R. (1991) *Economic Incentives and Plant Breeding Research.* North Carolina State University, Faculty Working Papers, DARE: 91-05, May.

Goldstein, J. (1985) Legal and administrative developments in depository practice – U.S. and abroad. *World Biotech Report,* Vol. 2, Online International, New York.

Hansen, L. and Knudson, M. (1996) Property rights protection of reproducible genetic materials. *Review of Agricultural Economy* 18, 403-414.

Harabi, N. (1995) Appropriability of technical innovations: an empirical analysis. *Research Policy* 24, 981-992.

Jaffé, W. and van Wijk, J. (1995) The Impact of Plant Breeders' Rights in Developing Countries. University of Amsterdam, Inter-American Institute for Cooperation on Agriculture, October.

Klemperer, P. (1990) How broad should the scope of patent protection be? *Rand Journal of Economics* 21, 113-130.

Knudson, M. and Hansen, L. (1991) *Intellectual Property Rights and the Private Seed Industry.* US Department of Agriculture, Econ. Res. Service, Ag. Econ. Report No. 654, November.

Lesser, W. (1986) Patenting seeds in the United States of America: what to expect. *Industrial Property* 9, 360-367.

Lesser, W. (1987) Anticipating UK plant variety patents. *European Intellectual Property Review* 9, 172-177.

Lesser, W. (1994) Valuation of plant variety protection certificates. *Review of Agricultural Economy* 16, 231-238.

Lesser, W. (1999) The Elements of an Effective *sui generis* System for the Protection of Plant Varieties. UPOV-WIPO-WTO/99/2. 29 January.

Machlup, F. (1958) *An Economic Review of the Patent System.* Study of the Subcommittee on Patents, Trademarks and Copyright, Committee on the Judiciary, US Senate, Study No. 15.

Merges, R.P. and Nelson, R.R. (1990) On the complex economics of patent scope. *Columbia Law Review* 90, 839-916.

Nijar, S. and Ling, C.Y. (1994) The implications of the intellectual property rights regime of the Convention on Biological Diversity and GATT on biodiversity conservation: a Third World perspective. In: Krattiger, A.F. *et al.* (eds), *Widening Perspectives on Biodiversity,* IAE and IUCN, Geneva and Gland, Chap. 5.4.

Nogues, J. (1989) *Notes on Patents, Distortions and Development.* World Bank, Washington DC.

Olufowote, J.O., Xu, Y., Chen, X., Park, W.D., Beachell, H.M., Dilday, R.H., Goto, M. and McCouch, S.R. (1997) Comparative evaluation of within-cultivar variation on rice (*Oryza sativa* L.) using microsatellite and RFLP markers. *Genome* 40, 370-378.

Reed, B.C. (1993) *A Practical Guide to Patent Law,* 2nd Edn. Sweet and Maxwell, London.

Schumpeter, J.A. (1950) *Capitalism, Socialism, and Democracy,* 2nd Edn. Harper, New York.

Straus, J. and Moufang, R. (1990) *Deposit and Release of Biological Materials for the Purpose of Patent Procedure,* Momos Verlagsgesellschaft, Baden-Baden.

United Nations Conference on Trade and Development (UNCTAD) (1975) *The Role of the Patent System in the Transfer of Technology to Developing Countries.* United Nations, New York, TD/B/AC.11/19/Rev. 1.

UPOV Administrative and Legal Committee (1989) *The Interface Between Patent Protection and Plant Breeders' Rights.* CAJ/XXIV/4, 3 April.

034 Q16

K11

Recent Intellectual Property Rights Controversies and Issues at the CGIAR

5

Susan H. Bragdon

*IPGRI – International Plants Genetic Resources Institute,
Via delle Sette Chiese 142, 00145 Rome, Italy*

The CGIAR's Relationship with Intellectual Property

Background

The Consultative Group on International Agricultural Research (CGIAR) was established in 1971 and is an informal association of public and private donors that supports a network of 16 International Agricultural Research Centres (IARCs), each of which has its own governing body. The CGIAR mission is to use science and technology, in partnership with other organizations, to increase food security, alleviate poverty and protect the environment. With a budget of approximately \$320 million per annum,[1] it oversees one of the largest agricultural research efforts in the developing world.

Because the CGIAR is one of the largest and most important institutions for the conservation and development of genetic resources, international policies and policy debates can and do have a profound impact on the CGIAR programmes, priorities and day-to-day work. Nowhere is this clearer than with the legal and policy developments related to intellectual property rights (IPR).

The CGIAR Policy-making Process

Because each Center has its own mandate and governing body, when it sets policy the CGIAR frequently acts not as one institution but as many. As will be discussed at length below, recent attempts to develop an official CGIAR intellectual property policy point to the difficulties of deriving a common policy where the individual members have different boards, mandates and constituencies.[2] Adding to the challenge, there are at least 14 'policy-making' fora within the CGIAR.[3] In 1997, the CGIAR initiated an External System Review which presented its recommendations in October 1998 at International Centers Week (ICW'98), a meeting held annually at the World Bank Headquarters at Washington DC.[4]

The Review Panel recommended that the Committee structure of the CGIAR system be streamlined to improve effectiveness and efficiency.[5] It also felt that an independent policy committee, such as the existing Genetic Resources Policy Committee, continued to be necessary. The Panel recommended the creation of a central Board to be incorporated as a non-profit public service organization.[6] It recommended the central Board be established after consideration of legal and other factors relevant to its effective functioning. The central Board should, according to the Panel, consist of Members, a Board of Directors and Executive Committee, the CGIAR Chair and a chief executive officer with membership drawn from the stakeholders of the CGIAR. Currently, a task force has been established and is examining these recommendations and their possible implementation within the System.

Developing CGIAR Guidelines on IPR

Over the last decade, a rapidly changing IPR environment and increasing privatization of agricultural research have forced the CGIAR to develop its own policies and procedures on IP. The process of policy development has been complicated by the fact that the CGIAR system has no legal status, and its members often represent opposing sides of the highly politicized IPR debate. Despite years of discussion and debate by numerous committees, the CGIAR system is still in the process of developing a coherent, comprehensive policy on IPR. At present, the CGIAR has adopted Guiding Principles for the CGIAR on IP and genetic resources as an 'interim working paper'.[7] 'Under the leadership of the Committee on Intellectual Property Rights,[8] it is hoped proposals to resolve outstanding issues will be reolved during 1999. Currently, the CGIAR's guiding principles on IPR:

1. Reaffirm the fundamental objective of the CGIAR is to ensure access to knowledge, technology and materials in the interest of developing countries.
2. Reaffirm materials from the Center genebanks will be freely available.
3. Recognize the sovereign rights of states over their genetic resources and that the acquisition of germplasm, after the coming into force of the Convention on Biological Diversity (CBD), is subject to the Convention's provisions.
4. Recognize both Plant Breeders' Rights (PBR) and Farmers' Rights in accordance with the International Undertaking for Plant Genetic Resources (IU).

5. State that Centers will not claim ownership nor apply intellectual property to the germplasm held in trust, and will require recipients to observe these same conditions.

6. Regard the results of their work as international public goods and thus disclosure of information is the preferred strategy. IPRs will only be sought for Center research products when this is in the best interests of developing countries. In all such cases the reasons for seeking protection will be disclosed.

7. State that plant variety protection may be sought by recipients who have used Center materials for breeding but this may not prevent others from using the original material in their own programmes.

8. Provide that material will be distributed only on the basis that recipients seek Center approval prior to patenting any cells, gene or other derivative.

9. State that Centers will enter into agreements with holders of protected materials which recognize restrictions on the use and distribution of such materials only when this is in the best interests of developing countries

As will be illustrated by example later, with no centralized policy authority, CGIAR Centers remain free to interpret and apply CGIAR policies as they deem fit.

IPR and the CGIAR 'In Trust' Collections

There is no dispute that the vast majority of crop germplasm held in the IARCs was collected from the fields and forests of the South's farming communities. But to whom the germplasm ultimately belongs, to whom CGIAR is accountable, and whether or not CGIAR's germplasm can be subject to intellectual property protection by any party, has been a topic of controversy and debate. The status of the collections of plant genetic resources for food and agriculture (PGRFA) made prior to the coming into force of the CBD was left as an outstanding matter in the negotiations.[9] Negotiators adopted Resolution 3, which requested that this (and other) issues be addressed through the Food and Agriculture Organization (FAO) Global System for the Conservation and Utilization of PGRFA. Two components of the FAO system are the International Undertaking for Plant Genetic Resources (IU) and the International Network of *Ex-Situ* Collections under the auspices of the FAO. The IU is a non-binding intergovernmental agreement to promote the conservation, exchange and utilization of plant genetic resources. It is currently under negotiation under the auspices of the FAO Commission to revise it to bring it into harmony with the CBD. The International Network of *Ex-Situ* Collections currently contains only the designated collections of the CGIAR though it is open to other members.[10] As most of the accessions held by CGIAR Centers were collected prior to the entry into force of the CBD, the status of these collections is somewhat dependent on the outcome of the ongoing negotiations on the IU. At present, questions of ownership, terms of access and benefit-sharing associated with these collections remain unanswered.[11]

As an interim measure, the FAO Commission and the CGIAR decided to develop Agreements that would keep Center-held material in the public domain for the benefit of all humanity in line with the mission of the CGIAR system.[12] In 1994, the CGIAR and FAO entered into agreements whereby most of the materials ('designated material') in the Centers are held in trust for the world community. By the terms of the FAO/CGIAR agreements, the Centers have agreed to conserve this genetic material in conditions meeting international standards, to not take out any form of intellectual property protection on them and to pass these obligations on if the material is transferred further. The agreements were designed to ensure the relatively unrestricted flow of germplasm to all countries in the new bilaterally oriented context reflected by the entry into force of the CBD. Without these agreements, the role of the Centers might well have been reduced to becoming brokers for individual countries in bilateral exchange transactions. It is understood that the agreements will be modified, if necessary, according to the outcome of the IU negotiations.

There was concern at the outset of the negotiation of the agreements that there be a common understanding on the meaning of terms used. Consequently, at the time of signing, the FAO and the CGIAR issued a joint statement stating its common understanding of the meaning of a number of the agreements' provisions. There was particular concern over the significance of the word 'ensure' in Article 10, which provides:

> Where samples of the designated germplasm and/or related information are transferred to any other person or institution, the Center shall *ensure* that such other person or institution, and any further entity receiving samples of the designated germplasm from such person or institution, are bound by the conditions set out in Article 3 (b) and, in the case of samples duplicated for safety purposes, to the provisions of Article 5 (a). [emphasis added]

The joint statement holds that the Centers' obligation to 'ensure' recipients of germplasm do not seek intellectual property rights over designated germplasm and/or related information would be satisfied by arrangements, such as Material Transfer Agreements (MTAs), that require the recipient not to seek IPR on the material and to pass this same obligation to any subsequent recipients.[13]

1997–1998: Alleged Violations of the 1994 Agreements

In late 1997 and early 1998, several cases came to light and were publicized wherein recipients of designated germplasm from a CGIAR Center sought PBR in alleged contravention of the 1994 Agreements. These cases raised serious questions about the Centers' effectiveness in implementing the 1994 Agreements and, in particular, their use of MTAs to implement those agreements. Nevertheless, the cases also illustrate the efficacy of the 1994 Agreements and the commitment of the Centers to implement them in a coherent and consistent manner.

The highlighted cases involved the transfer of germplasm from two Centers to private, quasi-private and public sector entities in Australia. The situations facing the two Centers were almost identical yet their responses were diametrically opposed. With one of the Centers, two accessions were sent to the recipient institution for testing in 1988/89. In 1997, the Center formally signed an MTA with the recipient institution for these two accessions. The MTA specifically recognized that the Center held the accessions in trust under the FAO/CGIAR Agreements and prohibited application of PBR to them. In addition, a 26 June, 1997 letter from the Center to the recipient that accompanied the MTA reiterated that the Center would not allow PBR to be applied to the accessions. On 10 July, 1997 the director of the recipient institution wrote to the Center asking it to reconsider its position on PBR for the accessions. The Center denied the request in a letter of 28 July, 1997. On 5 August, 1997, the recipient applied for PBR in Australia for the two accessions obtained from the Center. Upon learning of the applications in December 1997, the Center: (i) requested the recipient to withdraw its applications and (ii) notified the Australian PBR authorities of the application and its contravention of the MTA between the Center and the recipient institution. The recipient institution subsequently dropped its PBR claims on the two accessions.

At least three designated accessions from another Center were distributed to the same recipient institution as in the case outlined above. The material was originally distributed prior to their designation but, according to the SINGER database,[14] further distribution of one of the accessions to the recipient institution took place in 1996. An umbrella MTA was signed between this Center and the recipient institution in 1995. The recipient institution approached the Center in 1997 to request its agreement for the recipient institution to apply for PBR on the three accessions. Unlike, the earlier case, this Center agreed to the request but requested that the recipient institution ensure that the PBR be applied within Australia only.

Issues Raised by Alleged Violations

These cases highlighted the areas where the implementation of the 1994 Agreements needed immediate strengthening. These included the need for:

- Harmonization of the content and use of MTAs.
- An agreed procedure for Centers to handle violations of MTAs when these become apparent.

- A clear and shared understanding of the meaning and practical consequences of designation when material has been freely exchanged for a
  period of time prior to its designation.

Though not the clause at issue in the cases noted, in reviewing the
situation, it became apparent that at least one Center's MTA was inconsistent
with the requirements of Article 10 of the FAO/CGIAR Agreements. In a
good faith effort to implement the CBD, the MTA stated that a recipient
would not seek or obtain IPR 'without negotiating this with the proper
authority of the country of origin'. While the clause represented an effort to
reflect the requirements of the CBD, it is the FAO/CGIAR Agreement that
is the relevant legal instrument and not the CBD.[15]

CGIAR Response to the Allegations

Recommendations of Center Directors and Chairs

The events caught the attention of the Committees of Center Board Chairs
and of Center Directors (the CBC and the CDC) and stimulated the
production of several statements aimed at ensuring consistent CGIAR policies
and practices relating to genetic resources, biotechnology and IPR. In a joint
letter conveying the documents to the Chairman of the CGIAR,[16] Dr Ismail
Serageldin, the Committees wrote:

> The Centers are convinced of the need for consistent policies and
> procedures across the System, and are further convinced of the need
> to make public these policies. The Chairs and Directors would also
> like to entrust you or your designate to speak for and protect the
> rights of the Centers in relevant international fora.

Attached to the letter were:

- CGIAR-endorsed Ethical Principles Relating to Genetic Resources.
- A common Germplasm Acquisition Agreement.
- A common MTA (in two forms).
- Agreed procedures for handling alleged MTA violations.
- Guiding Principles on IPR.
- A statement on Principles involving Center interaction with the private
  sector and other owners of proprietary technology.
- An agreed position statement on biotechnology.

Harmonization of MTAs

The desirability of harmonization with regard to the content and use of
MTAs was noted by the Inter-Center Working Group on Genetic Resources
at its meeting in Kenya in January 1998. Accordingly, it requested one of the

Centers, the International Plant Genetic Resources Institute (IPGRI), to gather and analyse the MTAs currently in use. This was done and potential problems brought to the attention of the respective Centers.

A standard uniform MTA for system-wide use was approved by the CDC and CBC and endorsed at ICW'98. The endorsed MTA adopts a 'software' approach whereby the retention of the material constitutes acceptance of the terms and conditions of the MTA. This approach was considered by many to be the easier mechanism to execute and therefore the preferred option. Consultations with the legal counsel of the FAO approved the software approach as a feasible option prior to its submission to ICW'98. Because the validity of this approach may depend upon the recipient's actual awareness of the MTA's terms, it is likely that mechanisms by which Centers can ensure this awareness by recipients will be discussed by the CDC or Inter-Center Working Group on Genetic Resources.

Procedures to Address MTA Violations

Unfortunately, as with all legal instruments, fulfilling one's own obligations under an agreement cannot guarantee that others will not violate its terms. Even when fully in conformity with Article 10, violations of the Centers' MTAs may occur. Catalysed by the cases noted above, at the MTM'98 the Centers agreed to procedures that Centers will follow when an alleged violation of an MTA has occurred. When faced with an alleged violation, the Centers agreed to:

1. Request an explanation from the germplasm recipient. If a satisfactory and timely explanation for the situation is not received, the Center will notify the recipient that a violation is thought to have occurred and request that the recipient cease and desist in its efforts to obtain IPR over the material, or renounce such rights or ownership if they have already been granted or claimed.
2. Notify the proper regulatory body in the relevant country of the possibility that the MTA has been violated and the granting of IPR may, therefore, have been inappropriate in the case of the material obtained from the Center.
3. Notify IPGRI and the FAO Commission on Genetic Resources for Food and Agriculture, through its Secretariat, of the possible violation of the MTA and transgression of the Agreements with FAO.

The proposed procedure also reserves the Centers' right to take other actions, including legal actions, as they might deem feasible and appropriate to enforce the MTAs and preserve the integrity of the Agreement with the FAO. In this regard, the proposed procedure states the intent of the Centers to work in cooperation with the FAO. The statement explicitly states that it is understood that the FAO, through the Commission on Genetic Resources for Food and Agriculture, may also wish to take actions in support of the objectives of the Agreement between the CGIAR Centers and the FAO. The proposed statement of procedure notes that the CGIAR would welcome and support all such appropriate initiatives.

Determining the Meaning and Practical Consequences of Designation

These cases raise the critical issue of what designation means in practice when the material has already been distributed prior to its designation. This is an issue that will be addressed and hopefully resolved within the framework of the revised IU. Indeed, the Commission noted that the 1994 Agreements would need to be revisited in the context of a finalized IU.

To address the immediate problem, Dr Serageldin sent a letter on 4 February, 1998 to Henri Carsalade, Assistant Director-General, Sustainable Development Department, FAO suggesting that the FAO Commission might wish to recommend a moratorium to its member governments on the granting of plant variety protection to designated material *regardless* of when the material was distributed. Future requests for permission to apply for PBR on designated material distributed prior to the 1994 Agreements may come to Centers. Because contracts and other legal agreements do not apply retroactively (unless otherwise provided), the 1994 Agreements do not provide a legal basis for a Center denying a request for permission to submit a PBR application for germplasm distributed prior to the conclusion of those Agreements.[17] Nevertheless, a consistent approach to responding to such requests is desirable and the Chairman's recommendation for a moratorium on granting IPR on this material provides the basis for such consistency. If approached with such a request, a Center can draw the attention of the recipient to Dr Serageldin's letter to the FAO recommending a moratorium and further suggest that the recipient does not apply for IPR on the material in question (even though the Center has no legal authority to enforce such a suggestion).

Outstanding Issues

Despite the progress made by the CDC and CBC, outstanding issues remain that will need to be considered at an ICW or at some point in time. Some of these relate to matters not adequately addressed or clear in the Guiding Principles. Others are raised directly or indirectly by the cases described in this paper and relate to implementation of the 1994 Agreements.

The Guiding Principles

The Guiding Principles have evolved over time and given the nature of the IPR environment they will need to continue to be dynamic and responsive.[18]

Three areas of the Guiding Principles were recently identified by the CDC as requiring further clarification.[19] These are:

1. The definition of derivative.
2. The question of benefit-sharing in the case of IPRs being taken out on Center-bred material or on derivatives.
3. The question of if and when to allow for IPRs on Center-bred materials when there has been no significant intellectual input by the recipient, and the related question of how to handle when more than one recipient in a country requests permission to apply for IPRs.

Derivatives

IPGRI is currently developing its institutional IP policy and has been considering how to handle the definition of derivative. With biotechnology enabling potentially significant differences with less genetic distance, the degree of genetic distances may not be sufficient to define derivative. It may therefore be useful to require certain minimum certified steps - such as hybridization and subsequent selection – in order for something not to be considered as 'essentially derived' and thus ineligible for IPR protection. Simple selection from a designated accession would not be considered as sufficient input to allow the recipient of designated germplasm to apply for any form of IPR on that germplasm.[20]

Benefit-sharing in Cases of IPR Taken on Center-bred Material or on Derivatives

The Guidelines adopted at ICW'98 require a recipient to seek permission from the Center before taking out patent protection. Encouraging the exchange, use and development of material requires a degree of certainty about how IPR issues including benefit-sharing arrangements will be handled by a Center. Inclusion of a Guiding Principle that correlates the extent of benefit-sharing anticipated with the degree of involvement in the development of the product could help alleviate the uncertainty that might otherwise hinder exchange, use and development of the resources. The principle might simply state that benefit-sharing arrangements will be determined based on factors such as the degree of involvement – including intellectual effort and endeavour and level of additional investment required – in the development of the product such that the higher the involvement in the stages of development the higher the expected royalty rate. It may be useful to develop benefit-sharing guidelines in conjunction with the Guiding Principles.

Center permission is required when a recipient wishes to take out a patent. Due to the practical effects of patents and PBR (e.g. there is no breeders' exemption in the former), Center permission is not required with a recipient seeking PBR. It might be useful, however, for the Guidelines to require recipients to notify a Center when seeking PBR on material derived from the Center. Such a requirement would facilitate monitoring of designated and other material in relation to PBR whether this is done by the PBR authority, a non-governmental organization or the Centers.

When Permission is Sought on Center-bred Material Where no Additional Intellectual Input has been Made; the Case of Requests from More than one Institution Within a Country

Unless otherwise prescribed by the supplier, Centers have the discretion to allow recipients to protect Center-held non-designated breeding material. In order to provide some degree of predictability and consistency, the Guiding Principles may wish to state that when the breeding material is wholly derived from Center efforts and created through the use of public funds, the threshold for granting intellectual property protection will be high; and, when granted it is anticipated that it will take place with appropriate benefit-sharing arrangements. It may also state that when such permission will be granted it will be granted only when the protection applies solely within the country of the recipient.

A short set of ranked criteria might be useful to clarify how decisions will be taken when more than one recipient in a country requests permission to take out IPR. The decision should ultimately be based on which recipient(s) will most effectively get the material to farmers. The decision on to whom permission will be granted might, for example, be based on the extent to which the choice: (i) strengthens local capacity in the form of local seed businesses; and (ii) effectively gets material to farmers (including meeting market demand) with the appropriate quality standards met and at a reasonable price. The ability to provide other relevant services may also form part of the criteria. There may also be an issue of how to select among several local seed companies. There are several alternatives that could be considered. All local companies could be permitted to proceed; or, consortiums to sell the seed could be promoted. The simplest route might be an open lottery. These would all need to be assessed in terms of administrative cost and the objective of effectively getting material to the farmer.

MTAs

Software Approach

There are several issues that require further clarification in the development and use of MTAs. There are questions concerning the legality of the 'software' approach though the FAO's approval strengthens a case for its efficacy. Thus far there are no test cases in relation to plant genetic resources that challenge the legality of this approach. A review of case law in relation to software might prove useful for any conclusions drawn in an analogous situation.

Related Information

Another outstanding issue receiving attention and diverse interpretation is the meaning of the term 'related information' in the agreed MTA. The agreed MTA holds that the recipient of designated germplasm has no rights to obtain IPR 'on the germplasm or related information'. Proposed definitions range from related information signifying only passport information and other information about the germplasm to it including genetic information within the germplasm (e.g. the genetic code). The implications arising from the two interpretations are starkly different and an agreed interpretation is necessary to ensure consistent implementation of MTAs across the CGIAR system.

CGIAR Role in Monitoring and Enforcement

In addition, at some point, Centers will need to address the larger issue of the appropriate role they should play in monitoring MTA compliance, including the question of who should be responsible for monitoring and what it entails in terms of human and financial resources.

Other Outstanding IP Issues

In addition, the events described in this chapter have presented the Centers with the opportunity to clarify issues of critical importance to the CGIAR, particularly in the context of the re-negotiation of the IU. The fourth Extraordinary Session of the Commission in December 1997 generally accepted the need for a multilateral system of exchange for PGRFA. Nevertheless, important technical and legal issues have arisen and will continue to arise as the details of the system are discussed. Solutions need to be based in reality and the CGIAR has an obvious interest in developing a workable system capable of achieving the IU's objectives while supportive of the complementary mission and purpose of the CGIAR.

There are many issues of direct relevance to the CGIAR that the IU negotiators must address. Some of these have arisen already in the context of recent events or just generally in the course of Centers pursuing their work. For example, the negotiators at the IU need to:

- Decide how to handle duplicate accessions of designated material that have been distributed prior to entering into the multilateral system. This is the same question that faced the CGIAR in the case noted and resulted in its recommendation for a moratorium on IPR for designated material pending resolution of the issue in the context of the IU.
- Determine the obligations of international genebanks and national programmes with regard to monitoring adherence to the system. The role of Centers in monitoring MTA compliance has been an issue since the FAO and the CGIAR made a joint statement on the interpretation of the 1994 Agreements.
- Decide what are or should be the responsibilities of an international genebank when a recipient wishes to take out a PBR on the genebanks'

non-designated, improved material without further change. This is directly related to one of the outstanding issues of the CGIAR Guiding Principles identified by the Center Directors and discussed earlier.

• Decide what are or should be an international genebank's obligations when a recipient wishes to commercialize (without taking a PBR) – even if restricted geographically – designated germplasm unchanged from the Center. Again, this directly parallels an outstanding issue in the Guiding Principles identified by the Center Directors.

• Ascertain how IPRs should be handled within a multilateral system based on free exchange. This was and continues to be the crux of the matter in the development and evolution of the CGIAR Guiding Principles.

Conclusion

Legal regimes for ownership, control and intellectual property over genetic resources are in a state of flux. Agricultural research is increasingly being privatized through IPR and other means. This dynamic and rapidly changing environment is of direct relevance to the CGIAR's work and mission. Hence, in pursuing its mission, the CGIAR must determine how it relates and responds to IPR. Specifically, there is a need for:

1. *The CGIAR policy development process to be assessed, clarified and restructured as appropriate.* There is little consensus on the potential impacts of IP on biodiversity, food security and development. In addition, opinions differ sharply on the implications of new biotechnologies. Furthermore, IP as it applies to biomaterials continues to be controversial and characterized by confusion and uncertainty. The CGIAR's ability to identify and analyse these complex issues and create and implement appropriate policy is therefore critical to the effective pursuance of its mission.

2. *Strengthening and enforcing the international agreements that place the South's germplasm 'in trust' for the world community.* Questions about monitoring and enforcement, the definition of key terms, access, benefit-sharing and the relation of IP and a multilateral system must be addressed if the intentions of the international agreements are to be realized.

3. *Addressing the outstanding issues in the CGIAR Guiding Principles.* Given the nature of the issues involved, the Guiding Principles must necessarily be dynamic and continue to evolve in light of new developments. Nevertheless, they should also demonstrate to present and future partners as well as the general public, how the CGIAR views intellectual property issues. They should establish the basis for consistent decision-making and ensure that the taking, granting permission to take or use of IP will be closely tied to furthering its mission.

Notes

1. See CGIAR Annual Report 1997.
2. For more on the development of the Guidelines including outstanding issues, see Geoff Hawtin and Timothy Reeves (19XX) Intellectual property rights and access to genetic resources in the Consultative Group on International Agricultural Research (CGIAR). In Shands, Collins and Lower (eds) *Intellectual Property Rights. III. Global Genetic Resources, Access and Property Rights.* Crops Sciences Society of America, pp. 41–58.
3. For example, the members of the CGIAR, the co-sponsors, the Technical Advisory Committee, the individual Center Boards of Trustees, The Committee of Center Board Chairs, the Committee of Center Directors, individual Center Directors, the Genetic Resources Policy Committee, the Inter-Center Working Group on Genetic Resources, the System-wide Genetic Resources Program, IPGRI (as the 'lead' Center on genetic resources and biodiversity issues), the NGO Committee and the Private Sector Committee.
4. The CGIAR sponsors two meetings every year. The first, International Centers Week, takes place during the last week of October in Washington DC. The second, the CGIAR Mid-Term Meeting, takes places in May in a host country.
5. CGIAR, September 30, 1998, *Shaping the CGIAR's Future: CGIAR System Review Report*, ICW//98/06, Chapter 15, Recommendation 18.
6. CGIAR, September 30, 1998, Recommendation 18.
7. These were adopted at ICW'96.
8. The IPR Committee is a sub-committee of the Center Directors' Committee.
9. See, Bragdon and Downes (1998) 'Recent policy trends and developments related to the conservation, use and development of genetic resources. *Issues in Genetic Resources* No. 7, IPGRI, p. 5.
10. Some countries have expressed an interest in placing their *ex situ* in the Network. Final decisions will likely await the outcome of the negotiations to revise the IU.
11. It should be noted that these issues — together with IPR and the implementation of Farmers' Rights — are being discussed in several international fora including the World Trade Organization (in particular the Agreement on Trade-related Aspects of Intellectual Property Rights, the CBD and the negotiations to revise the IU).
12. Prior to these agreements, plant germplasm from the Centers was freely exchanged. It was the policy of the Centers '... that collections assembled as a result of international collaboration should not become the property of any single nation, but should be held in trust for the use of present and future generations of research workers in all countries throughout the world'. It was understood that collected or donated germplasm accessions would remain freely available for conservation and use in research on behalf of the world community, in particular developing countries. Essentially, the FAO/CGIAR Agreements re-affirmed and gave legal weight to the CGIAR's commitment to hold its collections in trust for the international community.
13. A second Joint Statement is currently under consideration by both bodies. It will address technical problems associated with implementation of the Agreements including meeting requests for large numbers of accessions or large

quantities of seed; supplying seeds of difficult and costly-to-multiply accessions; providing designated materials which might harbour diseases or pests etc.

14. The System-wide Information Network for Genetic Resources (SINGER) was implemented in the interests of transparency with regard to the origins and location of the genetic resources in the in-trust collections, and in recognition of the importance of information in facilitating access to and use of genetic resources. SINGER has put in place the institutional and technical links to allow simultaneous searches of the diverse, independently designed and managed databases of the CGIAR Center.

15. As noted earlier, the CBD does not address access to *ex situ* genetic resource collections in existence prior to its entry into force. For this reason, negotiators adopted Resolution 3 of the Nairobi Final Act in May 1992, which contains a provision on the need to consider the issue of access to *ex situ* collections not covered by the Convention within the FAO Global System for the Conservation and Utilization of Plant Genetic Resources. The FAO/CGIAR Agreements were negotiated and concluded as a response to Resolution 3. Furthermore, the Convention does not prevent any germplasm donor from providing material to a genebank under the same conditions as would prevail in the case of designated material.

16. The CGIAR Chairman is nominated by the President of the World Bank, in consultation with the CGIAR through the Oversight Committee, from among the World Bank's senior managers. Mr Ismail Serageldin, the Bank's Vice President for Special Programs, has been Chairman since January 1994.

17. It is possible that a legal argument will be raised that such an obligation was implicit in the CGIAR policy of holding its collections in trust for the world community. The argument may be difficult to maintain when the in-trust policy was linked to a policy of unrestricted access, its relatively new understanding and foray into the policy matters related to IPRs, the recent broadening and expansion of IPRs etc.

18. See, the section 'Developing CGIAR Guidelines on IPR'.

19. See, the Center Directors' Committee Statement to MTM'98 on Genetic Resources, Biotechnology and Proprietary Science.

20. The ideas in this and the following sections arose in the context of discussions with Geoff Hawtin, Cary Fowler and the author.

034
Q16

Economics of Intellectual Property Rights for Agricultural Technology

Robert E. Evenson

Economic Growth Center, Department of Economics, Yale University, New Haven, Connecticut, USA

Intellectual property rights (IPRs) predate the development of public sector agricultural research systems. The Patent Office (established in 1790) was one of the earliest agencies established in the USA. Patent and copyright protection were the chief means for providing incentives for invention for almost a century before the Hatch Act of 1878 formalized the State Agricultural Experiment Station (SAES) system in the USA. It was argued that the Patent Office was the oldest organization conducting research for agriculture in the USA and that it functioned as a predecessor organization to the USDA-SAES research system because it recognized that the traditional 'scope' of patent IPRs failed to encourage plant and animal improvements.[1]

This scope changed greatly in the USA in the last century. The 1930 Plant Patent Act introduced patent protection for asexually reproduced plants. In 1970 the Plant Variety Protection Act provided 'Breeders' Rights' to plant breeders. The major expansion of IPR scope has taken place since then through *case law* where court decisions have expanded plant and animal IPR protection.[2] Today stronger plant IPR protection and, to a lesser extent, stronger Breeders' Rights, combined with developments in biotechnology have brought biological invention into roughly the same IPR domain as traditionally provided to chemical, electrical and mechanical invention. The WTO-TRIPs negotiations attempt to extend much of this scope of protection expansion globally. US interests, in particular, would like to see a harmonized system of IPRs for all countries based on the US system.

This scope expansion is a source of concern to agricultural scientists generally as it threatens them in two ways. They are threatened by *competition* (from private breeders) and they are threatened by the *altered information disclosure* incentives associated with expanded IPR scope. Even though other fields of science have dealt with strong IPRs for decades, agricultural scientists have been poorly prepared for IPR changes.[3]

Similarly, this expansion of IPR scope is seen as a threat in low-income developing countries which have traditionally resisted strong (or any) IPRs because of buyer–seller asymmetry (see below). For many low-income countries, national agricultural research systems (NARS) (supported by International Agricultural Research Centres (IARCs)) constitute most of their inventive activity. The combination of agricultural scientists' concerns and low-income country concerns produces a heightened sense of threat regarding IPRs that, to date, has evoked policy debate but little policy analysis.[4]

The resistance to IPRs in low-income countries has resulted in weak or non-existent IPR systems. Modern biotechnology research techniques applied to agriculture are being produced predominately by private firms in high-income countries. These firms rely on IPR systems to provide incentives for research by enabling them to sell products in IPR-protected markets. Public sector research organizations, including the IARCs, have been very slow to respond to the scientific opportunities being exploited by the private sector. This creates additional uncertainty and an additional threat for low-income countries. They cannot rely fully on their public sector research organizations to bring modern biotechnology products to them (at least in the near future). Their access to this technology depends on their IPR systems and on the skills of their scientists.

In this chapter I will attempt to address some of the basic economic principles associated with IPRs (which, as noted, have been in place for most fields of non-biological inventions for decades) and to relate them to the growing policy concerns of the public sector agricultural sciences. In the following six sections I (i) review the technical aspects of the major IPRs; (ii) discuss single-economy invention cases; (iii) introduce intellectual and biological germplasm; (iv) discuss multi-country cases and buyer–seller asymmetry; (v) illustrate these issues with summary data for plant varieties (rice) and for agricultural inventions (patents and utility models) and (vi) offer a discussion of unresolved policy issues.

IPRs: A Summary

It is useful to have a taxonomy of IPRs to clarify several key points. Table 6.1 provides a brief summary of major IPRs, their scope of coverage, conditions for obtaining the IPR, international conventions, disclosure requirements, researcher rights and reproduction rights.

Consider the traditional (utility) patent covering inventions in the

Table 6.1. IPRs: a taxonomy.

IPRs	Scope	Period of protection	Conditions for obtaining IPR			International convention	Disclosure requirement	Research exemption	Reproduction rights
			Novelty	Usefulness	Inventive step				
Patent (original)	Inventions: chemical, electrical, mechanical	17–20 years	Yes (global)	Yes	Strong	Paris, TRIPs	Enabling	None (conceptual)	Negotiable
Patent (expanded)	Inventions genes plants and animals	17–20 years	Yes (global)	Yes	Strong	Paris, TRIPs	Enabling	None (germplasmic)	Negotiable
Utility model	Minor inventions	5–15 years	Yes (national)	Weak	Weak	None	Enabling	None (conceptual)	Negotiable
Industrial design	Designs	Permanent	Yes	None	None	None	None	None (conceptual)	None
Breeders' Rights	Plant varieties	5–16 years	Yes	Yes	Weaker none	UPOV, TRIPs	None deposit	Allowed	Limited (Farmers' Rights)
Appellation of origin	Food products	Permanent	Regional	None	None	Lisbon	Location of production	Allowed	None
Folkloric rights	Indigenous products	Permanent	Yes	None	None	FAO/UNESCO		Allowed	Negotiable
Farmers' Rights (CBD)	Genetic resources	Permanent	Yes	None	None	CBD undertaking	Location of genetic resource	None (use of rights)	(Use rights)
Copyrights	Written works	Life + 50 years	Yes	None	None	Berne, TRIPs	None	Allowed	None (limited)
Trademarks	Brand names	Permanent	Yes	None	None	TRIPs	None	Allowed	None
Trade secrecy	Trade secrets	Permanent	None	None	None	None	None	None	None

chemical, electrical and mechanical fields. The three basic requirements for obtaining patent protection are:

1. The invention must be genuinely novel (new) judged against global standards. The USA has a first-to-invent rule strictly respecting this standard. Most other countries use a first-to-file rule to reduce disputes.
2. The invention must be useful, i.e. have a clear potential use (gene fragments were not patentable because they did not meet this standard).
3. The invention must entail an 'inventive step', i.e. be unobvious to one trained in the art. (This is a court judgement.)

These requirements serve to prevent someone from obtaining IPR protection for an invention that they did not create. There is widespread fear in countries with little experience with IPRs that outsiders (e.g. multinational corporations) can obtain IPRs for inventions created domestically. This should not happen although the first-to-file rule may allow some of this to occur.[5] (One obvious policy implication is that inventors may need to obtain IPRs to protect the integrity of their invention even if they do not wish to exercise the right to exclude others from using or making the invention without permission for the period of protection.)

The inventor must provide a disclosure of her invention so that a person skilled in the field is enabled to replicate the invention. This enabling disclosure or 'removal from secrecy' is not intended to allow others to actually make or use the invention without a negotiated licensing arrangement, but it is intended to make public the conceptual or intellectual 'germplasm' associated with the invention. A researcher or inventor is free to use the conceptual germplasm in making a 'follow-on' invention, but not the invention (embodied in a product or process) itself.

In Table 6.1, a distinction is made between the traditional patent and the case law strengthened patent as it now exists in the USA. The expansion of US patent law now allows the patenting of plant varieties and animals (genetically engineered). Gene clones or constructs and microorganisms are protected in the USA and other countries.

The chief difference between the traditional and the expanded patent is in the research exemption. Gene constructs and plant varieties that serve as 'parental material' in the development of improved plants and animals are physically contained in the progeny (as opposed to conceptual germplasm). As a result the IPR owner has the right to exclude their use in breeding programmes. (See below for a fuller discussion.)

The utility model is a 'petty patent' with weak novelty and inventive step requirements. It has not been used extensively for biological invention but could be so used (see later).

Industrial designs are generally not used for biological materials.[6]

The chief alternative to patent rights for plants are Breeders' Rights. (I include the 1930 Plant Patent Act and the 1970 Plant Variety Protection Act in this category.[7]) These rights are relatively weak because of the short period of protection and the research exemption and farmers' exemption associated with them. They have a weak inventive step requirement. The protected plant varieties must meet certain requirements standard to most varietal release programmes. The laws call for the IPR holder to provide seeds for deposit in *ex situ* collections, but IPR holders attempt to restrict their use even though the research exemption allows another plant breeder to use the protected variety as a parent in a breeding programme. The farmers' exemption allows farmers to save seed for their own use and for restricted sales to neighbours.[8] This IPR is likely to be chosen by countries required to develop *sui generis* protection for plants under the WTO-TRIPs agreement.[9]

Appellation of Origin rights are becoming increasingly important in specialized food (and wine) markets. We will probably see an expansion of this IPR. Some version of this may be developed to provide certification for natural food products, non-genetically engineered products, etc.[10]

Folkloric rights are not fully developed at this time.[11] The Convention on Biological Diversity (CBD) calls for Farmers' Rights, recognizing rights associated with farmers' varieties or 'landraces' developed through farmers' selections over many centuries as they moved from one region to another.[12] There is a popular perception that these farmers' varieties were produced by 'indigenous' people as opposed to 'foreign' immigrants (especially in the Americas). But this is not necessarily the case. Indigenous minorities may preserve valuable genetic resource today while mainstream farmers opt for modern plant varieties, but that does not necessarily mean that they actually produced the landraces in question. (See below for evidence for this.)

Copyrights and trademarks are important IPRs and are the IPRs most frequently violated in countries charged with IPR piracy. This is unfortunate because invention incentives are the more important incentives in an economic growth context.[13]

Finally, it should be noted that trade secrecy laws protect trade secrets even though it is one of the principles of patent and other IPRs that disclosure of secrets be made.

The Basic Economics of IPR Protection for an Invention

All inventions are made at a particular time and place and inventors have available to them information or knowledge that is at least to some degree the result of prior invention. Figure 6.1 provides the basic analytic framework for an incremental invention(s) in a single economy.

Two invention types are depicted. In the upper three panels, the market for a major invention in the first period after invention (1), the terminal period of IPR protection (T) and the post-protection period (+T) are depicted. This is an invention that does not lose its market to subsequent inventions.

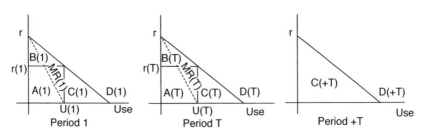

Type 1 Invention: Major Invention with Few Subsequent Substitutes

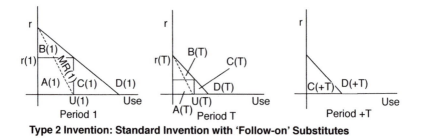

Type 2 Invention: Standard Invention with 'Follow-on' Substitutes

Fig. 6.1. Inventions in a single economy.

In period (1) the demand curve D(1) shows the quantity of use (denominated in dollar units) demanded as a function of a royalty rate, r. When an IPR monopoly is granted, the inventor will license U(1) units at royalty rate r(1). The area A(1) will be paid to the owners of the IPR. The area B(1) is the consumers' surplus associated with the invention. The area C(1) can be considered potential consumers' surplus because the marginal cost of replicating the invention is zero in this case. It is not correct to call this area a deadweight loss associated with IPRs because this invention may not have been made in the absence of the IPR incentive (i.e. the expectation of earning A(1) through A(T)).

In the case of the first (upper panel) invention, few substitutes have been created prior to the last period of IPR protection (T). The IPR holder in this case earns A(1), A(2), ... A(T) and consumers' surplus is B(1), B(2), ... B(T) and potential consumers' surplus C(1), C(2), ... C(T). In the period after IPR protection, the full consumers' surplus C(+T) is realized to the economy.

For the invention depicted in the lower panels, substitutes are quickly developed (they may even be inspired by the original invention – see below). As a result there is little or no demand for the invention by the end of the IPR period (T). For this invention the royalties A(T) will not justify paying the fee for maintaining IPR protection levied in most countries and the invention will become public property. European experience indicates that roughly 85% of inventions are not maintained until the terminal period of the IPR.

There are a number of policy issues associated with patent rights. These include:

1. Choice of T, the period of patent protection.
2. Rules regarding the 'breadth' of patent protection.
3. Options to 'buy-out' patent rights.
4. Recognition of foreigners' patent rights.
5. Public sector invention.

I address foreigners' patent rights and special germplasmic issues below. Here I will consider the length (and breadth) issues, public sector buy-outs and public sector R&D programmes (without IPRs).

Suppose we do not have a viable public sector R&D option and that we cannot figure out how to buy IPRs for A(1)–A(T) and then make them available at zero price to producers (and consumers). How can length and breadth be juggled to maximize producers' and/or consumers' surplus?

Consider changing length (given breadth rules). As the period of protection is lengthened for type 1 inventions, the present value of the A incentives goes up and the present value of C(+T), the post-IPR consumers' surplus, goes down. We thus have an incentive–consumers' surplus trade-off. If T is too short, it will provide insufficient incentives for inventions and consumers will lose B. The solution to the problem is to choose T so that the present value of B(1) + B(2) + ... + B(T) plus C(+T) is maximized.

This problem can also be addressed by expanding the size of the market by recognizing foreigners' rights (see below) in return for foreigner recognition of rights. With an expanded market, optimal T can be reduced.

Note, however, that for the type 2 inventions, changing T will have little effect (unless they are germplasmic – see below). For these inventions incentives can only be changed by changing breadth. (Since most are probably germplasmic, however, the germplasm analysis is relevant.)

Breadth of IPR coverage is determined by court decisions and by traditions regarding the 'inventive step'. When inventive step hurdles are low, IPR coverage is narrow, hence markets are small. Patent attorneys attempt to write patent applications to achieve maximum breadth for their clients. Expanding breadth does not necessarily expand the total market for inventions because, for a given amount of inventive effort, fewer inventions will be produced when IPR breadth is expanded. Breadth effectively has the same effect on incentives as length (see Nordhaus, 1969).

Before turning to germplasmic effects of invention, it is relevant to ask why governments have not used public sector R&D and/or public sector buy-outs to capture the Cs in Fig. 6.1.

The answer is that for much traditional agricultural plant and animal improvement research where IPRs have not been available, effective public sector R&D programmes have been developed. For mechanical, chemical and electrical fields of invention, some public sector R&D programmes have been developed but, in competition with private firm R&D, they have often not been as dynamic or effective. The public sector has been important in agriculture, in the health sector to some extent, and in some military- and space-related R&D. Even in agricultural research where public–private competition is observed (as with hybrid corn), public sector R&D cannot compete with private sector R&D.

In spite of the obvious benefits of public sector buy-outs, i.e. paying A to get C in Fig. 6.1, few governments have been effective in doing so. There are several problems. Perhaps the most serious is being able to tell the difference between type 1 and type 2 inventions. The market reveals this difference only over time. A buy-out of a type 2 invention is inefficient because the market loss will lead to public conversion of the invention. In addition, public sector buy-outs may create other incentive problems. It should be noted that for private sector inventions, most R&D is D (development) undertaken after the invention is made. IPR protection is required to justify the market development investments associated with invention. The buy-out could be delayed to deal with both problems, but then its value is reduced (i.e. C is lost by delay).[14]

The Germplasm Dimension

Legal scholars (more than economists) recognize two benefits to IPRs. The first is the incentive effect for inventive effort. The second is the disclosure or 'removal from secrecy' effect. In the absence of IPRs, trade secrecy strategies (protected to some extent by trade secrecy laws) provide incentives for R&D and inventive effort. When IPRs facilitate early removal from secrecy by requiring an 'enabling disclosure', this has at least two positive effects. First, it may weaken secrecy-based imperfections to competition between firms. More importantly, however, earlier disclosure may have germplasmic effects.

Germplasmic effects occur when one invention becomes a 'parent' to another. For plant and animal inventions this parentage is biological and an integral part of 'breeding' programmes. It can be easily identified. For chemical, mechanical and electrical inventions, germplasmic parentage is often more conceptual or intellectual in nature. It is less easily identified.[15] Consider the case where an inventor develops a plastic material with enhanced heat resistance. This invention will have a market and the inventor will collect royalties if the invention is patented. However, the very fact that this material is available for use in a communication device widens the potential for inventions in the communication device field. Alternatively, potential inventions may have 'puzzle' dimensions where the likelihood of an invention of a particular type depends on the number of other pieces of the puzzle that have been revealed.

There is a sense then that a parent invention 'lives on' in progeny inventions. This is depicted in Fig. 6.2 where the demand for progeny inventions G(T) and G(+T) is depicted for the inventions. (Note that the area G(T)–D(T) can be regarded as additional consumers' surplus.)

Now an important distinction emerges between the biological germplasm case and the conceptual germplasm case. It is that the biological germplasm parental components can be identified in biological progeny and that they can be regarded as IPR-protected components of the progeny inventions. This is not generally the case for conceptual germplasm. In fact, most patent protection laws explicitly provide for exemption of concepts and ideas from patent protection. This exemption is guided by the sense that concepts and ideas are 'common heritage' in nature and that IPRs should not impinge upon the exchange of knowledge in this form.

The principle of a 'research exemption' is also recognized in 'Breeders' Rights' laws though they may be 'strengthened' so as to change this. Emerging patent protection appears to be taking the form of patent protection of components in biological progeny. This includes single gene sources incorporated by genetic engineering techniques and of more complex parent plants and possibly animals. Another form of IPR strengthening is taking place in the granting of patents for genetic resources to be utilized for specific 'new' purposes even when the genetic resources have been known and available for other purposes.[16]

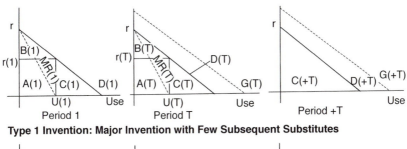

Type 1 Invention: Major Invention with Few Subsequent Substitutes

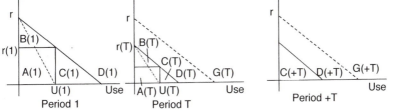

Type 2 Invention: Standard Invention with 'Follow-on' Substitutes

Fig. 6.2. Germplasmic effects of invention.

It is not clear at this time whether patent offices in OECD countries other than the USA will follow US practice in all regards. It is a pretty good bet though that they will (see V. Santaniello, Chapter 2, this volume) and that while developing countries will have the *sui generis* option (Breeders' Rights) for plant varieties, gene components will be considered subject to patent laws.

It should be noted that the progeny protection devices provide stronger incentives for private sector R&D. This added protection may also provide protection backward into pre-breeding and even genetic conservation activity (see final section).

Multi-country Recognition of IPRs

As noted earlier, most IPRs have negotiated international conventions which typically call for 'national treatment' of foreigners from member nations. That is, each member nation agrees to treat foreign citizens from other member nations on a par with domestic citizens. In addition, most countries have 'harmonized' their IPR laws and have been under increasing pressure to do so under the recent round of GATT-WTO-TRIPs negotiations.

This development of international recognition of foreigners' rights and harmonized IPRs has created essentially four 'blocks' of nations with different IPR policy interests. This is easy to see in empirical terms by referring to Table 6.2 which depicts international flows of inventions patented for most nations with patent protection systems. Three of the four blocks of countries are depicted in Table 6.2. The fourth includes the many countries which do not have functioning patent systems.

The three blocks are readily identified in Table 6.2 as the developed market economies, the recently industrialized (RIC) and the newly industrialized (NIC) developing countries (including a number of near NICs such as India).[17]

The upper left-hand part of Table 6.2 includes the OECD developed market economies. The data for this quadrant indicate that there are active international invention flows among the OECD block members. Substantial proportions of inventions originating in each country are protected in other OECD member countries.

The upper right-hand part of Table 6.2 shows inventions originating in the OECD countries that are protected in the block 2 RIC countries and the block 3 NIC (and near-NIC) countries. One can see that activity in this part is significant. OECD countries 'sell', i.e. obtain protection for, significant inventions, in all RIC and NIC (and near-NIC) countries.

The middle left-hand part of the table depicts sales of RIC origin inventions in OECD countries. This part shows limited activity. The lower left-hand part of Table 6.2 is empty. NIC and near-NIC countries are not able to sell their inventions in RIC or OECD countries.

The middle and lower right-hand part of Table 6.2 depicts international invention flows between RIC and NIC/near-NIC countries. It is essentially diagonal. RIC and NIC/near-NIC developing countries do produce inventions but they obtain little IPR protection in other countries.

This pattern of invention is consistent with a type of international product cycle and of technological dependence between countries. Developing countries import or buy (i.e. provide IPRs to) significant inventions originating in OECD countries. Traditional patent rights do not recognize germplasm rights but there is indirect evidence that many of the inventions in developing countries are germplasmic adaptations of OECD inventions. This explains why, for example, they are not valuable (i.e. not given IPRs) in OECD countries (the empty lower left quadrant). (See the next section for agricultural inventions.)[18]

Figure 6.3 provides some formalization to the data in Table 6.2 and relates this to Fig. 6.1. The upper panel of Fig. 6.3 depicts the market for an invention originating in an OECD country, in the origin country, in another OECD country and in a developing country. The demand for the invention in the other OECD countries is depicted as being less than in the origin countries (countries here are scaled to be of the same size) because of different economic, institutional and bio-physical conditions in the two countries. The expansion of the market to other OECD countries increases the incentives $(A_0 + A_1)$ for invention. Consumers' surplus per invention $(B_0 + B_1)$ and potential consumers' surplus $(C_0 + C_1)$ are also increased for each invention. The extent of the expansion depends on the spillover barriers associated with the invention.

There are actually two penalties for pirating IPRs and these are depicted in the market for OECD inventions in the developing countries (upper right panel) and in the market for developing country inventions in OECD countries (lower panels). One is the loss of market penalty. The loss of market penalty is critical for OECD countries but is small for developing countries. The operative penalty for developing countries is the supplier penalty depicted in the upper right panel. Here the OECD supplier is depicted as being in a position to impose costs reducing the demand in the developing country from D_w to D_{wo} if the developing country pirates. When the developing country offers IPR protection, the originating inventor actively seeks to market his/her invention in the country. He/she provides information and exposes the 'best technology'. He/she seeks to enter into agreements not only for the IPR but for related technical assistance. When the recipient developing country attempts to pirate, the supplier responds in a reverse fashion.

Until the recent GATT-WTO agreements and the Section 301 (and Super 301) actions by the USA, many developing countries concluded that piracy (and varying forms of cover-up) was the best route. Today, it is generally recognized that the best way to 'exploit foreigners' is probably to recognize their IPRs and then engage in adaptive imitative invention to hold down the payments for IPRs.[19]

Table 6.2. International patent flows, all sectors, 1990.

| | Granting | | | | | | | | | | | | |
| | Developed | | | | | | | | | | | | |
Applicant	AT 1990 Austria	CH 1990 Switzerland	DE 1990 Germany	DK 1990 Denmark	EP 1990 Europe	FR 1990 France	GB 1990 Britain	IT 1990 Italy	JP 1990 Japan	NL 1990 Netherlands	NO 1990 Norway	SE 1990 Sweden	US 1990 USA
AT	2,782	64	0	38	325	41	31	115	262	11	28	14	304
CH	137	1,892	15	149	777	105	84	176	1,067	53	79	40	1,074
DE	944	671	2,889	937	6,045	1,253	965	1,757	6,876	280	364	240	7,339
DK	5	3	0	766	89	16	27	17	69	11	43	18	116
EP	4	1	0	47	1,171	2	1	0	661	0	23	0	530
FR	66	0	11	353	2,486	7,653	149	409	2,515	124	210	45	2,625
GB	98	99	1	535	1,833	240	4,248	309	2,960	112	231	69	3,050
IT	71	88	4	146	730	207	181	16,591	901	49	62	41	1,127
JP	129	130	2	287	4,129	934	1,738	662	281,027	226	88	123	18,470
NL	41	5	0	135	688	48	21	19	745	180	51	11	769
NO	34	1	0	63	55	14	29	12	32	8	458	32	86
SE	40	9	0	375	529	60	51	28	488	39	275	1,506	653
US	222	202	1	928	5,643	905	1,507	1,161	14,917	411	650	320	59,692
ES	4	10	1	1	40	75	41	135	73	2	5	0	84
HU	92	35	1	53	58	52	50	77	85	6	18	30	80
IE	1	1	0	0	18	1	44	2	17	0	1	1	37
KR	1	1	1	0	6	6	26	61	340	0	1	1	194
PL	0	0	0	1	4	4	2	1	5	0	0	1	13
PT	3	0	0	0	2	1	1	3	0	0	1	1	6
TR	0	0	0	0	0	0	0	0	1	0	0	0	0
AR	0	0	0	0	1	0	0	6	3	0	0	0	13
BR	2	0	0	0	6	12	7	27	28	0	1	1	33
CN	0	0	0	0	8	1	3	2	6	0	0	0	36
EG	0	0	0	0	0	0	0	0	0	0	0	0	1
IN	0	0	0	0	1	0	3	0	1	0	0	0	1
MX	0	0	0	0	2	0	0	3	2	0	0	0	10
MY	0	0	0	0	0	0	0	0	1	0	0	0	0
PH	0	0	0	0	1	0	2	0	0	0	0	0	0
ZM	0	0	0	0	0	0	0	0	0	0	0	0	0

| | Granting | | | | | | | | | | | | | | | |
| | RIC | | | | | | | NIC | | | | | | | | |
Applicant	ES 1990 Spain	HU 1990 Hungary	IE 1990 Ireland	KR 1990 Korea	PL 1990 Poland	PT 1990 Portugal	TR 1990 Turkey	AR 1990 Argentina	BR 1990 Brazil	CN 1990 China	EG 1990 Egypt	IN 1992 India	MX 1992 Mexico	MY 1987 Malaysia	PH 1990 Philippines	ZM 1990 Zambia
AT	14	35	0	7	10	3	2	3	32	0	3	10	5	4	5	0
CH	38	52	27	46	21	43	18	13	131	184	8	66	27	46	40	0
DE	323	286	78	152	79	154	67	36	622	768	20	211	122	47	93	3
DK	27	15	8	3	3	8	0	0	19	45	2	6	3	2	12	0
EP	5	10	6	15	7	9	5	3	57	114	3	43	8	10	5	0
FR	136	61	92	122	21	119	20	33	288	434	36	138	62	12	21	0
GB	137	179	223	112	70	143	39	22	432	495	33	226	74	184	118	11
IT	144	28	22	63	18	33	16	21	161	158	12	49	29	4	11	0
JP	93	120	56	3,883	27	28	9	7	258	1,712	6	126	67	301	92	0
NL	5	27	14	54	6	8	9	2	40	225	3	19	7	7	12	0
NO	11	1	6	4	3	1	1	1	16	22	3	6	6	1	0	0
SE	63	20	26	26	7	14	2	2	89	88	6	20	10	18	8	0
US	543	307	378	1,410	90	320	83	138	1,783	2,486	90	602	872	266	500	11
ES	1,805	0	0	5	0	5	0	7	15	11	1	4	11	0	3	0
HU	20	1,496	3	4	35	10	1	9	14	44	5	9	2	2	12	0
IE	1	0	121	0	0	1	0	0	4	4	0	1	0	0	5	0
KR	2	0	0	3,294	0	0	1	1	3	40	1	4	0	0	0	0
PL	1	15	0	0	5,591	0	0	0	0	0	0	3	0	0	0	0
PT	1	1	0	3	0	16	0	0	2	6	0	0	0	0	0	0
TR	0	0	0	0	0	0	107	0	0	0	0	0	0	0	0	0
AR	3	0	0	0	0	0	0	201	15	73	0	0	0	1	0	0
BR	9	1	0	1	0	1	0	2	2,555	5	2	2	7	0	0	0
CN	1	1	0	0	0	0	0	0	3	7,339	0	2	0	0	0	0
EG	0	0	0	0	0	0	0	0	0	0	62	0	0	0	0	0
IN	3	0	0	0	0	0	0	0	0	0	0	616	0	0	0	0
MX	0	0	0	0	0	0	0	0	0	2	0	0	268	0	0	0
MY	3	0	0	0	0	0	0	0	2	2	0	0	0	17	0	0
PH	0	0	0	0	0	0	0	0	0	0	0	0	0	0	120	0
ZM	0	0	0	0	0	0	0	0	0	0	0	0	0	0	0	11

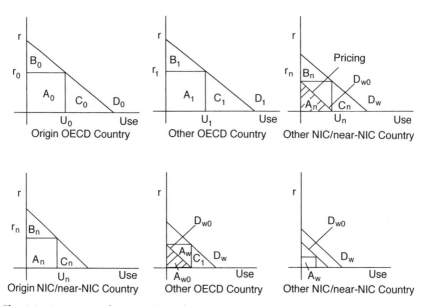

Fig. 6.3. International recognition of patent rights.

Agricultural Inventions: International Comparisons

In this section I report some international data for patented agricultural inventions intended for 'use' in several agricultural production and food production sectors.[20] I also report data for non-patented rice varieties to suggest where IPRs may matter in the future with extended IPR scope.

I begin by noting that a distinction can be made between the industry of manufacture (IOM) and the sector of use (SOU) for an invention. The agricultural production inventions discussed here are sector of use inventions since the agricultural sector itself is the industry of manufacture for very few inventions. The food production sectors, on the other hand, are both IOMs and SOUs for inventions. Chapter 12 addresses the measurement and interpretation of IOM–SOU invention assignments in the Yale Technology Concordance (YTC).

Patents and Utility Models in Developing Countries

The YTC uses Canadian Patent Office data to associate industry assignments with international patent classes (IPC). Despite the fact that the YTC is based on Canadian data, the industrial structure of Canadian inventions is not imposed when the YTC is applied to patent data for other nations. The probabilities of the YTC indicate a relationship between IPC (a product/process definition) and IOM or SOU (an industry definition), but permits flexibility for the data to display the industrial composition of patenting in other nations.

Invention information is presented in Table 6.3. Domestic-origin patents were chosen for this table to better identify the indigenous invention patterns by nation. Table 6.4 presents further information on the presence of domestic patenting as a share of all patents granted in each sector.

Domestic patenting mirrors the totals very closely, but is a little less agricultural and a little more food-oriented. American-origin patents follow the same pattern, but Japanese-origin patents tend to be more heavily agricultural (9% of Japanese-origin patents are destined for agricultural use) and less food-based (only 2% for food).

Within the agricultural sector, half of all inventions go directly to crops, with another 17% to crop services. Livestock averages another 14% of all agricultural use patents, and earns a further 10% through services to livestock. The remaining 10% is split evenly between fruits/vegetables and horticulture.

The food sector is less clearly defined, with 40% of all food-sector patents falling into the 'other food' category. Meat, beverages and tobacco each average 13% of the food sector total, dairy and cereals each compose another 8%, and 5% is contributed by patents for use in fruit/vegetable processing.

On average, domestic invention is less focused on livestock and tobacco, with more emphasis on horticulture and beverages. American-origin patents are weighted much more heavily towards tobacco, while Japanese-origin patents are heavily centred on crops and cereals.

Four nations in the sample (Brazil, China, Hungary and Korea) have used utility model protection at some point, although their emphasis has been different. Utility models give IPR to minor inventions or adaptations of existing technology and require a smaller inventive step to qualify for protection. Table 6.5 presents both the number of utility models by SOU and the ratio of utility models to full domestic patents in each SOU. All four nations saw between 5 and 7% of all utility models used in agriculture and food, a proportion slightly larger than seen for regular patents. All saw more use in the food sector than in agriculture, a trend not upheld in regular patents in the same nations.

There is a large difference among nations when we consider the reliance upon utility models for protection of domestic invention and use of full patents. Hungary had only one utility model for every three domestic patents, while China had twice as many utility models as domestic patents. While Hungary had relatively few utility models in agricultural use, Brazil, China and Korea had roughly as many as domestic patents. Both Brazil and Korea relied much more on utility models for livestock use than for crop use (relative to full patents). In counterpoint, China's highest relative reliance on utility models came in the crop services, while Hungary's greatest relative use of utility models was in the dairy and beverage sectors.

Table 6.3. Domestic-origin patents used in the agriculture and food sectors (all with IPCs).

Nation	Year	Agric. live-stock	Agric. crops	Agric. fruits and vegetables	Agric. horti-culture	Agric. services to livestock	Agric. services to crops	Agric. services other	Food meat	Food fruits and vegetables	Food dairy	Food cereals	Food beverages	Food tobacco	Food other	Agric. total	Food total	Ag + Food total	All patents
Argentina	1974	1	3	0	0	1	2	0	1	1	0	0	1	0	2	6	4	11	118
Argentina	1980	5	23	2	5	3	12	0	7	5	4	2	13	6	16	50	51	102	1,002
Argentina	1985	1	2	0	0	1	1	0	1	0	0	0	1	0	2	6	5	11	218
Argentina	1990	1	4	1	1	1	2	0	1	0	1	0	2	3	1	10	8	18	180
Brazil	1974	18	70	7	5	11	37	1	34	17	17	8	40	22	59	150	197	346	4,335
Brazil	1980	14	66	6	6	11	34	1	15	9	7	6	28	10	34	138	108	246	3,183
Brazil	1985	14	46	4	6	9	21	1	13	7	7	4	22	5	33	102	92	194	2,885
Brazil	1990	14	42	4	6	9	22	1	14	8	9	6	16	6	31	99	90	189	2,996
Brazil	1995	12	41	4	6	8	20	2	10	8	7	4	18	9	32	94	88	182	2,457
China	1990	69	136	15	30	39	45	13	65	34	26	38	76	43	228	347	510	857	10,426
China	1995	129	248	27	48	124	72	27	160	75	81	121	282	68	825	675	1,612	2,287	15,280
Egypt	1977	1	5	0	1	1	2	0	0	0	0	1	0	0	1	10	2	12	143
Egypt	1980	0	1	0	0	0	0	0	0	0	0	0	0	0	2	2	1	3	83
Egypt	1985	0	2	0	0	0	1	0	0	0	0	0	0	0	3	4	5	9	77
Egypt	1990	0	2	0	0	0	1	0	1	0	0	0	0	0	0	4	2	5	67
Egypt	1995	1	3	0	0	1	1	0	2	0	0	0	1	1	3	7	6	13	157
Hungary	1974	6	15	1	4	3	6	3	3	2	1	3	4	2	10	39	24	62	917
Hungary	1980	11	19	2	4	6	7	1	3	3	2	3	5	2	8	50	25	75	878
Hungary	1985	24	42	4	8	12	15	3	9	3	6	6	9	3	22	107	58	165	1,546
Hungary	1990	28	57	6	17	16	22	14	13	7	5	9	11	8	40	161	93	254	1,933
Hungary	1995	5	13	1	10	5	6	20	5	2	2	2	3	10	12	61	35	96	756
India	1976	2	8	1	1	1	4	1	3	2	4	3	9	2	18	18	41	59	1,239
India	1980	3	16	1	1	1	5	0	1	0	1	1	1	0	7	27	11	39	568
India	1985	4	15	1	1	2	5	0	6	2	4	2	3	4	17	27	38	66	1,021
India	1992	3	9	1	1	2	3	0	3	2	2	2	3	2	11	18	25	44	690
Kenya	1975–1989	0	0	0	0	0	0	0	0	0	0	0	0	0	0	0	0	0	1
Korea	1979	2	7	1	0	2	2	0	1	1	2	1	2	1	6	14	15	29	683
Korea	1985	4	8	1	3	2	3	1	7	4	3	2	8	1	35	22	62	84	1,275
Korea	1990	14	12	2	3	2	5	1	22	11	8	10	15	5	60	48	130	178	3,546
Korea	1995	23	33	4	11	12	15	4	29	17	13	17	27	19	108	103	230	333	8,988

Country	Year																	
Malaysia	1974	0	0	0	0	0	0	0	0	0	0	0	0	0	0	0	0	1
Malaysia	1980	0	0	0	0	0	0	0	0	0	0	0	0	0	0	0	0	0
Malaysia	1987	0	0	0	0	0	0	0	0	0	0	1	0	0	0	1	1	16
Mexico	1981	1	8	1	1	4	0	1	0	2	1	2	1	5	15	12	28	479
Mexico	1985	4	7	1	2	3	0	5	2	5	3	4	2	19	18	42	59	603
Mexico	1992	2	2	0	1	1	0	2	0	1	1	2	0	7	6	14	20	394
Philippines	1976	3	12	1	3	5	1	3	3	0	1	2	0	5	25	14	39	303
Philippines	1980	2	8	1	1	3	0	1	1	1	1	2	1	7	16	15	31	258
Philippines	1985	1	5	1	1	1	0	0	0	0	0	2	3	5	9	11	20	211
Philippines	1990	1	3	0	1	1	0	2	0	0	1	2	3	4	6	12	18	157
Poland	1974	18	31	3	10	13	1	24	10	5	8	9	3	34	80	94	175	5,047
Poland	1980	69	119	13	27	50	4	81	24	24	35	45	16	104	293	329	622	15,765
Poland	1985	43	104	15	19	46	4	66	15	19	24	25	14	87	240	249	489	11,391
Poland	1990	29	66	12	12	30	3	26	9	15	13	14	6	57	156	139	296	7,162
Poland	1995	30	67	8	13	28	2	21	11	24	10	12	4	53	155	135	290	5,212
Turkey	1979	1	0	0	0	0	0	0	0	0	0	0	0	0	0	0	0	1
Turkey	1985	1	4	0	0	1	1	0	0	0	0	0	2	2	7	4	11	116
Turkey	1990	0	2	0	0	1	0	0	0	0	0	1	3	2	4	6	9	118
Turkey	1995	1	1	0	0	0	0	0	1	0	0	0	1	1	3	3	6	132
Zambia	1968–1994	5	23	2	6	7	0	2	1	2	2	5	4	17	44	33	77	797
Canada	1978–1993	87	237	21	52	121	7	81	20	30	21	62	36	115	576	365	941	14,818
Japan	1990	713	1,847	354	469	815	119	930	403	470	447	776	249	2,921	4,514	6,197	10,710	432,599
USA	1990	323	599	70	267	260	28	305	91	203	93	345	140	694	1,614	1,871	3,485	74,056

Note: Values may not sum due to rounding.
IPC, International Patent Classification.

Table 6.4. Domestic share of patents for use in the agriculture and food subsectors.

Domestic/all	Year	Agric. live-stock	Agric. crops	Agric. fruits and vegetables	Agric. horti-culture	Agric. services to livestock	Agric. services to crops	Agric. other	Food meat	Food fruits and vegetables	Food dairy	Food cereals	Food beverages	Food tobacco	Food other	Domestic share of ag+ food	US share of ag+ food	Japan share of ag+ food	Other share of ag+ food	Domestic share of all patents
Argentina	1974	0.24	0.36	0.38	0.25	0.22	0.41	0.19	0.16	0.36	0.05	0.11	0.20	0.06	0.17	0.23	0.32	0.00	0.45	0.14
Argentina	1980	0.10	0.12	0.12	0.36	0.14	0.18	0.10	0.14	0.31	0.17	0.10	0.33	0.25	0.17	0.16	0.29	0.04	0.50	0.17
Argentina	1985	0.29	0.18	0.22	0.22	0.22	0.24	0.22	0.16	0.22	0.28	0.21	0.45	0.08	0.37	0.24	0.30	0.01	0.45	0.35
Argentina	1990	0.17	0.23	0.28	0.59	0.17	0.30	0.37	0.16	0.18	0.53	0.07	0.51	0.30	0.14	0.26	0.23	0.05	0.46	0.26
Brazil	1974	0.31	0.27	0.30	0.39	0.33	0.38	0.20	0.42	0.52	0.43	0.33	0.46	0.32	0.37	0.35	0.23	0.03	0.38	0.30
Brazil	1980	0.30	0.25	0.24	0.41	0.42	0.35	0.24	0.35	0.50	0.32	0.36	0.47	0.33	0.38	0.32	0.18	0.06	0.43	0.28
Brazil	1985	0.32	0.21	0.21	0.40	0.38	0.28	0.14	0.32	0.50	0.36	0.37	0.44	0.10	0.39	0.28	0.25	0.06	0.41	0.30
Brazil	1990	0.37	0.26	0.28	0.54	0.44	0.38	0.18	0.39	0.54	0.41	0.41	0.40	0.17	0.43	0.35	0.24	0.05	0.36	0.34
Brazil	1995	0.29	0.27	0.28	0.49	0.26	0.37	0.21	0.24	0.46	0.23	0.23	0.33	0.28	0.27	0.29	0.29	0.06	0.36	0.28
China	1990	0.71	0.61	0.62	0.76	0.62	0.61	0.66	0.63	0.72	0.52	0.68	0.67	0.47	0.64	0.63	0.16	0.08	0.13	0.48
China	1995	0.72	0.65	0.65	0.79	0.71	0.61	0.80	0.79	0.81	0.72	0.83	0.86	0.57	0.83	0.77	0.05	0.07	0.12	0.51
Egypt	1977	0.11	0.10	0.09	0.26	0.11	0.11	0.12	0.14	0.06	0.20	0.34	0.11	0.03	0.11	0.11	0.24	0.06	0.59	0.22
Egypt	1980	0.05	0.02	0.02	0.23	0.10	0.02	0.06	0.26	0.18	0.23	0.23	0.27	0.13	0.22	0.05	0.20	0.10	0.64	0.19
Egypt	1985	0.12	0.08	0.09	0.25	0.09	0.09	0.08	0.35	0.36	0.13	0.32	0.15	0.01	0.44	0.15	0.34	0.00	0.51	0.15
Egypt	1990	0.11	0.11	0.13	0.21	0.12	0.11	0.11	0.60	0.12	0.07	0.05	0.27	0.02	0.06	0.12	0.21	0.08	0.59	0.19
Egypt	1995	0.23	0.13	0.13	0.18	0.27	0.18	0.22	0.63	0.31	0.23	0.23	0.25	0.02	0.52	0.22	0.25	0.11	0.42	0.30
Hungary	1974	0.37	0.18	0.18	0.66	0.43	0.24	0.57	0.50	0.68	0.50	0.51	0.56	0.25	0.46	0.31	0.08	0.02	0.58	0.37
Hungary	1980	0.49	0.41	0.43	0.54	0.62	0.40	0.31	0.41	0.62	0.34	0.45	0.67	0.40	0.48	0.46	0.08	0.01	0.44	0.47
Hungary	1985	0.63	0.37	0.39	0.80	0.65	0.38	0.68	0.52	0.59	0.69	0.61	0.56	0.52	0.59	0.50	0.11	0.04	0.35	0.56
Hungary	1990	0.55	0.33	0.35	0.80	0.38	0.38	0.82	0.67	0.84	0.68	0.65	0.79	0.80	0.64	0.49	0.09	0.04	0.37	0.44
Hungary	1995	0.50	0.34	0.37	0.92	0.35	0.38	0.95	0.59	0.58	0.46	0.41	0.34	0.91	0.48	0.54	0.08	0.02	0.36	0.37
India	1976	0.26	0.30	0.31	0.36	0.38	0.38	0.50	0.40	0.57	0.43	0.35	0.54	0.25	0.42	0.39	0.22	0.05	0.34	0.40
India	1980	0.53	0.76	0.81	0.58	0.41	0.80	0.39	0.50	0.41	0.29	0.43	0.36	0.18	0.54	0.60	0.16	0.02	0.22	0.48
India	1985	0.46	0.55	0.47	0.48	0.32	0.54	0.37	0.50	0.43	0.61	0.44	0.39	0.28	0.47	0.47	0.20	0.03	0.30	0.43
India	1992	0.42	0.52	0.51	0.66	0.32	0.49	0.48	0.37	0.44	0.34	0.41	0.33	0.36	0.32	0.39	0.29	0.03	0.29	0.30
Kenya	1975–1989	0.00	0.00	0.00	0.00	0.00	0.00	0.00	0.00	0.00	0.00	0.00	0.00	0.00	0.00	0.00	0.27	0.03	0.70	0.00
Korea	1979	1.00	1.00	1.00	1.00	1.00	0.99	0.98	0.98	0.96	1.00	0.99	0.99	1.00	0.99	0.99	0.01	0.00	0.00	0.97
Korea	1985	0.75	0.52	0.59	0.76	0.66	0.54	0.73	0.83	0.89	0.79	0.85	0.79	0.48	0.88	0.77	0.11	0.10	0.03	0.55

	1	2	3	4	5	6	7	8	9	10	11	12	13	14	15	16	17	18	19
Korea 1990	0.48	0.33	0.45	0.53	0.45	0.34	0.44	0.55	0.64	0.54	0.53	0.54	0.45	0.51	0.49	0.12	0.32	0.07	0.34
Korea 1995	0.47	0.37	0.43	0.68	0.37	0.42	0.59	0.66	0.71	0.51	0.63	0.56	0.71	0.60	0.54	0.11	0.22	0.13	0.50
Malaysia 1974	0.00	0.00	0.00	0.00	0.00	0.00	0.00	0.00	0.00	0.00	0.00	0.00	0.00	0.00	0.00	0.36	0.22	0.42	0.00
Malaysia 1980	0.00	0.00	0.00	0.00	0.00	0.00	0.00	0.00	0.00	0.00	0.00	0.00	0.00	0.00	0.00	0.30	0.10	0.59	0.00
Malaysia 1987												0.15	0.00	0.00	0.01	0.32	0.21	0.46	0.01
Mexico 1981	0.20	0.36	0.22	0.38	0.14	0.32	0.21	0.08	0.12	0.27	0.22	0.18	0.09	0.29	0.23	0.49	0.01	0.27	0.18
Mexico 1985	0.39	0.31	0.33	0.43	0.39	0.31	0.35	0.42	0.60	0.52	0.45	0.33	0.31	0.49	0.41	0.43	0.05	0.12	0.30
Mexico 1992	0.15	0.08	0.08	0.05	0.07	0.08	0.04	0.09	0.07	0.10	0.17	0.08	0.03	0.14	0.10	0.79	0.02	0.09	0.10
Philippines 1976	0.29	0.27	0.29	0.47	0.41	0.34	0.45	0.50	0.65	0.25	0.26	0.41	0.12	0.25	0.32	0.36	0.07	0.24	0.30
Philippines 1980	0.22	0.16	0.17	0.30	0.13	0.22	0.21	0.27	0.58	0.25	0.27	0.30	0.03	0.35	0.22	0.38	0.08	0.32	0.22
Philippines 1985	0.07	0.08	0.08	0.20	0.06	0.08	0.09	0.12	0.15	0.08	0.15	0.21	0.07	0.16	0.10	0.45	0.11	0.34	0.13
Philippines 1990	0.07	0.07	0.06	0.04	0.07	0.08	0.03	0.20	0.09	0.05	0.12	0.29	0.28	0.11	0.11	0.47	0.07	0.35	0.09
Poland 1974	0.91	0.81	0.82	0.92	0.95	0.86	0.80	0.92	0.95	0.85	0.89	0.85	0.60	0.89	0.87	0.02	0.02	0.09	0.87
Poland 1980	0.69	0.38	0.37	0.70	0.68	0.46	0.50	0.85	0.80	0.72	0.80	0.79	0.64	0.77	0.60	0.08	0.02	0.30	0.78
Poland 1985	0.69	0.53	0.49	0.84	0.72	0.64	0.62	0.87	0.90	0.88	0.81	0.89	0.73	0.86	0.71	0.08	0.02	0.19	0.86
Poland 1990	0.82	0.64	0.68	0.89	0.83	0.68	0.77	0.85	0.95	0.96	0.89	0.94	0.83	0.91	0.79	0.05	0.04	0.12	0.92
Poland 1995	0.56	0.53	0.47	0.59	0.32	0.57	0.42	0.49	0.57	0.56	0.46	0.32	0.16	0.45	0.48	0.12	0.01	0.39	0.52
Turkey 1979	0.00	0.00	0.00	0.00	0.00	0.00	0.00	0.00	0.00	0.00	0.00	0.00	0.00	0.00	0.00	0.34	0.02	0.64	0.00
Turkey 1985	0.10	0.08	0.04	0.33	0.07	0.10	0.49	0.09	0.10	0.10	0.04	0.11	0.28	0.26	0.12	0.18	0.08	0.63	0.02
Turkey 1990	0.09	0.11	0.11	0.18	0.14	0.14	0.16	0.19	0.11	0.25	0.15	0.31	0.32	0.33	0.19	0.13	0.02	0.66	0.02
Turkey 1995	0.11	0.06	0.07	0.05	0.16	0.08	0.05	0.05	0.30	0.02	0.12	0.02	0.09	0.06	0.07	0.27	0.03	0.62	0.12
Zambia 1968–1994	0.30	0.31	0.30	0.31	0.24	0.31	0.28	0.46	0.46	0.42	0.35	0.28	0.17	0.57	0.32	0.19	0.01	0.48	0.27
LDC, NIC average	0.34	0.29	0.30	0.44	0.33	0.32	0.34	0.39	0.44	0.37	0.37	0.40	0.29	0.40	0.34	0.23	0.06	0.37	0.33

LDC, less developed countries.

Table 6.5. Utility models.

Nation	Year	Agric. livestock	Agric. crops	Agric. fruits and vegetables	Agric. horti-culture	Agric. services to livestock	Agric. services to crops	Agric. other	Food meat	Food fruits and vegetables	Food dairy	Food cereals	Food beverages	Food tobacco	Food other	Agric. total	Food total	Ag + Food total	All patents
Number of utility models																			
Brazil	1995	19.04	22.83	3.98	5.83	13.26	11.94	0.82	12.47	5.68	13.20	2.51	26.16	5.90	37.38	77.70	103.29	180.99	2,695
China	1995	135.88	257.32	36.11	63.96	103.14	140.50	9.10	101.59	62.35	58.73	46.05	170.78	95.27	355.79	746.02	890.56	1,636.58	34,106
Hungary	1995	1.00	1.78	0.25	0.83	0.59	0.91	0.06	0.95	0.36	0.94	0.66	1.79	0.22	3.44	5.42	8.36	13.78	257
Korea	1979	4.95	3.47	0.58	0.66	3.24	1.96	0.17	2.67	1.11	1.14	1.57	2.63	1.94	6.77	15.02	17.85	32.87	603
Proportion of utility models to domestic patents																			
Brazil	1995	1.57	0.55	0.89	0.95	1.61	0.60	0.51	1.28	0.68	1.84	0.56	1.47	0.64	1.18	0.83	1.17	0.99	1.10
China	1995	1.05	1.04	1.36	1.33	0.83	1.95	0.34	0.63	0.83	0.73	0.38	0.61	1.39	0.43	1.11	0.55	0.72	2.23
Hungary	1995	0.19	0.13	0.19	0.08	0.12	0.15	0.00	0.19	0.18	0.55	0.32	0.67	0.02	0.29	0.09	0.24	0.14	0.34
Korea	1979	2.93	0.48	0.86	1.36	1.66	0.93	0.62	1.80	2.01	0.56	1.40	1.33	1.33	1.07	1.05	1.19	1.12	0.88
Average		1.43	0.55	0.83	0.93	1.06	0.91	0.37	0.98	0.93	0.92	0.67	1.02	0.85	0.74	0.77	0.79	0.74	1.14

International Spillovers – Invention Data

For intersectoral spillovers, patent data not only provide domestic spillover indices, but international measures as well. When an inventor in country i decided to protect his/her invention by obtaining a patent in country i, he/she also has the option of obtaining (for a cost) patent protection in country j. Decisions regarding this option are informative regarding direct international spillovers between countries i and j. The inventor in country i (having already determined the invention to be worth protecting in country i will assess the likely market for the invention in country j. The probability of patenting in a second nation is higher for more universally important inventions (perceived

Table 6.6. Invention spill-in indexes by industrial class (eight countries – 1969–1987).

Industry	Spill-in indexes		Number of inventions	
	Manufacturing industry	Using industry	Manufacturing industry	Using industry
Electrical machinery	2.122	2.185	193,017	123,780
Electronic equipment	2.199	2.201	27,453	170,053
Instruments	2.015	2.239	15,253	52,841
Office machinery	2.071	4.345	46,416	25,225
Chemicals	2.854	2.788	251,203	154,047
Drugs	2.696	3.039	25,473	47,384
Petroleum refineries	2.179	2.264	5,449	19,998
Aerospace	1.876	1.929	10,415	15,116
Motor vehicles	2.009	2.044	89,415	123,828
Ships	1.664	1.779	7,509	9,287
Other transport	1.642	1.961	13,296	17,892
Ferrous metals	2.195	2.217	12,902	25,854
Non-ferrous metals	2.548	2.483	5,182	16,081
Fabricated metals	1.806	1.887	194,292	92,863
Food, drink and tobacco	2.271	2.106	15,652	53,146
Textiles and clothing	2.019	2.488	32,622	60,642
Rubber and plastics	1.952	2.381	72,086	58,526
Stone, clay and glass	2.093	2.260	27,366	28,162
Paper and printing	1.900	2.470	24,955	44,367
Wood and furniture	1.620	1.705	32,076	28,738
Other machinery	2.060	2.084	530,158	197,678
Other manufacturing	1.719	1.814	14,998	39,033
Agriculture		1.966		62,920
Mining	1.842	1.903	1,016	48,060
Construction		1.735		152,438
Transportation service	1.767		41,084	
Communication, utilities		2.002		79,992
Retail, wholesale trade	1.827		38,290	
Finance business		1.687		42,200
Government and education	1.694		27,679	
Health services		2.031		93,040
Other services		1.866		50,739

advantages over available substitutes) and for smaller biological, physical, economic and institutional barriers to technological spillovers.

Table 6.6 reports spill-in indexes for inventions by both IOM and SOU based on data for eight OECD countries. These indexes are the ratios of total patents obtained in the eight countries to domestic patents obtained. The message of this table is that agricultural invention (this does not include crop varieties) is not the least transferable technology. Sixteen SOUs have higher spillover indexes, eight have lower indexes.

Non-patented Inventions – Rice Varieties

Table 6.7 provides data for international development and exchange of rice varieties from a study of more than 1700 rice varieties (primarily indica types) released in the countries noted over the 1965–1991 period. The International Rice Research Institute (IRRI) is included as a 'source' in this table.

The salient points are:

1. IRRI produced (i.e. made the parental cross for) 17% of all rice varieties, 24% of all varieties used as parents and 97% of all ancestor varieties exchanged internationally.
2. NARs produced 83% of the varieties and of these 6% crossed international boundaries. NARs produced 76% of parent varieties and of these 18% crossed international boundaries.
3. Only 8% of all varieties released were fully national, i.e. based on national landraces.

These data are not strictly comparable to the invention-based data, but they show roughly the same indexes as reported for patented agricultural invention in Table 6.6. There is a high degree of location specificity to agricultural invention. This differs according to whether the inventions are chemical, where location specificity is low, or mechanical and biological, where location specificity is high.

The parental and ancestral data show that germplasmic effects are important and that they are less location-specific than is the case for inventions *per se*.

Gollin (1998) has computed the origin of landraces for rice. These are summarized in Table 6.8. There is a general impression that farmers in the 'new world' economies – the Americas and Oceania – created few farmers' varieties. But this is not necessarily the case. In fact, the most important farmers' varieties have been created by selection in new environments. For rice this has meant that farmers in the USA have contributed some of the most important landraces.

Table 6.7. Matrix of varietal exchange.

Releasing country	Source of varietal cross																				
	Other	Latin America	Oceania	Bangladesh	Africa	Burma	USA	China	India	Indonesia	IRRI	Korea	South-east Asia	Nepal	Pakistan	Philippines	Sri Lanka	Taiwan	Thailand	Vietnam	Total
Other	9	7	0	0	0	1	0	5 (2)	16	3 (2)	18 (9)	6	5	0	0	0	0	1	0	0	71 (13)
Latin America	3 (1)	185 (2)	0	0	1 (1)	0	5	0	2 (2)	0	39 (15)	1	0	0	0	2	1 (1)	0	0	0	239 (22)
Oceania	0	0	1	0	0	0	0	0	0	0	5	0	0	0	0	0	0	0	0	0	6 (0)
Bangladesh	0	0	0	17	0	0	0	1	4 (1)	0	11 (3)	0	0	0	0	1	0	0	0	0	34 (4)
Africa	1	0	0	0	69 (1)	0	0	1 (1)	1 (1)	0	26 (12)	0	0	0	0	1	2 (2)	0	0	0	101 (17)
Burma	2	0	0	1 (1)	0	33	0	1 (1)	1	1 (1)	18 (5)	0	2 (1)	0	0	1	2 (2)	0	12 (6)	2 (2)	76 (19)
USA	0	1	0	0	0	0	48	0	0	0	2 (2)	0	0	0	0	0	0	0	0	0	51 (2)
China	0	0	0	0	0	0	0	66	1	0	13 (8)	1	0	0	0	0	1 (1)	0	0	0	82 (9)
India	5	0	0	0	0	0	0	0	573	1	53 (33)	0	1	0	1	1	4 (3)	2	1 (1)	1	643 (37)
Indonesia	0	0	0	0	0	0	0	0	1	29	18 (13)	0	0	0	0	0	0	0	0	0	48 (13)
South-east Asia	0	0	0	0	0	0	0	0	1	0	7 (2)	0	21	0	0	0	0	0	0	0	29 (2)
Korea	0	0	0	0	0	0	0	0	0	0	1	105	0	0	0	0	0	0	0	0	106 (0)
Nepal	0	0	0	0	0	0	0	0	2	0	5 (2)	0	1	8	0	0	1 (1)	0	0	0	17 (3)
Pakistan	0	0	0	0	0	0	0	0	0	0	7	0	0	0	5	0	0	0	0	0	12 (0)
Philippines	0	0	0	0	0	0	0	0	0	0	25 (15)	0	0	0	0	26	0	0	0	1	52 (15)
Sri Lanka	0	0	0	0	0	0	0	0	0	0	2	0	0	0	0	0	51	0	0	0	53 (0)
Taiwan	0	0	0	0	0	0	0	0	0	0	0	0	0	0	0	0	0	6	0	0	6 (0)
Thailand	0	0	0	0	0	0	0	0	0	0	0	0	0	0	0	0	0	0	23	0	23 (0)
Vietnam	0	0	0	0	0	0	0	0	0	0	44 (27)	0	0	0	0	0	0	0	0	15	59 (27)
Total	20	194	1	18 (1)	71 (2)	34 (0)	53 (0)	73 (3)	601 (4)	34 (3)	294 (146)	113 (0)	31 (1)	8 (0)	6 (0)	32 (0)	62 (10)	9 (0)	36 (7)	19 (2)	1,709 (183)

Note: Numbers in parentheses represent borrowings through the International Network for the Genetic Evaluation of Rice (INGER); IRRI, International Rice Research Institute.

Policy Implications: Incentives

How will the expanded scope in patent rights, expansion of Breeders' Rights to more countries and the possible implementation of 'farmers' rights' in some form of users' rights affect incentives for private sector biological invention and related activities? I cannot do much more than to sketch out some of the more likely effects of these changing IPRs. Table 6.9 reflects my effort. It is important to note that these IPRs affect several activities associated with plant improvement. I have indicated several activities associated with genetic resource preservation and use with pre-breeding activities, with exchange and actual breeding activities.

Consider first the likely effects the stronger patent protection of plant cultivars has had or will have. The most direct effect will be to stimulate private breeding activities of conventional, hybrid and transgenic varieties. This in turn will stimulate the market for advanced breeding lines. Companies will sell breeding lines because they can protect them. This will stimulate some pre-breeding of advanced lines and this in turn will have modest incentive effects on genetic resource evaluation and *ex situ* conservation.

Perhaps the most important point to be made regarding the patenting of plant varieties is that the incentives will be modest and will not reach countries with weak IPRs. This means that the public sector role and responsibility in developing countries will be changed very little. This is because of limited spillover potential of plant varieties. The public sector will continue to bear a major responsibility to preserve, evaluate and exchange genetic resources, to engage in pre-breeding activities to support both public sector breeding in developing countries and to support private sector breeding in developed countries. The public will continue to have a role in providing a competitive alternative in all countries.

The strengthening of patenting for gene constructs has already created a market for cloned genes with specific trait contributions that can be genetically engineered into plant varieties. This will stimulate transgenic breeding and genetic evaluation of *ex situ* collections of genetic resources. It could stimulate widespread gene searches and could result in a modest increase in *in situ* conservation.

In situ conservation may be undertaken for two reasons. First, it may be an efficient means for conserving large numbers of potentially valuable species. An area might be preserved for purposes of systematic gene-searching based on geologic and other factors. The protected area might include formerly inhabited regions (or even currently inhabited regions) where some farmers' varieties might exist. In practice, however, these areas are probably not suited to large-scale conservation of farmers' varieties because these are widely scattered.

The second motive for *in situ* conservation of farmers' varieties is based on farmer breeding and selection. Natural evolutionary change in landrace is probably very slow. One can probably not justify *in situ* conservation simply

Table 6.8. Summary of international flows of landrace ancestors, selected countries.

Country	Total landrace progenitors in all released varieties	Own landraces	Borrowed landraces	Own landraces used in other countries	Net lending (borrowing), as share total landraces
Bangladesh	233	4	229	10	(0.940)
Brazil	460	80	380	43	(0.733)
Burma	442	31	411	9	(0.910)
China	888	157	731	2052	1.488
India	3917	1559	2358	1749	(0.155)
Indonesia	463	43	420	420	0.000
Nepal	142	2	140	0	(0.986)
Nigeria	195	15	180	0	(0.923)
Pakistan	195	0	195	10	(0.949)
Philippines	518	34	484	299	(0.357)
Sri Lanka	386	64	322	57	(0.687)
Taiwan	20	3	17	669	32.600
Thailand	154	27	127	220	0.604
USA	325	219	106	2420	7.120
Vietnam	517	20	497	89	(0.789)

Notes: In last column, all numbers are given as shares of landraces used in domestic varieties; figures in parentheses are negative numbers. Numbers may exceed one if a country is a large net lender of landraces. Positive numbers indicate that a country is a net lender; negative numbers indicate that a country is a net borrower.
Source: Gollin (1998).

for its evolutionary change benefits over *ex situ* conservation. Well-designed *in situ* farmer breeding selection programmes may have more promise.

Strengthening Breeders' Rights will have three major impacts through bringing more countries under IPRs. It appears that most OECD countries will opt for stronger plant patenting provisions while maintaining and strengthening Breeders' Rights. RIC and NIC/near-NIC countries will probably opt for weaker Breeders' Rights. Most poorer developing countries will adopt Breeders' Rights laws and provide little enforcement. This will, however, stimulate more private sector breeding activities in more countries.

This will have the largest effect on conventional varieties. Unless countries adopt reasonably strong patent rights for gene construct, given the high degree of location specificity, they will have little access to modern biotechnology.

Farmers' rights have yet to be fully developed. If they take the form of negotiated 'user rights' this will (and already has) impede the exchange of genetic resources in the short-run. If these rights can be negotiated, other IPRs can function. Countries will have an interest in inventorying and preserving genetic resources to earn these rights and this may stimulate more private sector preservation – *in situ* and *ex situ* activities.

Table 6.9. Incentives and private sector breeding activities.

Activities	Patenting plant cultivars	Patenting gene constructs	Stronger Breeders' Rights	Farmers' rights	Public responsibility*
Genetic resources					
Preservation					
in situ		+		++	++
ex situ	+	+	+	+	++
Evaluation					
Traditional	+		+	+	++
Genetic resources	+	++			+ (L)
Pre-breeding					
Advanced lines	+		+		+++
Gene cloning		+++			+ (L)
Exchange					
Landraces		+		−	++
Advanced lines	++		+	−	+ (L)
Gene constructs		+++			+ (L)
Breeding activity					
Conventional varieties	++		++		++ (L)
Hybrids	++	−	+		+
Transgenic	++	+++			+ (L)

*(L) indicates a strong responsibility in less-developed countries.

One cannot come away from a serious look at IPR impacts with the conclusion that the era of public sector conduct of plant improvement activities is over. It will be changed. In the OECD market economies it will be reduced in direct breeding where private firms will play a larger role. But even in OECD countries, pre-breeding and genetic resource preservation, evaluating and exchange will be as important as ever.

In the advanced developing economies, private breeding will be expanded, but not to the degree that it will in the OECD countries. The public sector will continue to play a role in all activities and should play a role in competitive breeding to provide farmers with a low-cost alternative to products provided in imperfect markets. The NARS and IARCs also bear a responsibility to bring science and the tools of the biotechnology revolution to these economies by supporting private sector activities through the provision of genes and advanced lines.

For the poorer developing economies where private sector R&D is not conducted and where IPRs are non-existent or non-functional, the NARS–IARC system provides their only access to modern technology. Little will spill-in to them. If the NARS and especially the IARCs do not bring modern science and biotechnology to these countries, they will not have modern plant varieties.

Implications for Genetic Resource Collection and Exchange

I have noted that the expansion in IPR protection will lead to more private sector activity in terms of collecting and maintaining germplasm collections. We will see expanded private holdings. The genetic resources in these holdings can be classified as:

1. GRs 'for sale' in gene markets.
2. GRs held in secrecy and used as breeding lines for IPR protected varieties.
3. GRs exchanged with collaborators.

Pertinent economic questions regarding these GRs include:

1. Will the IPR-induced private sector expansion result in more GRs held in secrecy by private firms?
2. Will original landrace-type GRs be held in secrecy?
3. Will public research programmes (IARCs and NARS) be encouraged to hold GRs in secrecy?
4. Will low-income countries be cut off from biotechnology flows if they continue to resist strong IPR systems?

The answer to the first question is that more privately held GRs will be held in secrecy. But it would appear that these GRs will be in the nature of breeding lines and not original or natural genetic stocks. GRs for sale will include landraces and other species that can be protected for specific uses or were discovered by a private firm.

The answer to the second question is that some of these may not be sold, but an IPR holder has some incentives to sell unless she has product sales sufficient to generate the monopoly revenue.

The third question speaks to both public and private sector behaviour. Public research firms have a public responsibility to facilitate maximum increases in welfare. Traditional public plant breeding has resulted in new varieties delivered 'free of charge' to certified-registered seed firms who reproduce and distribute the improved seeds. This is essentially equivalent to the granting of non-exclusive licences to users of inventions. Will public research programmes now begin to bargain for exclusive licensing of products that they obtain IPRs for (as private firms do)? If so, will they hold genetic resources in secrecy?

Optimal public research policy requires that several practical issues be dealt with. One is the international exchange issues. This is effectively the same as faced with international IPRs. Should a nation withhold technology from competing nations and presumably lose the option to import? In general, the answer is no. It should be possible for all countries to gain from market exchange of inventions whether they are priced or not. Many developed countries, however, have been reluctant to send technology freely to foreign nations.

A second issue is whether post-invention development requires protection.

With traditional varieties the post-invention work was undertaken by a seed industry that could collect rents. For some new IPR-protected genetic inventions, non-exclusive licensing may not provide incentives for post-invention market development. In such cases the appropriate procedure is to engage in exclusive licensing. This will generate revenue to the public research system. Curiously, most public sector research programmes in the USA offer scientists incentives that are much stronger than those of private firms. These incentives do lead to secrecy. Even when patents require removal from secrecy, the removal is far from complete. The secrecy problem is real, and research organizations need to address it effectively.

Finally, will low-income countries with little or no experience with IPRs and with political hostility to IPRs (and to foreigners) be disadvantaged as these changes take place? They almost surely will lose access to technology if they do not create markets protected by IPRs. Can the public system be relied upon to deliver the new technology to them even if they do not create these IPR markets? The answer appears to be that aggressive public systems could provide a partial remedy. But this requires a proactive policy stance where the public research system itself has to be market oriented to private firms and open to bargaining for low-income clients. We see little of this taking place in the IARCs and NARS in low-income countries at present.

Notes

1. The Patent Office organized searches for improved seeds and superior animals long before agricultural research systems were developed. Many early inventions were agriculturally related.
2. The critical cases were the Charbarty decision, establishing the case for patenting multicellular living organisms; the Hibbard decision, specifically expanding the scope of patents to plants; and the Allen decision, expanding the scope to animals.
3. Scientists in the fields of chemistry and pharmaceuticals, for example, have functioned for many decades in the presence of strong patent rights for chemicals and drugs.
4. See Siebeck et al. (1990) and Lesser (1994) for a treatment of IPRs in developing countries; also Siebeck et al. (1990).
5. The first-to-file rule does not allow the party to claim that he/she was the inventor when he/she was not the inventor.
6. Industrial designs protect shapes (e.g. furniture) etc. and are more like trademarks than patents.
7. The Plant Patent Act of 1930 protected asexually reproduced plants.
8. This provision is difficult to enforce and many advocates would like to see it eliminated.
9. The sui generis provision allows a country to develop its own IPRs for plants.

10. As food markets become more sensitive to specialized products, certification rules become more important.

11. See Lesser (1991).

12. It is somewhat ironic that the supporters of farmers' rights generally are opposed to other IPRs. Recent developments in Latin America, however, call for recognizing general use rights – farmers' rights associated with a given country. Once these rights are recognized (and payments negotiated), a country may recognize conventional IPRs. See Lesser (1994) and Jaffé and Van Wijk (1995).

13. The copying of videos, tapes, compact discs, perfumes, designer clothes, etc. constitutes the bulk of IPR piracy. Pirating of patent protected inventions is probably not widespread. Accusations of piracy in general go unchallenged and this almost certainly biases estimates of piracy losses to IPR holders.

14. See Nordhaus (1969).

15. US patents use a reference system that actually identifies some conceptual parentages. 'Front-page' cites (determined by the patent examiner) include prior patents, industrial publications and scientific publications. Science cites are growing in many fields (see final section).

16. It is argued that a patent could be granted for a previously unknown trait value use for a landrace even though the landrace itself is in a collection and has been used to impact for other traits.

17. This is because the NIC/near-NIC inventions are largely germplasmic adaptations of inventions originally developed in OECD countries. They are of value in the NIC/near-NIC countries but are not competitive with the original inventions and the follow-on inventions that they inspire in developed countries.

18. This can be described as a buy-then-imitate strategy. Deolaliker and Evenson (1990) provide studies of R&D and technology purchasing by developing countries.

19. This is based on Evenson and Johnson (1997).

20. Based on Evenson and Gollin (1997).

References

Deolalikar, A.B. and Evenson, R.E. (1990) Private inventive activity in Indian manufacturing: its extent and determinants. In: Evenson, R.E. and Ranis, G. (eds) *Science and Technology: Lessons for Development Policy.* Westview Press, Boulder, Colorado, Chap. 10.

Evenson, R.E. and Gollin, D. (1997) Genetic resources, international organizations and rice varietal improvement. *Economic Development and Cultural Change* 45(1), 7–33.

Evenson, R.E. and Johnson, D.K.N. (1997) Innovation and inventions in Canada. *Economic Systems Research* April 1997.

Gollin, D. (1998) Valuing farmers' rights. In: Evenson, R.E., Gollin, D. and Santaniello, V. (eds) *Agricultural Values of Plant Genetic Resources.* CAB International, Wallingford, UK, pp. 233–245.

Jaffé, W. and Van Wijk, J. (1995) *The Impact of Plant Breeders' Rights in Developing Countries: Debate and Experience in Argentina, Chile, Colombia, Mexico and Uruguay.* University of Amsterdam, Inter-American Institute for Cooperation on Agriculture, October.

Lesser, W. (1991) *Equitable Patent Protection in the Developing World: Issues and Approaches.* Eubios Ethics Institute, Tsukuba, Japan.

Lesser, W. (1994) Valuation of plant variety protection certificates. *Review of Agricultural Economics* 16, 231–238.

Nordhaus, W. (1969) *Invention, Growth and Welfare.* MIT Press, Cambridge, Massachusetts.

Siebeck, W.E., Evenson, R.E., Lesser, W. and Primo Braga, C.A. (1990) *Strengthening Protection of Intellectual Property in Developing Countries: A Survey of the Literature.* World Bank Discussion Papers No. 112. World Bank, Washington, DC.

414
L65
634

The Market Value of Farmers' Rights

Robert Mendelsohn

*School of Forestry and Environmental Studies, Yale University,
New Haven, Connecticut, USA*

Agriculture and pharmaceuticals are very large industries. Agricultural GNP in 1990 was estimated to be $1.2 trillion worldwide. If plants from native fields and forests account for even 10% of the value of these products, this would be $120 billion a year. The pharmaceutical industry is also very large. Judging from the fraction of revenues which came from natural plants and the magnitude of gross revenues, early analysts predicted that the drugs hidden in the tropical forest were worth from $400 to $900 billion (Gentry, 1993; Pearce and Puroshothaman, 1993). These studies imply that the ownership of the genetic rights to plants, Farmers' Rights, may provide vast market revenues to landowners if only legitimate property rights were established. The Farmers' Rights movement has been given added impetus because of the expectation that Farmers' Rights would provide desirable equity outcomes to poor small landowners and conservation incentives as well.

This chapter takes a critical look at Farmers' Rights by examining its market potential and institutional barriers. It is important to note that most plants are owned by several owners and usually lie in several countries. Pharmaceutical and agricultural companies, however, only need a few samples to take full advantage of the genetic material in a plant. With multiple sellers and but one product, the sellers are in direct competition with each other. In their enthusiasm to win a sale, they will bid the price down, essentially giving the plant away for the cost of collection. Joint ownership, in this case, leads to zero rent capture. Markets consequently have not placed significant value on Farmers' Rights. In essence, even if landowners were granted the right to sell samples from plants on their land, joint ownership would lead to market failure.

In order to overcome this deficiency, society needs to create a monopoly which acts in the best interest of all landowners. Only the monopoly would be allowed to sell samples. The proceeds from the sales would then be allocated back to the individual owners. No such monopoly yet exists, it would have to be created. Further, because most plants are not unique to one country, the institution would have to extend across national boundaries. There are, of course, few examples of international institutions being granted monopoly rights. Few countries wish to extend their sovereign rights to international institutions. This is consequently a major institutional hurdle for Farmers' Rights to overcome.

If a new institution were created to manage Farmers' Rights, it would have several major decisions to make. One problem the institution must face is how to sell the rights. Because the new drugs and farm products involve expensive and lengthy development, there are two key alternative strategies. The monopoly could sell samples. Companies could bid for the samples and the monopoly could then choose who to sell them to. This approach places all the risk of development on the shoulders of the companies as they must buy the rights before they know which plants will turn out to be successful. Alternatively, the companies could be given samples in return for a share of profits. This approach places the risk on the monopoly, who will have to wait to see if any of their samples turn out to be effective. The monopoly would then share in the resulting flow of net profits from successes. In principle, one could take a mixture of these two approaches by collecting only a fraction of the original sample fee and requesting a smaller share of eventual profits.

Some advocates for Farmers' Rights endorse being partners in the search for new drugs and plants because it appears that the drug and crop companies make a lot of money. However, sharing profits is not as attractive as it may first seem. First, sharing profits is not the same as sharing gross revenue. Profits are gross revenues minus costs. There are enormous costs associated with biotechnology and drug development. For example, it was estimated that a successful drug earned gross revenues from $3.2 to $4.7 billion. However, profits from a new drug could be as little as $96 million per drug. Profits are only a fraction of gross revenue. Second, it may be possible for drug and biotechnology companies to obscure where they got new ideas. Although one sample may have actually led to a new drug, companies may be able to claim that another plant with a similar compound was responsible. They just happen to already own the second plant. The technology is sufficiently complicated and international that it would be difficult to monitor the contribution of each sample. Third, it takes approximately 10 years to develop new drugs. Sharing in profits means there would be a long delay between providing samples and collecting returns. Many institutions would not be able to survive a long period where they earned nothing and yet had large expenses.

A second decision the monopoly must face to conduct sales is whether or not to grant exclusive monopolies to developers. For example, they could choose to sell a sample to just one drug company. This gives that company exclusive rights to the plant and therefore protects them from competition. They can invest in developing the plant's potential without fear that another company will beat them to eventual products. Of course, whether such monopoly rights are worth very much depends upon whether other plants could serve as reasonable substitutes. The definition of a species depends to some degree on what genetic attributes one considers significant. For example, whether a plant has a purple stain or a brown stain on each leaf may make it into two species. Each species may contain some important different chemicals. However, the chemical of interest to a drug company may be the same in both. Granting a company a monopoly to one species and not to related species may give little protection to the company. Exclusive rights to a sample, consequently, may not be worth a large premium.

There is a second reason why granting exclusive rights may not be an attractive principle. Each company has only a limited set of tests that it can conduct on each sample since the tests are often proprietary. Exclusive rights might condemn a sample to be tested only on a fraction of the tests in the market. By selling samples to multiple companies, one might introduce undesired competition for the same drug, but one would also be more assured that every sample will be exposed to the full set of available tests. That is, one would be more confident that the full development potential of each sample is being realized. Unfortunately, although the social value of selling samples to all companies is higher, the market value may not be. That is, companies may pay very little for samples which all competitors can buy as well. This would be a major conflict for a monopoly that on the one hand was created to raise money but on the other hand is intended to serve society.

Once the monopoly has successfully collected revenues from selling Farmers' Rights, the institution must face another challenge – distributing the funds back to owners. In principle, if every owner received their share of revenues, Farmers' Rights has the potential to create important conservation incentives and achieve equity outcomes. However, these outcomes depend upon how the money is allocated.

One alternative for the monopoly is to allocate one-time payments to all owners of plants sold each year. Unfortunately, one-time payments may provide poor conservation incentives. Technically, the conservation value of the successful plant will have been used up. The owner will have been paid for his plants and it is not likely there will be a second payment (additional payments are not necessarily ruled out with new technologies, etc. but it is a limited opportunity). Future conservation value would be limited. One-time payments may provide little conservation incentive.

Instead of paying a single lump sum payment, the monopoly agency may choose to provide a stream of revenues as long as the owner still possessed the plant. This would provide more of a conservation incentive since the payment is linked to the continuation of the plant on the owner's land.

However, it would also shrink the size of the payment since what could be given out as a single payment is now stretched over time. If the annual payments to landowners are supported by the interest income from the original sale of the Farmers' Rights, the annual payment (an annuity) would be equal to the real interest rate times the sale value. Given a long-term real interest rate of 4%, the annual payment would be the sale value of the Farmers' Rights times 4%. This strategy would also require that the agency keep track of whether the plants continue to exist throughout their territory. This would be a major undertaking.

Another issue the monopoly agency must cope with is determining who should receive the payments. Clearly, the rights belong to the landowners. How should they be allocated across multiple landowners? Should each landowner who has one example of the plant be given a share? Should landowners be given shares depending upon the number of hectares they have of the plant? Should shares be allocated based on the number of plants each landowner has? Should the money be allocated to help all landowners, regardless of whether they have the plant on their land or not?

Who gets compensated determines conservation values and equity outcomes. The closer compensation is tied to the number of plants, the more conservation value the programme will have. For example, if an owner just needs one plant to get full compensation, there is not much incentive to preserve any more than a small fraction of land in native species. However, if rights are allocated according to the amount of land with the relevant plant in ownership, wealthy owners may well be the primary beneficiary of Farmers' Rights. There may be a trade-off between conservation value and equity. Further, at least in many tropical forests, the official landowner is the government. Local people who may live in the forest may not have official rights. The government may not be inclined to share the revenues with the local people.

Of course, to operate a programme such as this would require resources. The monopoly agency would have to identify plants for sale and keep track of who buys them. The agency would have to identify where the plants come from and determine which landowners deserve compensation for each plant. Given that many plants have wide distributions, this could require an active programme keeping track of changes in ownership over time. The costs of operating this agency, of course, would come out of potential earnings to be disseminated.

What is the magnitude of the potential earning from Farmers' Rights? As discussed earlier, if Farmers' Rights were dispensed by individual owners, joint ownership would force owners to compete with one another. This would drive market values to zero. This market value of Farmers' Rights is likely to be negligible.

Monopoly rights could overcome this problem by having a single seller. How much revenue could a monopolist earn by selling future rights? In a recent set of papers, Mendelsohn and Balick (1995, 1997) attempt to estimate the value of hidden drugs in tropical forests. These hidden drugs are to tropical forest owners as crops are to farmers. Balick and Mendelsohn make two estimates of drug value. The first estimate assumes that the samples are sold to a single company with exclusive rights. The second estimate assumes that the samples are given to all companies and that the benefits are measured in social, not market terms. That is, the social benefits are measured as an increase in net consumer surplus, with no payments being made by drug companies.

The exclusive value of samples depends upon the revenues a successful drug would bring to a company, the probability that a sample would lead to a successful drug, and the cost of developing the drug. Mendelsohn and Balick estimate that a successful drug earns revenues of $3.2 to 4.7 billion. There is a one in one million chance that a sample will lead to a successful drug. The cost of searching through a million samples is $3.8 to 4.7 billion. Subtracting the expected costs from the expected revenue reveals that a sample costs more to find than it will return in income to a single company. Companies consequently will not pay much to receive new samples. In fact, with most existing arrangements, the companies have only paid for collection costs.

The social value of samples is more than the exclusive market rights. Social revenues can be as high as $147 billion for all the drugs hidden in tropical forests. These values are higher than the private returns to each company because each company only controls a limited number of tests. By sharing a sample across all companies, one can be more certain that all tests will be performed and all drugs will be found. Social values are also higher than market values because only a small fraction of the value of a new drug is actually captured in drug company revenues. Drug companies only have exclusive rights (patents) over new drugs for a limited time. When patents expire, revenues fall sharply as generic drugs compete with the original manufacturer. Even during the patent period, drug profits cannot capture all of the consumer surplus associated with the drug. Some of the benefits are lost from lost sales due to the higher monopoly price during this period. Some of the revenues are lost to uncollectible consumer surplus since companies are largely constrained to charge a single price. Mendelsohn and Balick estimate that the social value of all drugs hidden in the tropical forest is close to $100 billion.

If one were to sum all the potential hidden drugs in tropical forests and then allocate them to every hectare of tropical forest, the payment would amount to a one-time payment of $33. If these payments were sent out as an annuity for all time, the payment would be $1.32 per year per hectare. It is likely that similar estimates would apply to crop material as well.

This analysis suggests that Farmers' Rights are non-zero only if a social calculus is employed. That is, virtually all market mechanisms would price Farmers' Rights close to zero. In order to achieve non-zero revenues, Farmers' Rights would have to be defended by an extensive international institution.

This new institution would have to keep track of landowners for each sample sold. It would have to determine which samples led to new drugs. It would have to determine which patients benefited from each new drug. It would have to charge the government of those patients a fee for this service. Finally, it would have to allocate the funds back to the landowners. It will take considerable political will to create such an agency and give it the right to transfer large payments from the governments of the health recipients to landowners. Further, in the absence of a market, it will be controversial to establish what these payments from health recipients should be and who should get the resulting funds. Although Farmers' Rights sounds like a good principle, it will be very difficult to bring into practice.

References

Gentry, A. (1993) Tropical forest biodiversity and the potential for new medicinal plants. In: Kinghorn, A.D. and Balandrin, M.F. (eds) *Human Medicinal Agents from Plants*. American Chemical Society, Washington, DC.

Mendelsohn, R. and Balick, M. (1995) The value of undiscovered pharmaceuticals in tropical forests. *Economic Botany* 49, 223–228.

Mendelsohn, R. and Balick, M. (1997) Valuing undiscovered pharmaceuticals in tropical forests. *Economic Botany* 51, 328.

Pearce, D. and Puroshothaman, S. (1993) *Protecting Biological Diversity: The Economic Value of Pharmaceutical Plants*. CSERGE, University College, London.

QI6
634 032

[qlobal]

International Crop Breeding in a World of Proprietary Technology

8

Brian D. Wright

Department of Agricultural and Resource Economics, University of California, Berkeley, California, USA

In the last year, there has been growing recognition of the extent to which the business of crop breeding, public and private, is being transformed by the effects of new biotechnology and intellectual property rights (IPR). In this chapter I discuss some non-technical observations from an economist's viewpoint on unfolding events in this area, as observed in different fora over the past 12 months. I make no attempt to be comprehensive. This is more a 'report from the front line' than a review. Furthermore, I make almost no reference to the issues raised by the Convention on Biological Diversity (CBD), Farmers' Rights, TRIPs, and other issues I discussed during an earlier conference (Wright, 1998).

In what follows, I first sketch some background regarding the changes in the international research environment wrought by advances in biotechnology including, in particular, production of transgenic crops, and changes in IPR. I then note the very different sets of concerns regarding these changes that I have observed in different sets of participants in crop breeding, and suggest that international breeders may lag behind some private sector participants in grasping the full implications of these changes.

Third, I list some current uses of proprietary biotechnology as inputs, drawing on information regarding use by scientists in the Consultative Group on International Agricultural Research (CGIAR). Fourth, I discuss the implications of modern technology and property rights already manifest in the private agricultural seed breeding and crop protection industries. Then I touch on prospective uses of biotechnology in international crop breeding. In the next section, I draw attention to some implications of modern technology and property rights already manifest in the private agricultural seed-breeding and crop protection industries. In the final two sections, I discuss the challenges these revolutions pose for the international breeders, and follow with some alternative strategies to handle the access problem. Conclusions are given at the end.

Background

Protection of genetic resources is nothing new. Nations have been protecting their plants and animals against appropriation by foreigners for centuries. The Dutch long guarded the secret of the geographic origin of their 'Java' tea imports. The Saxons banned exports of their strain of fine-wool merino sheep, and the Australians, who managed to get hold of some indirectly from a flock given to the British Crown, later imposed a ban of their own on exports. Thomas Jefferson risked a death penalty when he smuggled some Piedmont rice out of Italy in the lining of his coat.

The assertion of Farmers' Rights to the varieties they have cultivated and selected over generations can be viewed as a return to that tradition. Now, as then, effective ownership is claimed for the state, not the farmers. The Farmers' Rights movement is in this sense an anachronism. Its emergence as a *quid pro quo* for recognition of the newly expanded proprietary rights of modern plant breeders heralds the demise of a system of open access to genetic resources that has supported unprecedented progress in crop yields.

The stunning institutional innovation in international crop breeding this century was the postwar establishment of the international crop breeding centres, the International Rice Research Institute (IRRI) and the International Center for the Improvement of Maize and Wheat (CIMMYT). They became founding members of the CGIAR, independent providers of agricultural research products as public goods, freely available on a non-exclusive basis to public and private users, without regard to national or colonial boundaries. Operations of members of the CGIAR were made feasible by the free availability of seeds and other germplasm from the world over, from collections maintained by breeders, who were largely located in the public sector, from collecting expeditions, and from genebanks of the type pioneered by Vavilov in Soviet Russia.

The whole operation required no negotiation for rights to use these crucial experimental inputs for screening and breeding on a large scale. Nor were there other significant inputs that required special arrangement for proprietary rights. Nor was there any significant expenditure of resources on negotiating rights transfers to clients. At most, all that was required was compliance with the terms of a Material Transfer Agreement including a commitment not to claim proprietary rights on the plant varieties received. This was usually no problem. The primary clients, the national agricultural research systems (NARS), were themselves public institutions with no intention of asserting rights to the seeds they provided to farmers.

The major impediments to exchange of germplasm were phytosanitary regulations and lack of information about what was needed, on the one hand, and what was available in accessions held in genebanks or working collections, on the other. Complaints about lack of complete characterization of genebank accessions figured prominently among the reasons genebanks were not used more frequently by breeders.

All this has now been changed by two related developments. The extension of IPR to life forms and their progeny, pioneered in the USA, has been spreading across the globe, in response to TRIPs provisions imposed by the World Trade Organization (WTO) for access to the benefits of liberalized trade. Partly in response to the extension of private property protection, there has been a revolution in the products and processes available to biologists in general. These biotechnology innovations have great potential for facilitating broader and faster progress in many areas including crop breeding.

But since many of these innovations are now generally subject to proprietary protection, permission from the rights holder may be required for legal access to the most advanced technology, as well as to genetic resources conserved *in situ* or in trust in genebanks. Failure to recognize proprietary rights is an increasingly serious issue, since biotechnology has also furnished the means of detection of violations. Both the creators and users of infringing products can be subject to legal action. Moreover, the new technology means that protection of outputs from copying may be feasible where it was not previously. The range of products that may be privatized is thus expanded both indirectly and directly by advances in biology.

The expanded privatization of intellectual property has taken place in an international environment in which privatization of formerly public entities, including many NARS, is proceeding apace. Remaining public organizations, including public universities and members of the CGIAR, are being tempted by budget cuts to look to the privatization of their outputs for revenues. Universities are already quite far down this road, with mixed results.

Public and private organizations are challenged with framing policies toward, and responding to the changes in, the property rights regime. Recently I have been involved in this process from three different vantage points. I will touch on my experience of each of these.

In 1997, I was an invited participant in the 'Intellectual Property Rights III Global Genetic Resources: Access and Property Rights Workshop' (IPR III), sponsored by the Crop Science Society of America, the American Society for Horticultural Science and the American Society of Agronomy. The overall goal was 'to review factors affecting global access to plant genetic resources and the effect of Intellectual Property Rights on the exchange of these materials' (Eberhart *et al.*, 1998, p. vii). The focus of the recommendations was on access to plant genetic resources, with recognition of the issues of appropriate incentives for conservation of germplasm and implementation of national policies on Farmers' Rights.

The problems experienced by US land grant university experiment stations were also discussed. Effects of IPR on exchange of research materials and on discouraging certain lines of research subject to actual or potential proprietary claims figured prominently in workshop discussions. But these problems were not the focus of the recommendations.

In September 1997, the Technical Advisory Committee (TAC) of the CGIAR addressed the question of how to handle biotechnology in the new legal and scientific environment. In particular, it sought to 'provide a strategy for the medium and long term, and an overarching policy framework' to 'provide a flexible environment for the centers of the CGIAR to manage biotechnology within their programs'. It appointed two Expert Panels, one on General Issues in Biotechnology, the other on Proprietary Science and Technology.

Key issues identified *ex ante* were:

- Interaction and collaboration with the private sector.
- Intellectual property.
- Harmonization with global agreements.
- Protection and promotion of international public goods.
- Flow of products to beneficiaries in developing countries.
- Biosafety.
- Ethics.
- Benefit sharing.
- Public awareness and perception.

The Expert Panel on Proprietary Science and Technology, of which I was the economist member, was given a charge that included:

1. Identify and examine issues of major concerns to the CGIAR in the area of proprietary science and technology and in the context of ongoing deliberations in the CBD, the FAO Commission on Genetic Resources for Food and Agriculture, and the WTO (with respect to Trade-Related Intellectual Property System or TRIPS).

2. Provide advice and recommendations on immediate and/or long-term needs with respect to such issues as:

- further refinement/resolution of CGIAR Guidelines for IPR;
- a central legal capability within the CGIAR for advising centres on proprietary matters;
- documenting and studying existing centre or inter-centre experiences in proprietary matters;
- tracking proprietary negotiations within the CGIAR for assessing future implications.

Recently the panels completed their reports for TAC. It so happened that while I was working on the Expert Panel on Proprietary Science and Technology, I became involved as an expert in litigation regarding patents related to technology for transgenic crops incorporating herbicide resistance genes and genes from *Bacillus thuringiensis* (Bt) for insect pest resistance, and their licensing.

The experience of involvement in both public and private aspects of proprietary agricultural biotechnology relating to crop breeding, following soon after my involvement in IPR III, gave me an interesting triple perspective on the problems involved. My remarks here reflect this experience, and are heavily indebted to what I learned from the work of others involved. But I should be clear that what I have to say here reflects my opinions alone. I speak for neither the CGIAR nor Berkeley nor any private entity here.

Some Relevant Facts About Current Use of Biotechnology

Current Uses of Biotechnology in Breeding

Scientists involved in international crop breeding, like their university and private-sector counterparts, are already using many biotechnology inputs in their research. As reported by ISNAR (1998), among the tools CGIAR researchers at seven centres surveyed are using are, in order of frequency of application of proprietary technology, selectable markers, promoters, transformation systems, insect-resistance genes, disease-resistance genes, genetic marker technology, diagnostic probes, and antisense.

Rapid Commercial Adoption of Transgenic Cultivars

In 1996, about 7 million acres were sown to transgenic cultivars, and this number jumped to over 31 million just a year later. In 1997, these acres were devoted to, in order of importance, soybean (40%), corn (25%), tobacco (13%), cotton (10%), canola (rapeseed) (10%) and tomato (1%). The most frequent commercialized transgenic traits are herbicide tolerance (40%), insect resistance (24%), product quality (21%), viral resistance (10%) and fungal resistance (4%).[1] Fairly spectacular early success in adoption is evident in glyphosate-resistant ('Roundup-Ready') soy and (some highly publicized glitches to the contrary) cotton, and in lepidopteran insect-resistant Bt cotton and corn. Though the earliest releases of commercial transgenes were viral-resistant tobacco and tomato in China, three-quarters of global transgenic acreage is now in developed countries. For 1998, it was reported that 45 million acres were planted to genetically engineered crops in the USA alone (Pollan, 1998).

Prospective Uses of Biotechnology in International Breeding

In transgenics, all players agree that the game has only just begun. Thus far it has been reported that 25,000 transgenic field trials have been carried out in 45 countries, 10,000 in just the past 2 years (ISNAR, 1998). Besides further developments in pest-resistance genes and combinations thereof to counter anticipated resistance build-up in the target pests, and in combinations with herbicide tolerance, there is great interest in output traits that add value to the final product. These include high oil or starch content, high protein, resistance to grain pest damage, and high digestibility of animal feeds (for example, low phytic acid reduces phosphorus pollution and improves animal nutrition).[2] Other traits on the horizon are products that eliminate food allergy problems and those that generate edible plant vaccines for human consumption.

Agricultural biotechnology research is dwarfed by research related to human health. In that research, the most pressing issues of intellectual property relate to research on the human genome. Companies are claiming patents on DNA sequence information including expressed sequence tags (ESTs), and single nucleotide polymorphisms (SNPs). Nobody knows whether these will be held to be patentable and whether public or private entities end up holding most of the rights. It is anticipated that this work on humans will provide a wealth of information for animal genetics. Whether the information will be efficiently shared is another matter (see Doll, 1988; Heller and Eisenberg, 1998).

Similarly, the phenomenon of 'synteny' makes information on one plant genome (e.g. rice) valuable for breeders of other plants (e.g. corn or wheat). I understand that much of this information for crops is being developed and held in the private sector, which is already making substantial investments complementary to the human genome work. Access to this information and related technology, and the terms of its use, will be crucial for breeders and genebank operators.

Effects of Transgenic Technology on the Structure of Seed Markets

The revolution in agricultural biotechnology and IPR has already transformed the market structure of the private seed industry in the developed world, even though most of the seed product is not yet transgenic. One way to understand what has happened is to begin with the fact that the first widely adopted transgenic traits have been substitutes for some other inputs, pesticides and herbicides, that are produced in chemical industries in which there are a small number of firms and high fiscal costs – in well-established oligopolies. Some firms (e.g. Monsanto) have realized much sooner than others (e.g. Dow) that selling traits to seed producers is not optimal for them. If they want to stay in the crop pest and weed control business, they had better integrate into the seed business. From the economic viewpoint, this could make sense. When an oligopolist sells an input at a price above marginal cost, it distorts the buyer's input choice, making the use of the input less efficient. Vertical integration deals with this problem.

The US seed industry has been transformed in just a few years. In the new seed industry, we have just a few players dominating certain markets. For example, the US cotton industry is now more than 80% controlled by Monsanto (if announced merger plans are approved). This case is particularly interesting. Monsanto has shown that a seed that can be saved and replanted can, in a developed economy, be effectively controlled by the seed company if the seed contains patented intellectual property of sufficient value to justify enforcement costs. The transgenic technology is leased, not sold, and the rights relate to acreage, not quantity of seed used. Where the legal structure gives insufficient protection, the notorious 'terminator' gene is a technical alternative designed to prevent seed-saving. But the prospect of such performance-suppressing technology has generated vocal opposition in India, apparently even before it was introduced in the country.

The US corn industry until recently had one large but independent and relatively benevolent leader, Pioneer, and numerous other substantially smaller firms, using foundation seed (pure lines that are parents of commercial hybrids) from a small but important and relatively benevolent seed supplier, Holden's. It is now an oligopoly, with Pioneer (in which DuPont has a minority interest) as one major player, and Monsanto, through ownership of DeKalb, Asgrow and Holden's, as another. Novartis is the third and smallest major player, with nearly 10% of the market, after comprising the merged assets of Ciba and Northrup King. Monsanto also licenses its transgenic technology to Novartis and smaller participants including Zeneca and Cargill, with which it recently formed a collaborative agreement for developing and marketing value-added traits. The major seed market players in the USA also are oligopolists elsewhere, especially in Europe and parts of Latin America, most notably Argentina and Brazil.

It is probably inevitable that transgenics and other innovations would increase the market concentration in the private seed industry. As in production of software, fixed costs are high and variable costs of reproducing the new technology are negligible, so competition with price near marginal cost is infeasible. Access to a large customer base is crucial for profitability and access acquired via purchase of established companies has become very costly. There is some logic to the notion that Monsanto aims to be the Microsoft of the seed industry.

Indeed even the current trend towards concentration leaves more major players in countries like the USA than are typical in agricultural markets for innovations in crop genetics. The privatized crop seed markets until fairly recently have existed only for some large-volume crops with intellectual property protection via use of hybrids. In wheat and rice and other food crops like beans and yams and cassava, there has typically been a virtual monopoly on innovation, held by the public sector. Farmers often saved their own seed. Now public international crop breeders are increasingly finding that their developed-country counterparts are private or have privatized intellectual property. They may now be less likely to be public monopolies but they are becoming private oligopolies integrated with the providers of inputs, both pesticides and herbicides.

The same trend is likely to occur in many developing countries that adopt enforceable IPR. Indeed the same companies are already prominent players in some less-developed countries. Integration will be not only vertical and horizontal but international as well. Dealing with these entities will be different from dealing with the prototypical NARS of old. Some of the latter are already in joint ventures with large, multinational corporations in this area.

Market Challenges for International Breeders

Operation with a Different Clientele

In the future, the public and private clients for international breeders including the CGIAR will more frequently be interested in using germplasm to make a profit. If clients find the international breeders' outputs useful, they may well be in a position to extract some oligopoly profits from using them in their breeding programmes. Members of the CGIAR have turned increasingly to provision of elite parent lines to NARS as their main objective rather than releasing cultivars from farmers. But if their clients turn to selling seed rather than giving it away, the CGIAR's policy of free distribution may subsidize the local seed industry rather than poor farmers or consumers.

If such situations arise, perhaps the best strategy for the CGIAR could be to leave all work on the crop relevant for that environment alone to the private sector. At present, hybrid corn research for temperate, high-quality soils seems to fit this category, as do modern controlled-environment poultry and swine operations.

How quickly this 'privatizable' category will expand is an open question. But two recent controversial cases are instructive. In one, an Australian seed company attempted to obtain plant variety protection for a cultivar obtained from the International Crop Research Institute for the Semi-arid Tropics (ICRISAT), with the intention of commercial sale. Very recently, Thailand has filed suit to prevent the patenting by Rice Technology, Inc. of a hybrid rice, 'Jasmatic', one of the parents of which is a Thai cultivar, jasmine rice type 105, obtained from the IRRI genebank (*Dow Jones Newswires*, 26 May, 1998, 'Thailand claims U.S. rice hybrid violated rights').

Even if international breeders exit from markets where breeders are profit-oriented, genebanks, the FAO as trustee, or the depositors, the countries of origin of the germplasm, will still have to confront the issue of how to transact with entities that want to use their products for profit. Such transactions are unlikely to be efficiently executed. The expected value of such breeding materials is likely to be quite modest in most cases, but in rare instances could be substantial. Western universities are notorious for overestimating the value of their technologies, and 'southern' negotiators are similarly likely to overvalue the prospects of their germplasm. 'Failure to transact' may be the safest, and most common outcome for the bureaucrat responsible for giving permission to use national germplasm, unless (as has happened in a select group of universities) institutional incentives structures can be appropriately reorganized.

Access to Modern Research Inputs

Modern crop breeding already offers a wealth of case studies on the complications that arise when more than one patent is involved in the production and marketing of a product. Overlapping intellectual property claims, conflicting claims, uncertainty in patent approval, high litigation expenses, and high regulation costs, and the uncertainty in the outcomes of litigation or negotiations are all very important influences on private and public plant breeders in the USA, the country where I have observed these problems first-hand. The above may be obvious to those who are private industry participants; but I have found the extent of the problems is more dimly understood by public breeders and academics.

I could go on at some length in justifying the above claims. But in the interests of brevity, I offer the following brief observations:

- The Chief Executive Officers of at least three top US participants in crop breeding biotechnology, Monsanto, DeKalb and Mycogen, are not biologists or agronomists by training – they are lawyers!
- Barton (1998, pp. 88–89, Table 8-1) shows more than a dozen instances of patent litigation related to transgenic applications of genes from *Bacillus thuringiensis* (Bt) as of May 1997.
- Members of a panel of patent attorneys involved in the biotechnology industry at a conference of the National Bureau of Economic Research that I attended in July 1997 stated that biotechnology firms have litigated when they thought their chances of success were only 25%. By contrast, it was claimed conventional pharmaceutical firms would settle if the chances of success were below 85%. The lawyers expressed a dim view of the current operation of the patent system in biotechnology.
- Patent litigation costs for one case typically run to millions of dollars for each side and take years of close managerial attention.

To conduct modern plant breeding, patent licences may be needed for markers, promoters, means of transformation, the transformed cells, the plants that are transformed, the genes inserted, the method of modification of the genes, and so on. Dozens of licences may be needed to produce one new cultivar. Often the relevant property rights claims are not yet public, or are under review or in litigation, so a prospective user may not know for years what must be licensed, and from whom; and licences may be unavailable if an exclusive licence has already been given to another entity.

How is an international breeder to get the processes and products needed for modern breeding?

Strategies to Handle the Access Problem

It is unlikely that the technology access problem will ever be 'solved'. The best we can hope for is to cope with it in a way that allows continued progress in plant breeding using modern technology. Alternatives for consideration include:

1. *Purchase the necessary licences.* One problem with this strategy is obvious: licences can be expensive, especially for an organization committed to distributing its output *gratis*. Moreover, even if right holders would like to grant 'special deals' for non-profits working in areas that do not infringe on its own market, 'most-favoured licensee' clauses in its commercial licences may preclude this (see Lanjouw, 1998, for the example of the Indian pharmaceutical market). To complicate matters further, just who to license from may remain unclear for years as patent applications work their way through the system and are subjected to legal challenges.

2. *Cross-license.* This assumes that the non-profit obtains patents on the technologies it offers for exchange with others (an expenditure of around a quarter of a million dollars for major markets) and restricts their use by others. It must also be prepared to defend its patents by prosecuting infringers, a costly and uncertain business (see above). Furthermore, the non-profit may have little technology of interest to a large, private company.

3. *Merge with a holder of necessary technology.* This alternative, often sensible in the private sector, is essentially out of the question for most non-profits.

4. *Get a research licence.* This removes the immediate legal hazard. But it introduces the danger of hold-up if a commercial licence is not guaranteed *ex ante*. After the non-profit finally has a successfully developed cultivar, the licensor can in effect hijack the research by controlling the conditions for grant of a commercial licence. The non-profit may find that it has in effect been toiling, unawares and unremunerated, as a branch of the private company's research arm.

5. *Ignore the problem and hope it will go away.* This has the advantage of allowing research to proceed, at least initially, without the inconvenience and cost associated with addressing the problem. A survey of seven CGIAR centres (ISNAR, 1988) showed this was a surprisingly popular option, if generally chosen by default rather than design. But the long-run risks are high. More benevolent infringees may simply cut off the supply of their technology when they find it is being used without permission. The most successful and potentially valuable outcomes may well be subject to infringement lawsuits which could easily be financially devastating to a CGIAR centre, and perhaps its clients.

6. *Make a market segmentation deal.* Where feasible, this may be most attractive. It is an option proposed in CGIAR (1998). The international breeder could offer a technology provider the rights to all improvements in developed-country markets in exchange for free use in applications relevant to poor countries, and for support in patenting the technology. Segmentation would require absence of competition for the technology licensor from exports of poor countries that use the technology. This may often be feasible. Binenbaum and Wright (1998) show that in CGIAR crops, poor countries have almost no significant exports at all.

Conclusions

Although changing regimes in biotechnology and IPR are only just beginning to show significant presence in farmers' fields, they are already transforming the private seed industry in the USA and other developed countries. Private corporations have anticipated the implications of the new regimes and have responded dramatically with innovation investments, takeovers, mergers and lawsuits. Public and international researchers and breeders are only now grasping the fact that they must at least assess the changes that have already occurred, and try to adapt to a world where much of the technology they will need is, or will soon be, owned by others.

Notes

1. The above facts are from ISNAR (1998).
2. Pioneer Hi-Bred International, News Release 3 February, 1998, 'Pioneer Hi-Bred will introduce hybrids that yield cleaner water'.

References

Barton, J.H. (1998) The impact of contemporary patent law on plant biotechnology research. In: Eberhart, S.A., Shands, H.L., Collins, W. and Lower, R.L. (eds) *Intellectual Property Rights III. Global Genetic Resources: Access and Property Rights.* CSSA Miscellaneous Publication, Crop Science Society of America, Madison, Wisconsin.

Binenbaum, E. and Wright, B.D. (1998) *On the Significance of South–North Trade in IARC Crops.* Report for the CGIAR Panel on Proprietary Science and Technology.

Consultative Group on International Agricultural Research (CGIAR) (1998) *Mobilizing Science for Global Food Security.* Report of the CGIAR Panel on Proprietary Science and Technology, Document No. SDR/TAC:IAR/98/7.1.

Doll, J.J. (1988) Biotechnology: the patenting of DNA. *Science* 280, 689–690.

Eberhart, S.A., Shands, H.L., Collins, W. and Lower, R.L. (1998) *Intellectual Property Rights III. Global Genetic Resources: Access and Property Rights.* CSSA Miscellaneous Publication, Crop Science Society of America, Madison, Wisconsin.

Heller, M.A. and Eisenberg, R.S. (1998) Can patents deter innovation? The anticommons in biomedical research. *Science* 280, 698–701.

International Service for National Agricultural Research (ISNAR) (1998) *The Use of Proprietary Biotechnology Research Inputs at Selected CGIAR Centers.* Report of an ISNAR study commissioned by the Panel on Proprietary Science and Technology for the CGIAR, ISNAR, Netherlands.

Lanjouw, J.O. (1998) *The Introduction of Pharmaceutical Product Patents in India: 'Heartless Exploitation of the Poor and Suffering'?* NBER Working Paper No. 6366.

Pollan, M. (1998) Playing God in the garden. *New York Times Magazine*, 25 October.

Wright, B.D. (1998) Intellectual property and Farmers' Rights. In: Evenson, R.E., Gollin, D. and Santaniello, V. (eds) *Agricultural Values of Plant Genetic Resources.* CAB International, Wallingford, UK.

9

Knowledge Management and the Economics of Agricultural Biotechnology [US]

David Zilberman,[1] Cherisa Yarkin[1] and Amir Heiman[2]

[1]Department of Agricultural and Resource Economics, University of California, Berkeley, California, USA; [2]Department of Agricultural Economics, Hebrew University, Rehovot, Israel

Biotechnology encompasses a wide array of innovations that stem from molecular biology including recombinant DNA techniques (genetic engineering). These innovations are the results of scientific discoveries that mainly occurred after 1950. Since the 1970s, these innovations have had significant impacts on medical diagnostics and therapeutics. In the late 1990s, there has also begun to be significant adoption of biotechnology innovations in agriculture. About 60 million acres worldwide were planted with transgenic seed in 1998.[1] Agricultural biotechnology, however, is still in its infancy, and although the production and sales of transgenic seed have been largely undertaken by private corporations, the pace and extent to which this technology is developed and utilized will be substantially affected by institutional arrangements and policies controlled by the public sector. Because biotechnology is knowledge and human capital intensive, the management of knowledge generation and technology transfer within and between the public and the private sectors will affect its ultimate future impact on agriculture.

This chapter reviews some of the institutional arrangements for the generation and transfer of knowledge in the USA and assesses their implications for the evolution and performance of agricultural biotechnology. The analysis leads to policy recommendations and proposals for institutional changes. The following section introduces the major categories of biotechnology innovations that affect agriculture and relates biotechnology innovations to another new wave of technologies, precision farming. It is followed by analysis of current and emerging institutional arrangements for technology transfer between the public and private sectors and their implications for agricultural biotechnology. In particular, we will present some of the lessons learned from the evolution of medical biotechnology and assess their implications for agricultural biotechnology.

The fourth section of the chapter includes an analysis of the impact of intellectual property rights arrangements and patent definitions on the evolution of agricultural biotechnology and the structure of agriculture. A concluding section will follow.

Categories of Agricultural Biotechnology and Their Relationships with Other Innovations

Agricultural activities utilize a vast number of species (e.g. animals, plants and fungi) and include a variety of stages (breeding, feeding, pest control, harvesting and processing) that are likely to be affected by biotechnology innovations. Taken as a whole, however, these innovations can be divided into several major categories.

Supply-enhancing Innovations

Biotechnology provides tools to accelerate and improve accuracy of traditional breeding systems. These molecular techniques have enabled faster identification of yield-increasing varieties and breeds and led to the discovery of growth-enhancing treatments and substances. One obvious example is recombinant bovine somatotrophin (rBST), which can substantially increase milk production, and has been widely adopted by US dairy farmers. Some innovations may enhance supply by overcoming environmental constraints on production. The use of genetically engineered 'ice-minus' bacteria, for example, can enhance the capacity of strawberries and other sensitive crops to survive in frost conditions. Research is currently under way for traits that will increase crop tolerance to heat, saline water and drought. Varieties that increase tolerance to adverse conditions may lead to expansion of supply by increasing acreage and may also reduce yield variability and uncertainty.

Pest Control Innovations

Many of the most widely used agricultural biotechnology innovations today belong to this category. They reduce pest damage by insertion of a genetic sequence so that plants express in their tissues proteins toxic to specific pests (e.g. Bt cotton) or by introducing genes that permit otherwise susceptible plants to tolerate specific proprietary herbicides such as Monsanto's 'Round-Up'. The former may substitute for more-toxic chemical pest controls, while the latter allow farmers to use less-toxic herbicides. Other genetic engineering research has resulted in crops resistant to infection by viruses, pests for which no chemical pesticide was previously available (e.g. UpJohn's summer squash resistant to tobacco mosaic virus). To the extent that reliance on toxic chemical pesticides is reduced, adoption of the biotechnology pest control innovation may have a beneficial environmental side-effect. Indeed, the adoption and the gain manufacturers obtain from pest control innovations are likely to be significantly enhanced by environmental regulations restricting the use of existing treatments.

Adoption of seed-based pest controls developed using biotechnology may also have adverse environmental side-effects, for example, by accelerating the build-up of pest populations resistant to the incorporated pesticide. It has also been suggested that herbicide tolerance genes may 'jump' in the field to weedy relatives, negating the value of this trait. These factors must be considered in evaluating the products of biotechnology, the alternatives and the management of these products in the field.

Quality-enhancing Biotechnologies

For most of the 20th century, excess supply, and consequently low commodity prices, was the main cause of the 'agricultural problem'. In recent decades, it has become clear that consumers are often willing to pay higher prices for agricultural commodities of better quality. Hedonic techniques, which provide a means to estimate the contribution of particular characteristics to a products' value, have been used to estimate the value of specific quality traits. Parker and Zilberman (1993), for example, show that the price of peaches may triple as a result of increases in size, sugar content or availability in 'off season' periods. Quality-enhancing innovations that enhance the nutritional value of agricultural commodities (reduced cholesterol in eggs, increased vitamin content of fruits and vegetables, etc.) may be of special value to particular subpopulations, and their availability may increase the use of food items as therapeutics. Other quality-enhancing innovations improve the attributes of agricultural commodity relevant to processing or product distribution (e.g. tomatoes with increased shelf-life, greater concentrations of solids, etc.) or add value by making consumption of certain food items more convenient (e.g. personal-sized seedless watermelons). This pattern of product differentiation aimed at consumers follows that established by food technologists, who have engineered processing techniques that have allowed a proliferation of varieties of cereals, breads, snack foods, etc. Quality-enhancing biotechnology innovations may have the same impact through direct modification of agricultural commodities.

New Products

Biotechnology is likely to permit the expansion of the set of species utilized and the range of output produced by agricultural systems. Gene-splicing techniques can be used to cause plants to produce materials and substances that are now derived chemically and may permit introduction of a range of completely new substances. Plants have already been modified to express therapeutic substances, fine chemicals, nutrients, specialized oils, etc. Application of biotechnology to plant and animal aquaculture has begun to increase the range of products available from these species and holds great promise for future development that may eventually relieve pressure on world fisheries.

Improved Diagnostic Detection and Monitoring Procedures

Biotechnology has opened a vast array of possibilities to tag movements of living organisms and related genetic substances. It may lead to procedures that will improve efficiency of resource allocation in agriculture that is currently hampered by externalities and free rider problems. For example, assignment of precise liability to agricultural pollution is difficult because of limited ability to trace movement of waste products and identify sources of polluting substances. Similarly, efficient pricing of genetic materials (say, seeds) may be impossible without the capacity to assign output value to component source materials.

We now examine three technological features of biotechnology that have important implications for the development, adoption and value of these technologies in agriculture. These features relate specifically to the modification of crop plants, which can be loosely thought of as seed-based biotechnology innovations. These features are:

Stacking

Agricultural production takes place in a diverse array of complex environmental settings, so that crop quality and yield depend on a broad set of factors. The biotechnology crops currently marketed generally incorporate a single novel genetic trait or, at most, two. However, to realize the full potential of this technology, seed suppliers will need to develop the capacity to cost-effectively incorporate a large number of genetic modifications in a given crop variety. This is a research challenge because of the vast complexities involved in introducing multiple traits.

If the number of genetic alterations of a seed is not a substantial constraint, one may expect that, over time, many of the functions that are carried out today by pesticides and fertilizers will be substituted by modified genetic materials. To a large extent, that will simplify agricultural production practices and increase the value of modified seeds to reflect the reduction in the cost of alternative inputs as well as the increase in yield and quality that a modified seed may provide. If there are constraints on the conduct of simultaneous multiple genetic alterations, one of the challenges of seed designers will be to determine what traits and which crop varieties should be modified. When the number of feasible alterations is constrained, the effective use of genetic materials will be, to a larger extent, dependent on effective multi-input management techniques that include effective combinations of seeds with other inputs such as chemical.

Introduction of complex stacks of novel genetic materials may also cause larger environmental and regulatory health costs. Regulators will need to test for possible side-effects of individual genetic modifications and, at the same time, investigate the possibilities of negative effects from interaction of multiple modifications. Thus, both the technical cost of trait-stacking and some of the regulatory challenges that it poses imply that the introduction of seeds with multiple novel traits will be gradual. At least in the foreseeable future (the next 10–20 years), it does not seem that advances in biotechnology will substantially reduce the need for synthetic inputs such as chemical pesticides and fertilizers. On the contrary, some of the early applications of biotechnology in agriculture have been complements to chemical herbicides.

Terminator Genes

With biotechnology, the value of genetic materials will significantly increase as they both substitute and complement other inputs and provide new sources of value added. This value will be reflected by increased prices of seeds and other plant propagation materials, making it very tempting to farmers to save the progeny of transgenic seeds whenever possible, even if it conflicts with agreed-upon contracts. The saving of seed for future on-farm use has long been a legal right of farmers, so there are strong traditions supporting seed-saving. Seed companies are able to easily detect such activities using biotechnology-based diagnostic methods. However, the cost of monitoring, both directly and indirectly through legal costs and perhaps unsympathetic courts, may limit the usefulness of these approaches. The alternative is the design of genetic materials with ineffective progenies. One method is to introduce a novel genetic trait that prevents viable second generations of modified seed, the so-called 'terminator gene' developed by the US Department of Agriculture in cooperation with the Delta Pine and Land Company, now owned by Monsanto. Terminator genes may not be acceptable in some locations; the Indian Parliament, for example, is considering legislation against their use. The likelihood of inconsistencies in regulation of genetic materials across different countries suggests that companies may discriminate in the type of products that they develop and sell in different markets. Regions that place greater restrictions reduce the ability of seed suppliers to capture the value added by their innovations, and these companies may therefore choose not to sell advanced materials in those markets. Difficulty in capturing benefits of introducing novel traits in various markets may thus lead to *de facto* trade barriers and to an overall reduction of efficiency realizing the benefits from biotechnology.

The Complementarity Between Biotechnology and Precision Farming

Information technologies, including both computers and remote sensing, are the other advanced technologies that have become prominent at the end of the 20th century. Computer technologies played a fundamental role in the evolution and progress of biotechnology by facilitating gene sequencing and functional genomics, and information technology has offered new avenues to improve productivity through other means in agriculture as well.

Precision technologies are a set of innovations that rely on remote sensing, geographical information systems and related computer technologies to improve the accuracy of application of agricultural inputs. Precision agriculture is a generic term that includes use of satellite-aided technologies such as the Geographic Positioning System (GPS) as well as advanced application of monitoring technologies, e.g. computerized irrigation based on weather data with drip and sprinkler irrigation (see Parker and Zilberman, 1996).

Precision technologies are likely to reduce the environmental damage associated with application of chemicals and, thus, may reduce the value of biotechnology innovations that provide alternatives to these chemicals. To that extent, precision farming provides substitutes to biotechnology.

Note, however, that precision farming may require higher human capital and management skills than biotechnology, and adoption of new seed varieties is likely to be easier and faster than adoption of improved management practices. On the other hand, in precision farming one may develop more refined seeding methods that can profitably use slightly modified varieties within a field to take account of variations in land quality and other environmental conditions. This capacity of precision technology complements biotechnology because it may increase the demand for differentiated seeds and increase their productivity. Precision technology will also enable a more careful output measure of different genetic materials and performance of species in various ecosystems, thus enhancing productivity of research that attempts to identify the properties of various genetic substances. The improved monitoring capacity that precision technologies provide may enhance the productivity of biotechnology research and generation of new biotechnology innovations.

Intellectual Property Rights and the Structure and Pricing of Biotechnology Products

Expansion and differentiation of products that biotechnology provides, as well as its capacity to substitute chemicals and other inputs with improved seeds, are likely to affect the structure of agricultural industry. However, the price for seed evolution and input of biotechnology products depends on the capacity of the innovators and producers of this product to capture their benefits, and that depends on the definition of intellectual property rights (IPR).

Wright (1998) argues that policy-makers are faced with the challenge of determining the exact breadth of patents, especially if these patents are crucial for future discoveries and enhancement of a technology. These patents are defined more broadly. They will increase immediate investment in research since they make returns on the discoveries and innovations higher. On the other hand, they may retard future innovative activities by increasing the cost of future research that is contingent on the knowledge and techniques protected by the patent. These types of trade-off are very important in agricultural biotechnology. Regulators have to define what type of discovery and invention activities are entitled to patent protection and to what extent to enforce these patent rights. One can distinguish between several types of knowledge that are especially important for agricultural biotechnology.

Genomics

This study maps the genetic structure of specific organisms. The Human Genome Project, funded largely by the US National Institutes of Health with collaborators in Britain, France and other countries, is expected to complete its work of identifying the approximately 100,000 genes that make up the genetic 'blueprint' of the human species in less than 2 years. There are significant projects under way to map the genomes of some of the major plants and animal species used in agriculture.

Functional Genomics

This area of study builds on the knowledge about gene sequences derived from genomics, seeking to identify the role and functions of specific genes. Under this category, for example, is research that has resulted in identification of genes that are responsible for certain types of plant growth and protection against particular insects such as corn rootworm and cotton boll-worm. It also encompasses studies examining how changes in the structure of these genes may affect performance and outcomes.

Biotechnology Processes

This category encompasses a wide variety of research efforts that examine alternative means of genetic modification (e.g. techniques for incorporating novel genetic material into plant, animal or microbial cells).

Biotechnology Products

This category is composed of research that focuses on developing innovative products through incorporation of novel genetic materials into various organisms and scale up of production to commercially viable quantities. The incentive for private companies to pursue development of biotechnology products hinges upon the ability of innovators to protect their inventions (e.g. novel genetic traits as well as transgenic organisms). The definition of the kinds of innovations that qualify for patent protection has become quite murky in recent years. Theoretically, patents cover discoveries of new ways to do things or new products and not discoveries of basic knowledge such as mathematical formulas or basic laws of nature. In this regard, results of genomic research may be considered by some to represent discoveries of natural phenomena.[2] While in earlier times genomic discovery required significant investment and ingenuity, in recent years these activities have become highly automated and do not, in themselves, require much ingenuity. Genomic knowledge has public goods properties, and patent protection may create legal barriers that will retard significantly the development of biotechnology innovations in the future. Therefore, policy-makers have to seriously consider the breadth of patent protection granted for genomic discoveries.

Private genomics enterprises such as PE Biosystems and InCyte have invested heavily in generating genomic knowledge, securing their investment by building databases that they charge users to access, through a variety of contractual arrangements. If fundamental elements of new genetic knowledge are to remain in the public domain, government support will be required for some research in genomics. Public sector support is also important because an organism's genetic structure may not have an apparent economic value but may be valuable as part of larger research agendas.

The case for providing patent protection for functional genomic knowledge is more substantial than that for basic genetic discoveries. Such knowledge may have immediate implications for development of products, and its generation is not straightforward, as it requires relating the performance of organisms to their genetic structure. Because of the complexity and the high risk of undertaking functional genomics research, the private sector may under-invest in this type of endeavour, an area that may justify some form of public sector support.[3]

There is a straightforward case for providing patent protection to biotechnology processes. However, if the patented activities or materials are crucial to the development of future innovations and discoveries, the ability to restrict access afforded by patent protection may lead to significant monopolization and inefficiency in the system. Therefore, government intervention, using incentives and/or regulations, is necessary to ensure that important innovations are made available for a reasonable fee to researchers and developers of new technologies that rely on them.

One example of sound licensing practices that enhance the utilization of key biotechnology innovations is the Cohn-Boyer patent. Jointly held by the University of California at San Francisco and Stanford University, this patent covers a key technique for combining genetic materials. Rights for this patent were not sold exclusively but were available to anyone for a reasonable fee. This patent brought the universities more than $100 million in licensing revenues over the years and has been widely credited with the emergence of the biotechnology industry. Assigning the rights to the patent to one company, say, Genentech, might have slowed the evolution and commercialization of biotechnology.

Strict patent protection for particular products is the most obviously justifiable. These inventions meet the economic criteria of requiring investment of resources and ingenuity. Yet, it may be important that governments encourage markets for the right to use these patents rather than allowing systems to exist that limit their use to a small number of organizations without capacity to trade.

Outcomes Under Alternative Trading Arrangements and IPR in Biotechnology

The extent to which individuals and firms can trade the rights to utilize the biotechnology patents will shape the structure of the industry and efficiency use of biotechnology. Several scenarios may evolve:[4]

Effective Protection of IPR with Smooth Flow of Information

Under this scenario, companies will engage in research and claim patents for various biotechnology processes and products. Companies will pay royalties to produce genetic materials and seeds. One means to achieve this system would be to set up a clearinghouse to distribute royalties and fees among companies. The sale of seeds will result in the distribution of proceeds from the seller to all the entities whose patents were used in the production of the seeds.

A similar clearinghouse arrangement exists in the music and movie industries. The much broader set of sellers and users of agricultural biotechnology products may make establishment of such arrangements more difficult, but in principle it is feasible. This type of arrangement would be especially useful for biotechnology products that are incorporated into commodities such as wheat. If the market for seeds is competitive for a large variety of available products, we expect (following the hedonic price model) that the price of each seed will be the sum of the prices of each of its attributes. In an ideal setting, the hedonic prices of the characteristics provide the bases for determining royalties to owners of IPR. Of course, the value of a particular characteristic varies by crop, location and other market considerations. In situations where IPR are well defined and protected, and the cost of enforcement is relatively low, then the free flow of information within the industry is likely to result in a proliferation of specifically adjusted seed varieties. It also may lead to preservation of biodiversity since many of the original varieties that are locationally adapted could be slightly modified to a desirable trait, rather than replaced with a more uniform seed variety (Zilberman *et al.*, 1998).

No Trading Among Firms of the Right to Use Intellectual Property for Biotechnology

Under this extreme scenario, companies will not be able to obtain the rights to use others' innovations, a situation likely to lead to consolidation in the industry, resulting in a small number of companies, each with its own parallel line of products. Under such scenarios, some of the major companies will take over small companies with large seed stocks in order to obtain their proprietary varieties. In this case, farmers will have to make decisions about major lines of products. Overall, the set of products will not be as diverse as under the first arrangements, since some valuable combinations will not be possible, reflecting the efficiency loss associated with lack of trade. With this type of arrangement, a reduction in biodiversity may be observed because some locally adopted varieties that are not associated with organizations with, say, a strong set of biotechnology products, will be dominated by mainline transgenic varieties.

The reality will probably be between these two extremes. We expect that, for some traits, there will be effective mechanisms for accounting and payment for IPR. Yet, the trade may be limited. There will be some major parallel lines of products, and the rights to use some desirable traits may be strongly restricted, hampering efficiency.

Prevalence of Contracting

The introduction of biotechnology is likely to enhance vertical integration and contracting in agriculture. This is especially the case for new products. The developers of these products must find farmers to produce them, but farmers may hesitate to adopt a new product based on a new technology for which the ultimate market value may be unclear. Thus, developers of the genetic materials may also become the marketers of the product that it produces. That was the history of integration in the broiler sector, where seed companies (feed suppliers) signed contracts with chicken growers to buy their livestock. Thus, we may observe that seed companies, food processors and others will in the future invest in biotechnology, generate genetic materials and contract with growers to produce the products which they will then sell. We may also have a situation where several companies, the biotechnology manufacturer and a food distributor will work together so that the biotechnology company will produce a genetic material and the food distributor will be engaged in contracting.

One of the main issues that will determine the diffusion of biotechnology around the world and the structure of international agriculture is the ability to protect IPR internationally. If these rights are rigorously protected only in the USA and some of the other developed countries, there will be a larger number of companies that trade for rights to IPR in those countries than elsewhere. In countries where IPR are less protected, a smaller number of companies exist, which will provide genetic materials only to contractors. Despite the strong efficiency arguments for intellectual property protections, some exemptions on royalty payments may be required for developing and subsistence farmers. For example, subsistence farmers may be granted access to biotechnology processes and innovations either for a minimum fee or in exchange for the right to use the materials that belong to CGIAR centres. However, the pace and the evolution of new biotechnology innovations depend on the extent and the distribution of finance for research and transfer of research knowledge, and that will be the topic that we will discuss below.

Knowledge Generation and Transfer for Biotechnology

Introduction of new biotechnology products generally is the result of several stages of effort. They include, first, research that may be led by discoveries that provide the essential elements of new products. If appropriate, the discovery is *patented*, and then a development process ensues. During this process, innovations are scaled up from the laboratory to the field, their health and environmental implications are evaluated, and procedures for commercialization are developed. Once a product is ready to be introduced commercially, it is promoted and marketed, produced, sold, adopted and utilized by the final users. The various stages in the evolution of a product may be carried out by different organizations, and the key feature of innovative society is that smooth mechanisms are introduced to enable transfer of responsibilities to the product evolutions between entities in a smooth and efficient manner. The experience of medical biotechnology and a short history of agricultural biotechnology have indicated several important patents regarding product evolution.

The Important Role of Universities and Research Institutes in Research and Discovery

Until the 20th century, most innovations were originated by practitioners who found a new way to do things or came up with new concepts. Even today practitioners play a very important role in innovations. However, in the case of information technologies and, in particular, medical biotechnology, academic scientists conducted most of the crucial innovations and discoveries that provide the foundation of fundamental discoveries. Many of the basic procedures of biotechnology were introduced by scientists conducting research in molecular and cell biology in universities and research institute laboratories, using the funds of public agencies, in particular the National Institutes of Health (NIH). Universities in most cases patented these new discoveries. The Bayh-Dole Act of 1980 provided an institutional structure that allowed universities for the first time to sell the rights to discoveries arising from publicly funded research to private entities. It laid the foundation for a very intensive process of technology transfer from research institutes and universities to the private sector.

Emergence of Offices of Technology Transfer (OTTs) as Major Institutions

Some OTTs existed from the 1940s and played an important role in commercializing discoveries made by researchers at MIT, Stanford and certain other universities. Their role, however, has become more important over the last 25 years. OTTs have professionals who screen university researchers' discoveries, help to patent them, search for parties interested in licensing the rights to the innovations, monitor and enforce technology transfer contracts, and manage royalties (Parker *et al.*, 1998). Royalties typically range from 2 to 10% of product sales. Also, at least in principle, royalty rates increase as the relative contribution of the university research to the value added of the product rises. Royalties are shared among the university, the department where the discovery was made and the inventor. Universities may also obtain a signing fee, and technology transfer contracts may require a minimal annual fee to protect against situations where companies buy patents and do not utilize them, e.g. to prevent companies from buying patent rights in order to suppress innovations that would compete with their existing products.

OTT Revenues Cover a Very Small Share of University Research Expenditures

While technology transfer played an important role in the introduction of biotechnology and other innovations, the revenues of OTTs, while substantial, may provide less than 5% of the universities' research income. They provide much less than 1% of the university's overall budget. In 1996, OTT revenues in the USA were approximately $550 million. A significant portion of these revenues covered OTT costs including patenting expenditures and salaries for staff. Annual research budgets of universities and research institutes in the USA exceeded $10 billion, and the total budget of higher education in the USA exceeded $100 billion. Thus, one does not expect university research royalties to pay for the research. Note also that only a small fraction of the revenues from patents went to the researchers. The economic surplus generated by patents is divided among research institutes, researchers, producers, distributors and final consumers. Thus, the multiplier of university innovations is quite large (some have argued that it is at least $40 for each dollar spent).

One also has to recognize that patents have a finite life. It takes between 5 and 7 years to develop a patented invention to the point that it can be fully utilized. The revenue-accumulation process is slow and reflects an S-shaped diffusion curve. Thus, profits from patents do not capture much of the benefits of new innovations that in many cases are long lasting, since past innovations provide the key element of knowledge that leads to future discoveries and products.

OTTs have established working relationships with industries and, thus, are useful in raising other sources of private income to support university research. They include grants, contracts and donations. In some important cases, universities have taken equity stakes in companies as compensation for technology transfer. While some private universities oppose this type of arrangement, MIT and other private universities have used it, and it may have a better potential for sharing risk and increasing university revenues in the long run.

Technology Transfer Revenues at the Universities are Skewed and Random

The distribution of technology transfer royalties among universities is very uneven. The top 10 universities obtain roughly 50% of revenues (Zilberman *et al.*, 1998). Only a few key innovations generate licensing revenues in the tens of millions of dollars (the Cohen-Boyer innovation captures more than $100 million in revenues), while university revenues from most income-making patents are $10,000 or even less. Zilberman *et al.* (1998) argue, however, that the factors that explain the OTTs' income are the age of the office (since it takes time to build the infrastructure and a patent portfolio to generate revenues), quality reputation of the university (the highest earning universities include the University of California, Stanford and MIT), and some stochastic process. Universities that were fortunate enough to have one or two big successes (e.g. the University of Florida, which owns the rights to Gatorade) may earn large incomes for a while.

Critical Innovations Have Been Transferred from Universities to Start-up Companies

Major international corporations were not ready to buy the rights to develop some of the most creative university innovations, so one of the critical roles of OTTs has been to develop alliances between university researchers and the entrepreneurial business sector, especially venture capitalists, that has resulted in start-up companies to develop the technologies. Major biotechnology companies were established in this way, including Genentech, Chiron, Amgen, Calgene, etc. Over time, major corporations have taken over some of these start-up companies and incorporated them into their own operations. For example, Monsanto bought Calgene, DuPont bought Mycogen and Roche owns a majority share of Genentech.

Major companies have research centres that generate many important innovations of their own, but most of the research within major companies is targeted to short-term projects. Much money is spent to bring products to market, including the costs of meeting regulatory criteria to assess side-effects, and often less emphasis is given to new and creative ideas. Researchers at universities aim towards original and unique discoveries that will result in promotions, prestige and an increase in income. Thus, research conducted in universities and research in corporations, to a large extent, are complementary. University and research institutes, at least in the case of medical biotechnology, give rise to new ideas. Typically, start-up companies incubate them, and major companies commercialize, market and produce them. When research companies take over some of the start-up companies and develop their own research capacity, we may witness an increase of original innovations in the private sector. The private sector may also have better laboratories and equipment, giving them an edge. Furthermore, some companies get ahead in the innovative process by providing contract money to university researchers in exchange for rights of first refusal to license innovations. This type of arrangement can also provide companies with better access to the knowledge and personnel at the universities.

Conclusions

The introduction and adoption of biotechnology promise improvement in agricultural productivity, food quality, nutritional status and health, and may also contribute to environmental quality improvement and biodiversity preservation. Biotechnology applications may also present risks to the environment and biodiversity. The extent to which the potential of biotechnology will be realized depends on the policies and regulatory framework that will affect its evolution. This chapter argues that the basic feature of desired policies is their capacity to enhance the generation and transfer of knowledge and, in particular, it suggests:

1. *Public support of research in biotechnology and related fields.* University research is the source of major biotechnology breakthroughs and cannot be substituted by private sector research. University innovations enhance change and competitiveness in the biotechnology industry.
2. *Fine-tuned criteria for patent protection.* Discoveries of basic, natural facts (gene structures) should not be given patent protection. They would be limited to biotechnology discoveries that are novel and related to meaningful applications.

3. *Framework for smooth trading and effective enforcement of IPR in biotechnology.* Such legal and institutional frameworks will consist of transparent pricing as well as quick access and efficient execution of monetary transactions associated with the use of biotechnology IPR. Fast access to product and process innovations will enable effective generation of a diversified and extensive set of biotechnology products and the capacity to adjust to heterogeneity and preserve biodiversity.

4. *Differentiated pricing of biotechnology products and IPR to intensify its use in research and encourage activities benefiting the poor.* Harmonization of biotechnology pricing across locations may limit their adoption and hurt poorer users. Research activities and genetic materials for subsistence farmers should receive preferential pricing.

5. *Knowledge of the side-effects of biotechnology products should be continuously monitored, analysed and acted upon in regulation and product design.* Our analysis suggests that the introduction of biotechnology is likely to contribute to change in the structure and conduct of the agricultural sector. In particular,

(a) Gradual transition from production of small numbers of commodities to a large number of differentiated products.

(b) Increased reliance on contracting (and vertical integration) rather than markets in the interaction among farmers, input suppliers and buyers.

(c) The competitive models become less insightful and relevant in the analysis of agriculture, and the use of monopolistic competitive models becomes more appropriate.

(d) The agricultural product range is expanding and will likely encompass more than food and fibre products.

6. The impacts of biotechnology in agriculture depend on the adoption and use of other new types of innovations, especially information technology.

Notes

1. Carl Pray, paper presented at the NC-208 meeting in Tucson, Arizona, 25 February, 1998.

2. Wright's discussion was presented at the NC-208 meeting in Tucson, Arizona, 25 February, 1998.

3. Parker and Zilberman (1993) argue that generally a private sector tends to under-invest in research that may lead to patentable innovations because they take into account only the gains of producer surplus (profit to producers) and ignore the gains to consumers that exceed the cost of the product that reflects lower prices and availability of new products and amenities.

4. For more details, see Zilberman (1998).

References

Parker, D. and Zilberman, D. (1993) Hedonic estimation of quality factors affecting the farm–retail margin. *American Journal of Agricultural Economics* 75, 458–466.

Parker, D. and Zilberman, D. (1996) The use of information services: the case of CIMIS. *Agribusiness* 12, 209-218.

Parker, D., Zilberman, D. and Castillo, F. (1998) Office of Technology Transfer, the privatization of university innovations, and agriculture. *Choices* 19-25.

Wright, B. (1998) Public germplasm development at a crossroads: biotechnology and intellectual property. *California Agriculture* 52, 8-13.

Zilberman, D. (1998) Value and pricing of agricultural biotechnology products under alternative regimes of intellectual property rights. In: *Promoting Agricultural Innovations in Developing Countries: Implications for the Conservation of Genetic Resources and the Economy.* Report submitted to FAO, University of California at Berkeley.

Zilberman, D., Yarkin, C. and Heiman, A. (1998) Intellectual property rights, technology transfer, and genetic resource utilization. In: Smale, M. (ed.) *Farmers, Gene Banks and Crop Breeding: Economic Analyses of Diversity in Wheat, Maize, and Rice.* Kluwer Academic Publisher, Boston, Massachusetts, Chap. 12.

Q16
632

Comparing Allocation of Resources in Public and Private Research[*]

10

Stéphane Lemarié

INRA-SERD, Université Pierre-Mendès France, Grenoble, France

During the last 30 years, a large number of studies have been devoted to agricultural research. At the same time, its organization has changed dramatically, the major role of public research being replaced partially by private firms. This chapter is devoted to the comparison of the efficiency of public and private research for the management of a given research activity in agriculture.

The economic literature produces a paradoxical view on the subject. On the one hand, private expenditure on agricultural research (in industrialized countries) now represents two-thirds of total expenditure instead of one-half some decades ago. On the other hand, productivity growth on research expenditure leads to estimates[1] of the social rates of return of about 35% for public research and 20% for private research. How can this contradiction be interpreted?

First, it can be argued that these two rates of return are non-relevant when comparing public and private research because the activities managed by both sectors are very different.[2] In particular, public research generally manages a larger part of the fundamental research while private research manages a larger part of the development of new products. For a given innovation, it is generally accepted that development costs represent several times the research costs. Consequently, it would be logical to observe a lower rate social rate of return for the most costly activity.

Second, a series of arguments can be proposed to explain that the social rate of return to private research is less than the private rate of return.

*The first version of this paper was prepared for the workshop on 'Systems and Trajectories of Agricultural Innovation: Institutions, Technology and Conventions in Agricultural Regulation', held 23–25 April, 1998 at Berkeley, California.

- The private investments in research are oriented by expected private return. The expected private rate of return is not fully correlated with the social rate of return, because appropriability conditions vary from case to case. For example, investments in corn breeding in the USA represent more than 10 times the investment in wheat breeding (Frey, 1996) mainly because the appropriation is more important in the first case (hybrid seed), and not because the market for wheat seeds is negligible.
- The private incentives to invest in research exist only if there is some way to obtain market power thereafter. Private firms' innovations are consequently associated with some loss of social surplus because of restriction of demand (Moschini and Lapan, 1997).
- Finally, the contradiction can be explained by the efficiency of the allocation of resources in research. The allocation process can be driven by different rules: maximization of private profit or social surplus, or individual career of researcher. Even if the process in both the public and the private parts is a mix of all these determinants, there is no doubt that some variation exists between these two institutional configurations.

This chapter focuses more particularly on this last argument. The discussion will be based on both a review of theoretical works analysing allocation of resources in research, and a series of illustrations taken from agriculture. Until now very few economists have proposed such a comparison, one exception being the work by Wright (1983). The main reason is probably that public and private research are generally considered as complementary. Consequently, there is no interest in comparing the efficiency of managing two different activities by two different types of actor. However, recent history shows a substitution of some public research activities by private research. The problems studied in this chapter then become important because, in the long term, public and private research are considered as partial substitutes. Before addressing this problem, the rest of this introduction is dedicated to the presentation of the conceptual framework used in this chapter.

Public and private research are distinguished by their goal. Private research is oriented towards improving the profit of the firm, while public research is oriented towards the improvement of the social surplus (or welfare). Social surplus needs to be defined in a broad sense, different public research institutions having quite different behaviours. Basically, these institutions can be evaluated with two criteria: the value of the innovation directly provided to society or the value of the scientific production. In the first case, the social surplus is directly affected, while in the second case, the variation of social surplus is more hypothetical, but we can reasonably consider that a larger scientific production will increase social surplus in the long run. The weights of these two criteria are different from one public institution to the other: in France, for example, the 'innovation' criterion is more weighted for institutions such as INRA and CEA compared to CNRS where 'scientific production' is more weighted.

Research is seen as a set of uncertain activities producing objects of different nature: publications, material, instruments, persons, etc. Objects can be the input of other research activities, and/or can be released and delivered to production activities. Some objects are intentionally produced while others should be considered as by-products. Each activity is defined by the subject of the research. Several actors (public and/or private) are generally involved in the same activity. No particular distinction is made between the more applied and the more fundamental research activities.

The different types of research activities produce a large range of objects: for example, scientific research generally produces publication, but may also produce genetic material (possibly protected by patents). No particular association is made between some activities and some types of institution. As it was said before, some public institutions can be involved in applied research, while some companies might be doing fundamental research. The type of object produced by two laboratories, and its status (public/private good), can be different depending on the type of institution, or even more individual strategies (e.g. the strategy of the director of one laboratory).

Finally, the general framework proposed here is broad enough to represent any kind of institutional involvement in research.[3] However, we will see that the criteria proposed in this chapter for the analysis of efficiency of allocation of resources can virtually be applied to any kind of situation. In the first part of the chapter, I will present the static criteria with the following question in mind 'for a given result, is the involvement of actors optimal?'. In the second part of the chapter, I will present the dynamic criteria with another question in mind 'How does the involvement of actors affect the accumulation of knowledge and consequently the different results in the long term?'. In the conclusion, I will discuss a series of problems which might emerge with the application of these criteria.

The Static Criteria Based on the Non-rivalry and the Appropriation Properties

The Central Dilemma

All the discussion in this part is based on two properties of the objects produced by research activities.

1. *Non-rivalry.* Once an object is produced, it can be used several times with very little additional costs. Non-rivalry is observable when simultaneous uses are possible, or when the uses can be done sequentially without damage to the object, or even when duplication of the object can be done with very low costs.

2. *Exclusivity of use.* There are different means for one actor to restrict the use of the object he/she has produced. The simplest way is the secret: the

creator will not show the object and give any information on it.[4] The other way is to use property rights (e.g. patent, copyright): the creator will be allowed to restrict the use made by other actors. Note that not all property rights give complete power to restrict use (e.g. Breeders' Right).

These two properties lead to a central dilemma:

- If there is no way to restrict the use, the incentive to produce the object by doing research could be very low, because it is better to let someone else produce it first, and then duplicate it for a very low cost (Arrow, 1962).
- If there is some way to restrict the use, then there is some incentive to invest in research, but the object will probably be produced several times by several actors competing in the same research activities. If this happens, it can be argued that too much money has been spent to produce the second object, because this second unit could have been produced by a simple duplication of the first one.

These two arguments have been intensively discussed in the literature. Here we will confront them with illustrations taken from agricultural research. Before going further, we have to be conscious that the discussion is limited here to the static properties: the production of one and only one innovation is considered here. The aspects referring to the dynamic properties will be discussed in the second part. For example, duplication may favour the accumulation of knowledge in the long run and may then be less problematic than indicated in this part.

The Lack of Incentive Problem

In this section, I will discuss successively a one-activity case and a two-activities case. In the first case, the lack of incentive problem is revisited, by considering other aspects such as time length for duplication and experimental design constraints. In the two-activities case, I analyse the effect of spillovers on incentives and propose some solutions to limit these negative effects.

Production of One Object

This case is the one considered by Arrow (1962): as long as there is no way to control the use of the object, nobody will have enough incentive to produce it. Two solutions are then possible: the enforcement of property rights in order to create private incentives, or the public commitment in research. Two illustrations are proposed here to reconsider these conclusions and underline other important factors influencing the private incentive to invest.

First, we can consider the case of plant breeding. In their original form, Breeders' Rights give a monopoly for the commercialization of the product but do not forbid the farmer from saving seed or competitors from using the protected variety as an input in their own research programmes. Seed-saving is attractive as long as the variety is not a hybrid. If the farmer saves his/her own seed (e.g. wheat), the time for duplication is one year, and the evidence shows that this time is too short to give enough private incentives to invest in research.[5] Conversely, when the duplication comes only by the imitation (e.g. hybrid corn), evidence shows that the time length for the imitation is long enough to create incentives. Interestingly, this time length has been diminishing over time because of technique improvements: the possibility of making several generations in one year has reduced this length from more than 5 years to probably less than 4 years. This phenomenon has given legitimacy to the leading breeders negotiating a revision of the UPOV convention at the beginning of the 1990s. As a result, duplication has been restricted by constraining a new protected variety to be genetically different enough from previous varieties. To summarize, this case shows that incentives to invest in research exist even with low restriction, as long as the time length for imitation is long enough. Appropriation occurs then by 'being the first in the race'.[6]

In other cases, research costs compared with the volume of the market can eliminate any incentives to invest in research, whatever the restriction imposed on the use of innovation. The bovine selection case illustrates that point. To simplify the purpose, we consider only the improvement on the male side. Thanks to artificial insemination, the value of one bull can largely be increased, because it can have larger numbers of offspring. No restriction problems exist because the diffusion of sperm is controlled, the strict duplication of the bull is impossible and the time lag between generations is long enough. However, the production of offspring from a particular cow specifically for research purposes is too expensive and cancels any incentive. The solution adopted is a compromise where the cows have a double status: first, they are owned by farmers and used for milk and/or meat production, second the information obtained on their performance is used to evaluate the value of the parents, and possibly select the best ones. In France, the programme for the collection and exploitation of this information is largely supported by the public.

Production of Two Objects with Spillovers
Spillovers are externalities (generally positive in research) between two research activities: the production of one object by the first research activity unintentionally affects the production of a second object by another research activity.

Figure 10.1a and b gives two simple representations of this situation. In both cases, two innovations are produced for two areas (A and B), and the use of the innovation can be controlled, so there are incentives to invest in the research activity A and B (cf. previous paragraph). In Fig. 10.1b, these two activities are linked with a particular upstream activity A' and B', whose results cannot be controlled. In some cases the actor investing in A will have

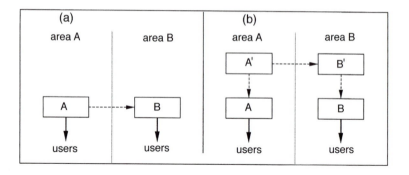

Fig. 10.1. Two simple representations of production of two research objects with spillovers.

some interest in integrating A′ and restrict the use of the object produced by A′ by secret (the same being possible in area B). Conversely, if there is no interest in integrating A′, we suppose that public research is willing to commit on these activities.

Externalities are represented from A to B in Fig. 10.1a and from A′ to B′ in Fig. 10.1b. In Fig. 10.1a, externality leads to under-investment in activity A because the actor only considers the effect in area A, and ignores the positive effect on area B. In Fig. 10.1b, an under-investment exists also, but for activity A′. The interesting point to observe is that public research can lead to under-investment since its investment is rationalized with respect to a limited area (generally a country). Two solutions can then attenuate this problem:

- The integration of activity under the same umbrella: multinational companies or international public research centres.
- The enforcement of property rights on the object circulating between the two areas. The investment in activity A (Fig. 10.1a) or A′ (Fig. 10.1b) will then increase because the effect on area B can then generate profit (via licensing fees, for example).

Different *ex post* analyses of rates of return to research activities have shown that spillovers between countries are generally positive and significant. As a consequence, different interesting illustrations of the simple representation in Fig. 10.1 can be found.

Evenson (1996) discusses the link between national agricultural research systems (NARS) and International Agricultural Research Centers (IARC). The idea is to underline the interest of the division of labour between the IARC and the NARS: the IARC provide germplasm innovations which can be used in several countries, while the NARS use these germplasm innovations and try to adapt them to local climates. The IARC are supported by the international community, so we might expect not too much distortion in favour of one particular country. Finally, the centralization of this research appears to be more efficient compared to a situation where each country invests in its own germplasm innovations. These principles are illustrated with empirical analysis on genealogies of rice (Evenson and Gollin, 1997). An equivalent problem appears also in the history of US agricultural research, with the relationship between the State Agricultural Experiment Stations (SAES) and the US Department of Agriculture (USDA).[7]

Enforcement of property rights can be found in the management of genetic resources, after the Convention on Biological Diversity (Rio, 1992). The idea is to give rights to developing countries (Farmers' Rights) on their genetic resources, in order to give the incentive to preserve. Clearly, this solution has to be compared with the IARC/NARS solution discussed previously. The case of conservation of genetic resources does not provide any answers, since there is still a large debate between the multilateral system (IARC/NARS) and the bilateral system (Farmers' Rights).

Synthesis
The discussion on the lack of incentives criteria can be summarized with three propositions:

1. A non-restriction of use may lead to a lack of incentive to invest in research, which is a form of misallocation of resources. It can happen with private research when the use of the innovation cannot be restricted. It can also happen with public research when there are some spillovers towards other countries. Public incentives can be lower than private incentives if the spillovers between countries are important (multinational companies may internalize the spillovers).
2. For private research, the restriction of use is not strictly equivalent to incentives to invest in research. On the one hand, the incentives can be generated by 'being the first in the race', even with low restriction of use. On the other hand, research costs can lower incentives, even when restriction of use is possible.
3. A lack of private incentives can possibly be overtaken by an enforcement of property rights. If such a solution is possible, we then need to compare efficacy of allocation of resources in both public and private research in the new setting, by using the other arguments (duplication and accumulation of knowledge). Conversely, when lack of incentive persists even with enforcement of property rights, then public research is generally justified.

The Duplication Problem (in a Static Context)

On the Optimal Level of Duplication
As observed earlier, because of the non-rival nature of objects produced by research, we can suspect an excessive level of duplication as soon as more

than two units of one object are produced by two parallel research projects. The reason is that the second unit could have been produced by simply duplicating the first one. However, three main reasons lead us to be very careful when dealing with duplication.

1. *Duplication depends on the substitutability between objects.* If two objects produced by two different research activities are good substitutes, removing one activity has less effect, because the object produced by the other activity makes a compensation. Such a case can also be interpreted as a partial duplication between activities. If we go back to the representations given in Fig. 10.1, we can wonder how far the activity in region B duplicates the activity in region A. As a matter of fact, we could also represent the activities A' and B' as only one activity (say C) producing objects both for A and B. We would then observe a duplication of activity C in the areas A and B.[8] To summarize this point, duplication is appreciated differently depending on the way we represent the structure of research activities, and consequently we can only give an indication of level of duplication.

2. *Research activities are uncertain.* We do not know precisely *ex ante* the project which will be successful *ex post*. Uncertainty concerns the technical result (success/failure) and the date of the innovation. Duplication can increase the expected profit by increasing the probability of success or bringing forwards the date of the discovery. Generally, the marginal gains in terms of probability of success or discovery date are decreasing (at least after some level), so there is generally a certain level of duplication over which marginal cost (i.e. the cost of one supplementary programme) exceeds the marginal gain.[9] Duplication combined with uncertainty can also lead to unexpected results: the value of the objects produced by all the programmes is greater as the number of programmes increases (but probably with decreasing returns also).

3. *Duplication is a consequence of competition.* Competition has not been discussed until now. At the beginning of this first part, the discussion was centred on the effect of exclusion on the incentives to invest in research. Exclusion leads to some monopoly powers, and a decrease of competition level. When exclusion is not complete, externalities can lead to under-investment in research. One solution is to internalize the externalities by grouping the activities under the same umbrella. These propositions converge to underline the interest of the large hierarchies which can control a lot of research activities. Different arguments can, however, be proposed to show the limits of concentrating activities within one organization, and conversely the interest of introducing some competition (see next paragraph). A certain level of duplication is consequently useful when introducing interesting effects of competition.

Main Properties of Competition in Research Activities

Competition in research has mostly been studied in the industrial context, with both empirical and theoretical contributions. The empirical contribution has addressed many subjects but rarely duplication.[10] One of the main reasons is probably that databases provide data at the sectoral level while duplication is appreciated at the smaller level of the research activities.

Numerous theoretical contributions have analysed the effect of competition on the incentive to invest, and studied the welfare properties of the level of investment in research at the equilibrium.[11] The theoretical results can be classified in three main propositions:

- The *common pool* problem (Dasgupta and Stiglitz, 1980). In a one-period symmetric game, the marginal gain when increasing the level of investment is generally more important at the firm level compared to the social level. This property leads to an excessive level of investment in research, which can be interpreted here as an excessive level of duplication

- The *pre-emption* problem (Fudenberg and Tirole, 1985). In an asymmetric game (one actor has more knowledge than its competitors at the beginning of the first period), there is no interest for the followers to invest in research since the leader will always be able to have the same result with less investment. Consequently, a small advance in research can be equivalent to a monopoly position and leads to under-investment in research.

- The *asymmetry of information* problem. Wright (1983) has compared three modes for allocating resources in research (patent, prize and contract) with asymmetric information. The researcher has more precise information on the technical parameters compared to the central administrator who decides the mode of allocation of resources. The hierarchy (i.e. the contract in Wright's paper) is generally less efficient compared to the more competitive situations (prize or patent).

This short and selective review is enough to show that there is no unique relationship between competition and duplication. Competition has to be studied in several contexts to provide more robust results about duplication.

Recently, different contributions have addressed the analysis of competition in more fundamental research. Dasgupta and David (1994) made the distinction between two polar forms of regulations: Science and Technology, considered as institutional frameworks. Briefly, competition can be represented as a patent race in Technology and a publication race in Science. Both systems lead to some disclosure, without entailing property rights. Finally, the carrier at the researcher level is evaluated on the basis of the effect on profit in Technology and on publications in Science. Technology is the dominant mode of regulation in private research and Science is dominant in public research. Although interesting work has been proposed on the analysis of regulation in science activities,[12] no analysis has addressed the problem of duplication. The parallel between patent races and the race for publication leads us to the intuition that excessive duplication may be possible in some particular case because of the common pool problems. However, in the public sector the decision is a result of a combination of decentralization and hierarchical regulation. Certain public research institutions are mainly regulated by the hierarchical system, leading probably to less internal duplication.

The Applicability of the Duplication Criteria

This section shows clearly that the evaluation of duplication can rapidly become an onerous task for two reasons:

- With a positive perspective (how much publication is there?), duplication has to be evaluated for each research activity, and this will require intensive work for collecting data.
- With a normative perspective (is there not enough or too much duplication?), the optimal level of duplication is difficult to appreciate since it depends on different factors which are difficult to estimate (uncertainty, value of expected and unexpected results, positive effect of competition). Note that the estimation is probably harder, the more fundamental the research is. An interesting example is given in the genomic domain by Jourdan (1993). At the time his laboratory was researching chromosome X, he explained that there were more than 20 laboratories in the world doing very similar research. Should we interpret this number as excessive?

The Dynamic Criteria Based on the Accumulation and the Diffusion of Knowledge

Linked Innovation and Dependency

The patent has some positive effects on the diffusion of knowledge because the rewards are always associated with the disclosure. However, some differences with a publication race model appear when a related innovation is made thereafter. In the publication race model, as long as citation is correctly made, the reward to the first one who publishes does not prevent the other publications. On the other hand, to prevent imitation (innovation invented around the first patent), the patent system introduces a notion of dependency: if the second patent is within the domain of revendication of the first patent, then the second innovator will need a licence from the first innovator if he/she wants to benefit from the innovation. Scotchmer (1991) shows that even when the broadness of the patent is chosen optimally, there is some lack of incentive either because the first innovator will be easily imitated (too narrow), or because the second innovator depends too much on the first one (too broad).

As described earlier, the evolution of property rights in the seed industry shows that the effect of dependency is getting more important. In the original version of the Breeders' Rights based on the first UPOV convention (1961), an exemption for research was included: any variety can be used as a source of germplasm in the research programme of a competitor. The revision of this convention at the beginning of the 1990s has reduced this exemption: any variety with more than $x\%$ of genes common with an older one will depend on it. At the same time, the patent system was introduced to protect genes.

The Diffusion and the Use of Knowledge

Until now, we have supposed that once an actor invests in research, there is some probability of producing an interesting innovation. Failures are explained by the uncertainty which is an intrinsic characteristic of research activities. We turn now to an alternative concept, in which the circulation, the absorption and the use of the knowledge are constrained. More precisely, two hypotheses can be made:[13]

1. The knowledge is embodied in different kinds of objects, and the nature of this support has an influence on the way knowledge is diffused. The simplest conception is to distinguish between hardly transmissible tacit knowledge embodied in individual know-how, and easily transmissible codified knowledge embodied in publications or some instruments.
2. The ability to use the knowledge produced by the environment depends on the absorptive capacity of the actor. In a first approximation, absorptive capacity is represented by the knowledge base of the firm: the more we know, the easier it will be to understand what is produced elsewhere. Absorptive capacity is also determined by other factors, as for example the internal organization of the firm.

This framework leads to two interesting observations for the purpose of this chapter:

- R&D has an indirect effect linked with the enforcement of absorptive capacity. The cases where duplication was considered as excessive when using the criteria discussed before have to be reconsidered because duplication makes absorption easier.
- The way the knowledge is embodied in objects is not independent from the actors' strategy. In particular, when appropriation strategy is based on secrecy (i.e. to make knowledge as unusable as possible by competitors), the diffusion of knowledge is very limited. Patent (in the institution Technology) and publication (in the institution Science) are then interesting solutions because property rights are associated with disclosure.

The characteristics of the learning process lead to special properties when several emerging technologies are competing. The central characteristic is the learning curve: the performance of each technology will progressively be improved as the number of actors investing or using it increases. When several technologies are competing, several equilibria may be possible and the selection of the equilibrium depends on the path (Arthur, 1989). With this context in mind, several authors have suggested that a private system may select an unfavourable equilibrium. Conversely, some technology policy may be oriented towards the selection of more favourable equilibria. One orientation of public research would then be to maintain a certain level of technological diversity, to prevent rapid lock-in (Callon, 1993).

Conclusion

In this chapter, I have discussed a series of criteria for the comparison of efficiency of allocation of resources in public and private research. As underlined in the introduction, these questions have rarely been addressed in the literature, the main reason being that these two modes are generally considered as complementary. The development proposed here leads to three main lessons.

First, even if criteria appear to be very simple, the instrumentation for measurement can rapidly become an arduous task. This problem is particularly important in the two following cases: the duplication in public research and the accumulation of knowledge in private research.

Second, even when measurement issues can be solved, the application for prescription can bring new troubles. This problem was especially important concerning duplication: even if a satisfying measure of duplication can be found, should we consider this level as insufficient or excessive? Actually, a lot of factors influence the optimal level of duplication (uncertainty, unexpected results, competition) and no robust properties have been found to manage them.

Third, criteria can lead to contradictory prescriptions. The lack of incentives criteria lead one to say that public research should invest when there is a social interest but no private interest. Such a rule can lead to investment in applied research, while the last criterion on the accumulation of knowledge underlines the importance of public research for emerging technologies. Another contradictory case appears also about the size of the institutions: the problem of externalities leads to very centralized institutions, but these centralized decisions can be inefficient in a context of asymmetric information. The last contradictory point concerns property rights which are encouraged when using the lack of incentive criteria but are questionable in a dynamic context.

Acknowledgement

I thank my colleagues from INRA/SERD for their helpful comments. However, I am the only one responsible for this text.

Notes

1. See Huffman and Evenson (1993) for more evidence on this finding.
2. Two other reasons can be given to reject this comparison. (1) The database on private research expenditures is generally weak compared to the database on public research. However, if this incompleteness means that private research expenditures are underestimated, the rates of return should then be lower than the estimation, and the gap between both rates of return should be greater. (2) The emergence of new research activity (biotechnology) will affect the social rate of return. Consequently, rates of return in the past might not be relevant to predict rates of return in the future.
3. This conception is compatible with the one proposed by authors such as Rosenberg and Pavitt who clearly showed the limit of the linear model (Kline and Rosenberg, 1986; Pavitt, 1991).
4. This strategy is generally possible for process innovation. See Levin *et al.* (1987) for more evidence on appropriation strategies in different sectors.
5. See Frey (1996) for precise and recent data on the public and private investments in research in the different varieties in the USA.
6. See Levin *et al.* (1987) for more analysis on this argument, and its weight in different sectors.
7. See chapter 2 in Alston and Pardey (1996) for more details.
8. This case shows also that duplication can be combined with under-investment in research.
9. For example, if we consider a series of identical programmes represented by a Bernoulli trial with the same probability. The expected profit is then: $E(\pi) = v(1 - (1 - p)^n) - n$ with v the value of the innovation (the cost of one programme being one unit), p the probability of innovation and n the number of programmes. The optimal number of programmes is the closest integer to the integer around the the the real $n^* = [\ln(v) + \ln(-\ln(1 - p))]/-\ln(1 - p)$ which provides the best profit. This integer is generally greater than 1.
10. In his survey of empirical studies, Cohen (1995) distinguished five determinants of research expenses and research outputs (e.g. patents): industrial structure, appropriability, demand, technological opportunities and organizational structure.
11. Note that these contributions consider research as a stochastic process. My remark about the interest of duplication in order to overcome uncertainty is taken into account.
12. See Stephan (1996) for a recent survey on the economics of science.
13. See Cohen and Levinthal (1990) for a detailed presentation of this framework.

References

Alston, J.M. and Pardey, P.G. (1996) *Making Science Pay – The Economics of Agricultural R&D Policy.* AEI Press, Washington, DC.

Arrow, K.J. (1962) Economic welfare and the allocation of resources for invention. In: National Bureau of Economics Research (NBER) (ed.) *The Rate and Direction of Inventive Activity: Economic and Social Factors.* Princeton University Press, Princeton, pp. 609–626.

Arthur, W.B. (1989) Competing technologies, increasing returns, and lock-in by historical events. *Economic Journal* 99, 116–131.

Callon, M. (1993) Is science a public good? *Science, Technology and Human Values* 19, 395–424.

Cohen, W. (1995) Empirical studies of innovative activities. In: Stoneman, P. (ed.) *Handbook of the Economics of Innovation and Technical Change*. Blackwell Publisher, Oxford, pp. 182–264.

Cohen, W.M. and Levinthal, D.A. (1990) Absorptive capacity: a new perspective on learning and innovation. *Administrative Science Quarterly* 35, 128–152.

Dasgupta, P. and David, P.A. (1994) Toward a new economics of science. *Research Policy* 23, 487–521.

Dasgupta, P. and Stiglitz, J. (1980) Uncertainty, industrial structure, and the speed of R&D. *Bell Journal of Economics* 11, 1–28.

Evenson, R.E. (1996) The economic principles of research resource allocation. In: Evenson, R.E., Herdt, R.W. and Hossain, M. (eds) *Rice Research in Asia: Progress and Priorities*. CAB International (in association with IRRI), Wallingford, UK, pp. 73–90.

Evenson, R.E. and Gollin, D. (1997) Genetic resources, international organizations, and rice varietal improvement. *Economic Development and Cultural Change* 45, 471–500.

Frey, K.J. (1996) *National Plant Breeding Study – I: Human and Financial Resources Devoted to Plant Breeding Research and Development in the United States in 1994*. Special Report 98. Iowa State University, Iowa Agriculture and Home Economics Experiment Station, Ames, Iowa.

Fudenberg, D. and Tirole, J. (1985) Preemption and rent equalization in the adoption of new technology. *Review of Economic Studies* 52, 383–401.

Huffman, W.E. and Evenson, R.E. (1993) *Science for Agriculture: a Long Term Perspective*. Iowa State University Press, Ames, Iowa.

Jourdan, B. (1993) *Voyage autour du génome: le tour du monde en 80 labos*. J. Libbey, Paris, 180 pp.

Kline, S.J. and Rosenberg, N. (1986) An overview on innovation. In: Landau, R. and Rosenberg, N. (eds) *The Positive Sum Strategy: Harnessing Technology for Economic Growth*. National Academy Press, Washington, DC, pp. 275–305.

Levin, R.C., Klevorick, A.K., Nelson, R.R. and Winter, S.G. (1987) Appropriating the returns from industrial research and development. *Brookings Papers on Economic Activity* 3, 783–820.

Moschini, G. and Lapan, H. (1997) Intellectual property rights and the welfare effects of agricultural R&D. *American Journal of Agricultural Economics* 79, 1229–1242.

Pavitt, K. (1991) What makes basic research economically useful? *Research Policy* 20, 109–119.

Scotchmer, S. (1991) Standing on the shoulders of giants: cumulative research and patent law. *Journal of Economic Perspectives* 5, 29–41.

Stephan, P.E. (1996) The economics of science. *Journal of Economic Literature* 34(3), 1199–1235.

Wright, B.D. (1983) The economics of invention incentives: patents, prizes, and research contracts. *American Economic Review* 73, 691–707.

Biotechnology Inventions: What Can We Learn from Patents?

Daniel K.N. Johnson[1] and Vittorio Santaniello[2]

[1] *Department of Economics, Wellesley College, Wellesley, Massachusetts, USA;* [2] *Dipartimento di Economia ed Istituzioni, Università degli Studi di Roma 'Tor Vergata', Rome, Italy*

Intellectual property rights (IPR) cover most forms of patented knowledge in a similar fashion, regardless of the type of technology, its origins or uses. That is, the application process, the tenure of granted patents and the protected rights granted to a patent do not vary with the type of technology protected. This chapter explores several characteristics of patents in the biotechnology field, comparing and contrasting them to patents in other fields of research. Since protection is essential to the financial success of most knowledge-creating ventures, the differences we describe below may predict the direction and intensity of future biotechnology patent applications, and research in general.

It is well established in the literature that patent counts are imperfect measures of innovation (Jaffe, 1986; Griliches, 1990; Trajtenberg, 1990; Johnson and Evenson, 1997). However, most studies also recognize the difficulties involved in obtaining better measures. Surveys of professionals in the field are extremely expensive (Johnson and Evenson, 1997), while patent data are relatively cheap or even free to obtain. The accuracy of patents as a measure can be improved by distinguishing between important inventions and less important patents, a distinction which has been achieved using data on subsequent citations (Jaffe and Trajtenberg, 1995), renewal fees (Schankerman and Pakes, 1986) and international family size, the set of nations in which similar patent rights are protected (Lanjouw *et al.*, 1996).

This chapter relies on several datasets as indicators of biotechnology invention, but all measure patents (or the applications for patents). We use all patents granted by the US Patent and Trademark Office (USPTO) between 1975 and 1994, since they represent an international array of applications, are included in most international patent families, and are easy to analyse in their entirety. A random sample of over 1600 patents granted by the European Patent Office (EPO) between 1984 and 1998 was analysed by hand to supplement and compare with the US data in key sections.

Five fundamental attributes of patent applications will be examined in order to shed light on the differences between biotechnology and other fields of research. The next section explores the lag between application and grant dates of patents. The third section presents biotechnology patents by their industries of manufacture and sectors of use. The fourth section examines the references listed by granted patents, for information on the contributions of foreign patents, scientific literature and domestic patents, as well as the ages and technological fields of those references where possible. The following section presents data on subsequent citations or references to each patent. Finally, the sixth section maps the geographical concentration (both foreign and domestic) of patent applicants before the final section concludes with some comments about the importance of the differences between biotechnology patents and IPR in other fields of research.

There is no universally accepted definition of biotechnology, only the recognition that it encompasses parts of a number of disciplines, including most notably molecular biology and chemistry (Acharya, 1999). It is 'not an industrial sector, but a set of techniques for the manipulation of living organisms which comprises several disciplines' (Saviotti, 1998). For that reason, the definition used here includes inventions in a number of fields of research, as described by product or process instead of by industry.

Since 1972, most nations have registered and counted patents by International Patent Classification (IPC), information which is valuable in distinguishing the product or process involved in a patent, but which is only indirectly helpful in identifying the industries creating inventions or sectors using them. The definition of biotechnology used in this chapter therefore differs slightly for the EPO and US patent samples (see Table 1.1). Acting upon EPO advice, in calculations of European data we include five IPCs as a definition of biotechnology. The US Patent Office offers no official definition of biotechnology, but seven IPCs were included in the US definition, for two reasons.

First, all had high proportions of patents which contained some variant of the word 'biotech' embedded in their text. While this is only a rough indicator of content, in 1998/99, over 20% of all patents granted in four of the seven classes included that term. At least 6% of patents in each class had the term in their text. Since presumably only a fraction of all biotechnological inventions include the term 'biotech' itself, a much higher proportion of each IPC is biotechnology-related. The one IPC included in the EPO definition but not considered in the US was excluded because less than 0.7% of US patents in that class (A01K) included any text indicator of 'biotech'.

Second, a publication on biotechnology inventors by the Office of Technology Assessment and Forecast at the US Patent Office (1998) suggests a list of 478 US patent subclasses related to biotechnology. To facilitate international comparisons, this chapter chose to use international patent classes instead. However, a recent concordance developed to compare the two

Table 11.1. European and US sample composition.

IPC	Description	Number of patents in European sample	Number of US patents, 1975–1994
A01K		75	None included
A61K	Preparations for medical, dental, or toilet purposes	946	47,480
C07H	Sugar derivatives, nucleosides, nucleotides and nucleic acids	None sampled	3718
C07K	Peptides	187	3841
C12N	Microorganisms or enzymes	291	7404
C12P	Fermentation or enzyme-using processes	None sampled	4685
C12Q	Measuring or testing processes involving enzymes or microorganisms	113	3080
G01N	Investigating or analysing materials	None sampled	30,857

classifications (Johnson, 1999), indicates that over 75% of all patents in the list map directly into the seven IPCs chosen for study here.

Given the slight difference in definitions, all international comparisons in this chapter must be interpreted with care. Differences may be attributed to the composition of biotechnology as reflected in the definitions, to the use of a random sample for the EPO while using the full population of US patents or to real underlying differences between the nature of biotechnology in each region.

Figure 11.1 presents data on all patents granted in the USA between 1975 and 1994, showing the total number of biotechnology patent applications granted (the line, as measured against the right-hand axis) and their share of all applications granted (the bars, as measured against the left-hand axis). Rising from 4% of the total in 1975, then falling to below 3% in 1977 and 1978, biotechnology remained steadily between 5.5 and 6% of all applications between 1979 and 1992. The marked drop in 1993 and 1994 in both series is an artefact of the data, since the data are only presented for patents *granted* between 1975 and 1994. The number of patent applications in 1993 and 1994 which were also granted by the end of 1994 is low for all fields, but, for a reason which we will show in the next section, it is especially low for biotechnology-related applications.

The Application-to-grant Lag

In order to avoid the distortion seen in Fig. 11.1, similar information is presented in the line of Fig. 11.2, but data are here presented by their *grant* year cohort. The line (as measured against the right-hand axis) shows that as

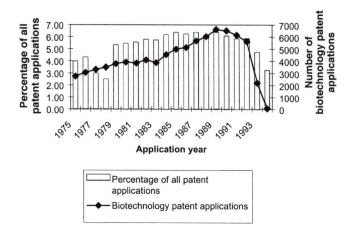

Fig. 11.1. Biotechnology patent applications in the USA (and percentage of all US applications), granted 1975–1994.

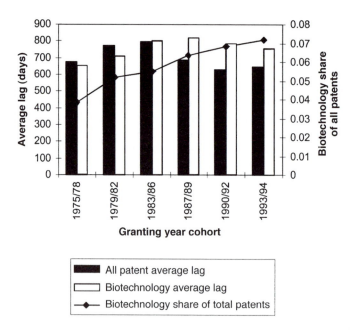

Fig. 11.2. Application-to-grant lags and importance of biotechnology, US patents granted 1975–1994.

a percentage of grants, biotechnology has been increasing in importance, and in fact reached over 7% of all patents granted in the USA in 1993/94.

The reason for the sizable difference between the patterns shown for 1993 and 1994 on Figs 11.1 and 11.2 is simple, and is shown by the bars on Fig. 11.2. The average application-to-grant lag is over 600 days for all patents. Since we are considering only patents granted between 1975 and 1994, there are a relatively low number of patents with application dates in 1993 or 1994 in any field, because few of them will be granted by the end of 1994. However, biotechnology patents have an even longer lag than the average patent, averaging 109 days longer in 1993-1994. So proportionally fewer of their 1993 and 1994 applications were granted by 1994.

It is interesting to note that biotechnology patents have not always been subject to a longer lag between application and grant. In fact, in the 1970s, biotechnology patents were granted more quickly than other patents. However, in the late 1980s, when average lags were cut markedly by the USPTO, there was no similar cut in the lag for biotechnology applications. The result was a gap that reached an average of 154 days longer for biotechnology grants between 1990 and 1992.

Of course, the results presented so far have been averages, so individual results could vary quite widely. Figure 11.3 displays the full distributions of the granting lag for all patents by granting cohort. While the average lag for the cohorts granted in 1975-1978, 1987-1989, 1990-1992 and 1993-1994 are all quite similar (see Fig. 11.2), their distributions look quite different. In fact, the variance is much higher in 1993-1994 than it was in 1975-1978.

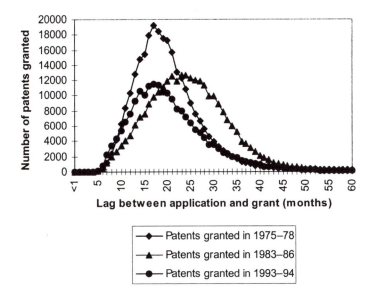

Fig. 11.3. All patents granted in the USA between 1975 and 1994, by application-to-grant lag.

Figure 11.4 presents the same information for biotechnology patents alone, and shows that the variance did not vary much over time although the average rose during 1983–1986 and has fallen slightly since then.

An interesting comparison can be made using the cumulative distributions of all patents and biotechnology patents on the same graph. Figure 11.5 shows that between 1975 and 1978, the probability that a patent would be granted after a certain number of months did not vary depending on its biotechnological nature. However, between 1979 and 1982, biotechnology stochastically dominated other patents, meaning that for any given lag, a greater percentage of biotechnology patents would have been granted (Fig. 11.6). That is, not only was the *average* lag shorter for biotechnology, but other things held equal, even long or short lag patents were granted more quickly if they were biotechnological.

By 1983–1986, the distributions were close to equal again, as Fig. 11.7 shows. However, since then, biotechnology has had a longer lag and has been stochastically dominated by other patents. Figures 11.8–11.10 clearly show that biotechnology patents take longer to be granted than other patents do.

The longer lags experienced by biotechnology patent applications are perhaps a benefit to biotechnology inventors in the USA, because applications are not published until they are granted. Thus, secrecy is maintained longer for biotechnology patents than for other applications, and where secrecy is valuable to maintaining a knowledge-based edge over competitors, biotechnology inventors may prefer to have a longer lag before grant.

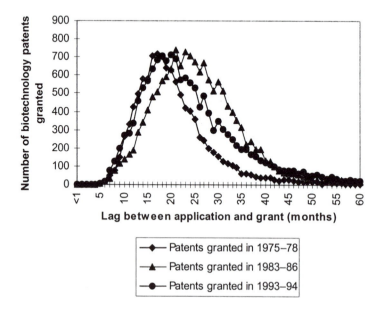

Fig. 11.4. Biotechnology patents granted in the USA between 1975 and 1994, by application-to-grant lag.

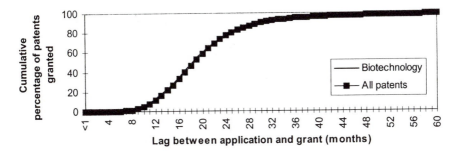

Fig. 11.5. Application-to-grant lags for biotechnology and all patents granted in the USA between 1975 and 1978, as cumulative distributions.

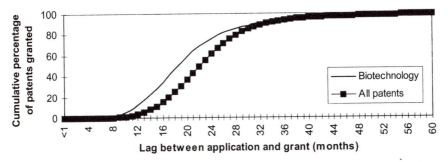

Fig. 11.6. Application-to-grant lags for biotechnology and all patents granted in the USA between 1979 and 1982, as cumulative distributions.

However, in the rest of the world, and in the USA soon if current pressures to conform to international standards succeed, applications are published 18 months (545 days) after application, regardless of grant status. Given the data presented here, if implemented in the USA this change would

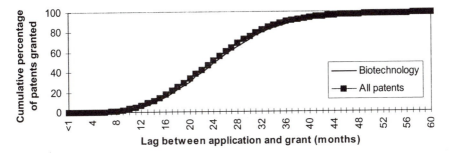

Fig. 11.7. Application-to-grant lags for biotechnology and all patents granted in the USA between 1983 and 1986, as cumulative distributions.

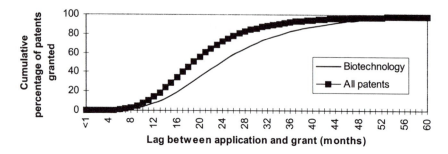

Fig. 11.8. Application-to-grant lags for biotechnology and all patents granted in the USA between 1987 and 1989, as cumulative distributions.

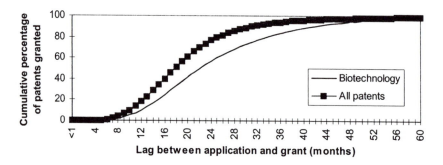

Fig. 11.9. Application-to-grant lags for biotechnology and all patents granted in the USA between 1990 and 1992, as cumulative distributions.

affect many inventors by publicizing details of patent applications after 575 days instead of after an average grant lag of 645 days. It would affect biotechnology inventors even more dramatically, reducing their secrecy period after application to 575 days from an average of over 750. Thus, if post-application secrecy is

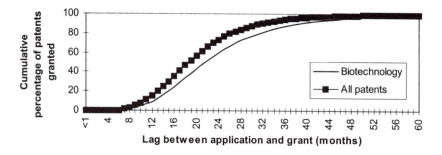

Fig. 11.10. Application-to-grant lags for biotechnology and all patents granted in the USA between 1993 and 1994, as cumulative distributions.

valuable to all inventors, biotechnology inventors in particular will prefer to keep the US patent system unchanged.

In addition, since the rest of the world already adheres to the 18-month publication rule, we might expect fewer biotechnology applications in the rest of the world compared to the USA. Since applying in the USA grants a longer period of secrecy, inventors may forego applications elsewhere if the fear of early publication in another nation poses a serious risk to future profits. This will probably only affect marginal cases, but will be more pronounced in biotechnology than in other fields.

Industries of Manufacture and Sectors of Use

While the categories of the IPC system are helpful in distinguishing the product or process involved in a patent, the industries involved in the production and use of new technology are often interesting to policy-makers or economists. The newest version of the Yale Technology Concordance (YTC) was designed to simultaneously assign industries of manufacture (IOM) and sectors of use (SOU) to IPC patent counts using a probabilistic structure.

The Yale Technology Concordance (YTC) provides a probability-based assignment of inventions, given an IPC designation, assigning them to IOM and SOU. Probabilities are based on assignments made by the Canadian Patent Office over a period of 25 years, during which time IPC, IOM and SOU codes were attached to over 300,000 patents. While previous work has used the YTC,[1] this research develops a new version of the YTC which not only updates the probabilities to include more data, but considers simultaneous IOM and SOU probabilities. Therefore, where previous studies were limited to calculations of total patents by IOM or total patents by SOU, this work is able to make full IOM–SOU tables, or input–output tables of inventions based on patent data originally listed only by IPC. Details on the construction and tests of the accuracy of the YTC can be found in Evenson and Johnson (1997) and Kortum and Putnam (1997).

It is important to recognize that although Canadian data were used to calculate probabilities, in using the YTC the only structural constraint imposed is a technical one between IPC (i.e. products/processes) and IOM or SOU (i.e. sectors). It does not assume the same industrial structure for other nations or time periods, just that the same product as defined by IPC comes from the same industries and is used in the same sectors.

The full IOM–SOU table for biotechnology patents granted in the USA between 1975 and 1994 is available from the authors, and a summary is presented in Table 11.2. Table 11.2 emphasizes the obvious importance of the chemical, drug and instrument IOMs, which produce over 93% of all biotechnology patents. The instrument industry has declined in share over the last 15 years, with its share absorbed by the chemical and drug industries. Turning to SOUs, health is by far the largest using sector, accounting for over half of

Table 11.2. Distribution of biotechnology patents by IOM and SOU (% of total).

	1975–1994		1978–1982		1990–1994	
	IOM	SOU	IOM	SOU	IOM	SOU
Agriculture	0.08	3.05	0.04	3.09	0.12	3.03
Forestry and fishing	0.00	0.06	0.00	0.06	0.00	0.06
Mining	0.01	0.75	0.00	0.78	0.01	0.70
Electrical appliances	0.00	0.00	0.00	0.00	0.00	0.00
Electrical lighting	0.03	0.01	0.03	0.01	0.02	0.01
Radio and television	0.02	0.02	0.02	0.02	0.02	0.02
Electrical industrial equipment	1.12	0.23	1.27	0.26	0.93	0.19
Other electrical equipment	0.14	0.08	0.16	0.09	0.12	0.06
Electronic equipment	2.34	0.51	2.67	0.58	1.95	0.42
Chemicals	11.79	3.01	10.60	2.59	13.39	3.40
Drugs	60.69	13.91	58.58	10.77	62.85	17.19
Petroleum	0.00	0.14	0.00	0.12	0.00	0.15
Transport	0.04	0.67	0.05	0.77	0.04	0.56
Ferrous metals	0.01	0.25	0.01	0.29	0.01	0.21
Non-ferrous metals	0.02	0.13	0.02	0.14	0.02	0.10
Fabricated metals	0.04	0.19	0.05	0.22	0.04	0.16
Instruments	21.17	6.76	23.88	7.70	18.10	5.68
Computers and peripherals	0.17	0.12	0.20	0.14	0.15	0.10
Other office machinery	0.00	0.02	0.00	0.02	0.00	0.02
Other machinery	0.76	0.99	0.79	1.11	0.71	0.84
Food	0.32	1.50	0.27	1.14	0.38	1.83
Textiles	0.00	0.05	0.00	0.06	0.00	0.05
Rubber and plastic	0.13	0.16	0.14	0.18	0.12	0.14
Non-metallic minerals	0.03	0.17	0.04	0.19	0.03	0.15
Paper	0.02	0.45	0.02	0.49	0.02	0.40
Wood	0.00	0.09	0.00	0.10	0.00	0.07
Other manufacturing	1.06	0.39	1.16	0.43	0.98	0.36
Construction	n/a	0.28	n/a	0.32	n/a	0.24
Transportation and storage	n/a	0.16	n/a	0.19	n/a	0.14
Communication	n/a	0.32	n/a	0.32	n/a	0.30
Trade	n/a	0.89	n/a	0.98	n/a	0.82
Finance	n/a	7.40	n/a	8.39	n/a	6.25
Government and education	n/a	0.26	n/a	0.30	n/a	0.23
Health	n/a	55.73	n/a	56.76	n/a	54.96
Other services	n/a	1.26	n/a	1.38	n/a	1.16

all biotechnology inventions used. Drugs and instruments are also large users, as biotechnology invents for its own use. There is an anomalous result showing the finance sector as a user of 7% of all biotechnological inventions, a result which must be explored more closely in future work.

As a test of the accuracy of the YTC, and for international comparison, 1600 EPO patents in biotechnology were individually assigned to IOMs and SOUs by scientists for this project. A summary of the full IOM–SOU table for their work, along with the YTC version, which is calculated based on IPC information from the same patents, is reported in Table 11.3. A summary is in Table 11.3.

Table 11.3. Distribution of biotechnology patents by IOM and SOU (% of total).

	EPO by hand		EPO by YTC		USA by YTC	
	IOM	SOU	IOM	SOU	IOM	SOU
Agriculture	1.92	6.57	0.21	6.16	0.08	3.05
Forestry and fishing	0.50	1.36	0.01	1.96	0.00	0.06
Mining	0.00	0.12	0.02	0.11	0.01	0.75
Electrical appliances	0.00	0.00	0.01	0.00	0.00	0.00
Electrical lighting	0.00	0.00	0.01	0.00	0.03	0.01
Radio and television	0.00	0.00	0.00	0.00	0.02	0.02
Electrical industrial equipment	0.00	0.00	0.04	0.00	1.12	0.23
Other electrical equipment	0.25	0.00	0.01	0.00	0.14	0.08
Electronic equipment	0.31	1.30	0.04	0.01	2.34	0.51
Chemicals	17.78	0.00	12.90	3.56	11.79	3.01
Drugs	43.93	14.62	78.16	19.47	60.69	13.91
Petroleum	0.00	0.00	0.00	0.09	0.00	0.14
Transport	0.12	0.00	0.02	0.00	0.04	0.67
Ferrous metals	0.00	0.00	0.01	0.00	0.01	0.25
Non-ferrous metals	0.00	0.00	0.03	0.00	0.02	0.13
Fabricated metals	0.81	0.00	0.33	0.01	0.04	0.19
Instruments	0.06	0.00	2.27	0.15	21.17	6.76
Computers and peripherals	0.00	0.00	0.03	0.01	0.17	0.12
Other office machinery	0.00	0.00	0.00	0.00	0.00	0.02
Other machinery	0.25	0.00	1.86	0.09	0.76	0.99
Food	0.93	0.99	0.46	1.91	0.32	1.50
Textiles	0.06	0.00	0.11	0.01	0.00	0.05
Rubber and plastic	0.06	0.00	0.24	0.09	0.13	0.16
Non-metallic minerals	0.12	0.06	0.11	0.05	0.03	0.17
Paper	0.00	0.12	0.04	0.08	0.02	0.45
Wood	0.06	0.00	0.10	0.00	0.00	0.09
Other manufacturing	0.43	0.00	3.01	0.47	1.06	0.39
Construction	0.12	0.06	n/a	0.06	n/a	0.28
Transportation and storage	0.00	0.00	n/a	0.01	n/a	0.16
Communication	0.00	0.00	n/a	0.18	n/a	0.32
Trade	0.00	0.31	n/a	0.98	n/a	0.89
Finance	0.00	0.00	n/a	0.34	n/a	7.40
Government and education	0.00	0.00	n/a	0.10	n/a	0.26
Health	31.60	62.76	n/a	62.48	n/a	55.73
Other services	0.68	11.71	n/a	1.63	n/a	1.26

The comparison illuminates one shortcoming of the YTC results, namely the health sector. Canadian patent officials did not consider the health sector to be an originator of inventions so YTC calculations do not permit inventions to have health as an IOM. A case-by-case reading of biotechnology patents shows that many have been developed in health research institutes. Unfortunately, this means that the individual assignment of patents and the YTC results are not strictly comparable.

However, if the health sector IOM is included as part of the drug IOM, the results of individual assignment by hand and those done using the YTC are remarkably similar. In fact, the correlation between results is over 0.98

for both IOM and SOU assignments. This is astounding, considering the enormous time savings involved in using the YTC. The YTC assignment took less than 1 minute to complete and could be accomplished by anyone with minimal computer expertise, while the assignment by hand required weeks of painstaking work by specialists.

References

Overall Patterns

Every patent application is required to prove its novelty, usefulness and unobvious nature through supporting materials including references to previous literature and patents upon which the application improves or from which it diverges. Data on references provide interesting information about the underlying knowledge which supports new inventions as well, and provides a striking contrast between biotechnology and other fields. Figure 11.11 compares the average references of patents by their year of grant. Notice that the number of total references has been steadily increasing over time, a phenomenon known as 'citation inflation'. This has been attributed in part to the computerization of patent records, making it easier to find (and therefore, reference) earlier patents. In the 1970s, biotechnology patents averaged fewer citations than other patents, but have increased much more rapidly, and by 1993–1994 they averaged three *more* references than other patents.

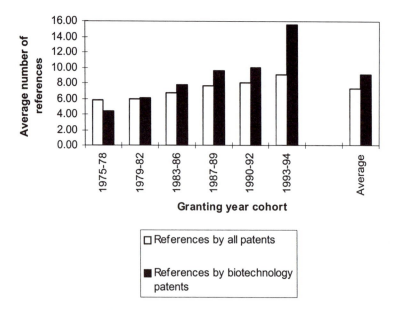

Fig. 11.11. References by all patents compared to biotechnology patents alone.

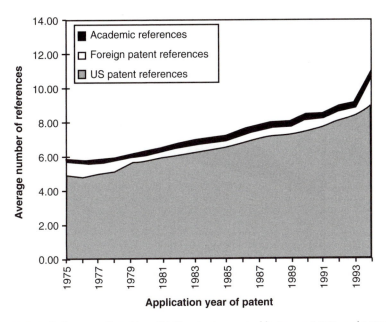

Fig. 11.12. References listed by all US patents granted between 1975 and 1994.

Even more striking is biotechnology's much greater reliance on foreign patents and academic literature. Only 3% of all references in the average patent are to academic or scientific literature, while in contrast, biotechnology patents regularly list 30% academic references. Patents average less than 8% foreign patent references, while biotechnology usually exceeds 12%. Figures 11.12 and 11.13 present the same data by year of application for greater clarity, and to avoid the truncation bias for patents granted in 1993-1994 as noted earlier. Notice, in particular, the increasing relative importance of US patent references for all patents (as they increase in number while academic and foreign references do not) while exactly the opposite trend holds true for biotechnology patents.

American References

Due to the wealth of information available on US patents, it is possible to further examine the references to US patents listed by biotechnology and other patents. This section will explore the age of the average reference to a US patent, and the patent classes (IPCs) or industries (IOMs and SOUs) that generate the knowledge referred to by biotechnology patent applications.

It is noteworthy that biotechnology patents use a much younger reference base for their knowledge than other patents do. Figure 11.14 shows the average length between the application date of the referring patent and the grant dates of the US patents to which it referred. The graph shows that an

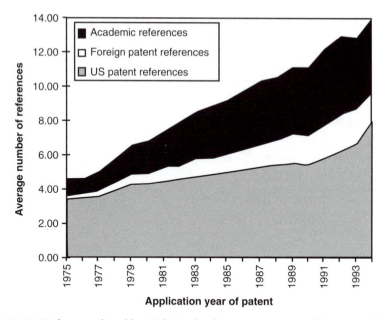

Fig. 11.13. References listed by US biotechnology patents granted between 1975 and 1994.

average patent refers to other US patents which were typically granted about 17 years before the current application. However, biotechnology applications refer to patents granted only 12 years previously. This supports the common intuition that biotechnology is a quickly moving field for inventors.

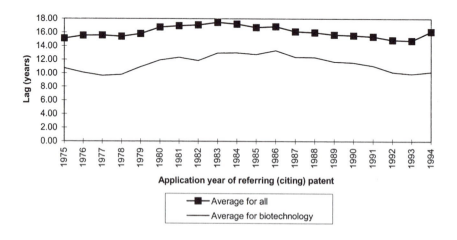

Fig. 11.14. Reference lag between application of citing patent and grant date of US references, for patents granted between 1975 and 1994.

To determine the nature of flows of knowledge between fields of research, it is interesting to identify the products which biotechnology patents reference and which reference biotechnology patents in return. As a first step at that study, all references by biotechnology patents granted in the USA between 1990 and 1992 to other US patents were collected. Unfortunately, before the IPC system was devised in 1976, national patent offices assigned only their own version of the patent classification system. Therefore, references were sorted into USPC (or US Patent Classification) groups, and the Wellesley Technology Concordance (WTC) was applied to calculate totals by IPC. The WTC is a concordance similar to the YTC, but uses all 1.5 million US patents granted between 1975 and 1994 to build a probability-based relationship between IPC and USPC systems. Details of its construction and some applications are given in Johnson (1999).

There were 19,054 patents granted in fields of biotechnology between 1990 and 1992, and a total of 91,116 references to prior US patents which had viable USPC codes attached. Interestingly, the WTC indicates that biotechnology refers to a wide range of IPCs. Half of all references are made to other biotechnology patents; 37% are made to patents in the same biotechnology field, patents in IPC A61K to other patents in A61K, etc. and another 11% are made to patents in the other biotechnology fields we considered. Other highly cited patent classes that may contain biotechnological patents are also shown in Fig. 11.15. However, 40% of all references are taken from other fields of research.

Since references have now been tabulated by IPC, we can apply the YTC to present them tabulated by IOM or SOU. Figures 11.16 and 11.17 show the same references as Fig. 11.15, but now decomposed into IOM (Fig. 11.16) and SOU (Fig. 11.17). The drug and chemical industries (as well as health as a SOU) are the most referenced by biotechnology patents, followed by instruments, non-electrical machinery and electronic equipment. Fabricated metals, rubber and plastics also receive significant references, each comprising about 1% of all biotechnology references. Notice also that 88% of all references come from the top five IOM, but SOU are more dispersed, with only 65% from the top five.

As further evidence of biotechnology's reliance on previous patents in the same industries, we can compare the IOM–SOU distributions of references and the patents themselves. The correlations are extremely high (0.87 between IOM totals and 0.97 between SOU totals), confirming that biotechnology applications reference patents with very similar origins and uses to those of the referring patents themselves.

Foreign References

References from US patents to foreign patents deserve attention as well, because they reflect a measure of the speed and direction of technology

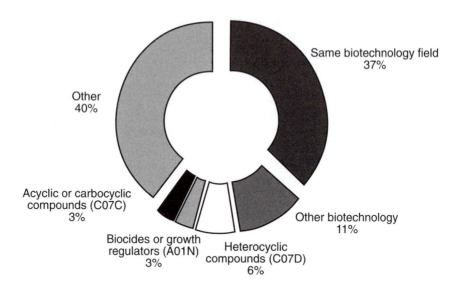

Fig. 11.15. References from biotechnology patents, by IPC product.

transfer between nations. Figures 11.18 and 11.19 summarize those spillovers for all patents granted in the USA between 1975 and 1994, showing that the main foreign donors of intellectual capital were (unsurprisingly) Germany,

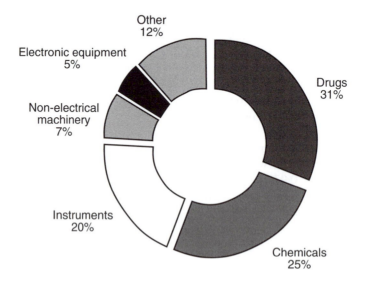

Fig. 11.16. References from biotechnology patents, by industry of manufacture.

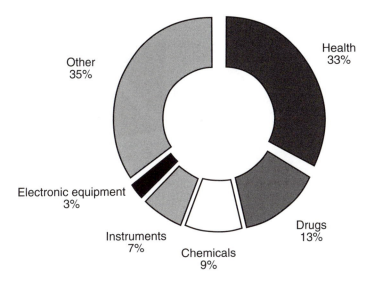

Fig. 11.17. References from biotechnology patents, by sector of use.

Japan and Britain, with the EPO contributing on behalf of Western Europe as well. Together these four accounted for 75% of all citations to foreign patents.

While biotechnology patents have the same top four sources accounting for 75% of the total, the EPO and Britain are more important at the

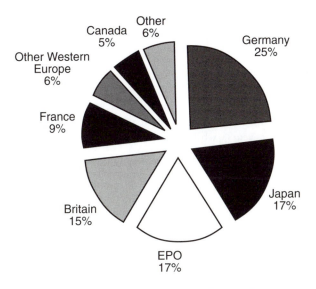

Fig. 11.18. Foreign references by all US patents, 1975–1994.

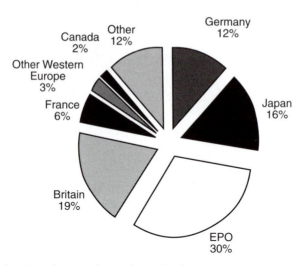

Fig. 11.19. Foreign references by US biotechnology patents, 1975–1994.

expense of Germany. Notice also that nations outside of Western Europe, Canada and Japan increase dramatically in importance for biotechnology references.

It is also instructive to look at the age of the references coming from each nation, to get an indication of the speed of technology transmission. Figures 11.20, 11.21 and 11.22 present data for all references for eight nations (or groups of nations) with some interesting results.

Patents granted under the EPO or World Patent Office (WPO) are referenced very quickly, with 90% of all citations occurring within 9 years. References to patents in other developed nations are slower, but vary greatly by nation. Ninety per cent of all references to Japanese patents occur within 13 years, but for Canada that same level takes 40 years. References to France are generally very old, with only one-third less than 13 years old, and only 85% less than 60 years old.

References to newly industrialized nations are relatively infrequent, but also vary by nation. Citations to Korean patents are quick, with 90% occurring within 7 years, while citations to Brazilian patents are slower, looking more like the French model.

Graphs for biotechnology references to foreign nations have been omitted, since they closely resemble the graphs for all patents, but have much quicker citation periods. EPO, WPO and Japanese references are roughly 1 year quicker, while Canadian and French references are more than 10 years quicker. Not only are foreign references quicker for biotechnology, but the quicker citation nations (like the EPO) are more important while slower citation nations (like France and Germany) are less important.

The result is an average of 14.6-year-old foreign references for all patents, but an average age of 7.4 years for foreign references from biotechnology

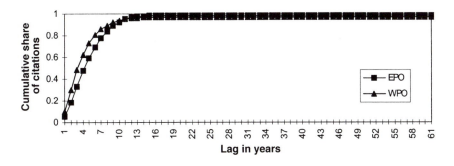

Fig. 11.20. Cumulative distribution of US patent citations to foreign patents, 1975–1994.

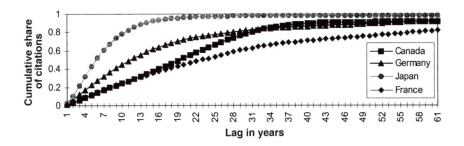

Fig. 11.21. Cumulative distribution of US patent citations to foreign patents, 1975–1994.

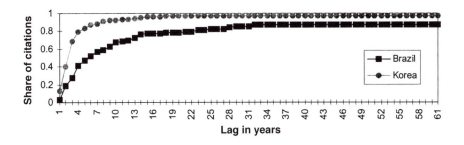

Fig. 11.22. Cumulative distribution of US patent citations to foreign patents, 1975–1994.

patents. Comparing this to reference speeds in the last section on US patents, it means that on average, all patents cite foreign patents as quickly as they cite US patents. However, *biotechnology* patents actually cite foreign patents more quickly than they cite US patents.

These data suggest that there are certain key nations which provide intellectual capital for patent applications in the USA, which naturally have varying speeds of knowledge transmission. All transmission speeds are faster in biotechnology, and the nations with faster transmission speeds are more important, once again emphasizing the special nature of biotechnology patents.

In summary, biotechnology patents cite much more academic literature than other patents do, indicating a closer link to the forefront of science. They refer to more foreign patents, indicating greater reliance on, and recognition of, an international community progressing in the field. Furthermore, their references are more recent by a substantial degree, averaging citations between one-half and two-thirds the age of their peers in other fields. Finally, biotechnology patents rely on other biotechnology patents for a large portion of their references, meaning that the germplasm they use also has a quick rate of growth and change.

Subsequent Citations

After examining the references that biotechnology patents make to other patents, it seems logical to consider the references that other patents make to them. This would offer some measure of the new knowledge germplasm that biotechnology offers to other inventors. However, the difficulty in measuring subsequent citations is that every patent has a different number of subsequent patents capable of referring to it, since a patent cannot be cited until it is published. In addition, there has been citation inflation over the period 1975–1994, as mentioned earlier.

To overcome those difficulties, a citation deflation index was constructed based on the average number of citations made by patents in any given application year, and this deflator was applied to all patents to create a 'real' 1978-based number of references to other patents and literature. In addition, all results will be stated in 'per subsequent patent' figures. That is, we created a citability index, or probability of citation, which rates patents on how many inflation-adjusted citations they received for each patent that could have cited them, a procedure inspired by the work of Jaffe and Trajtenberg (1995).

Figure 11.23 gives the probabilities of subsequent citation at certain key intervals after granting of the patent. For example, patents with applications in 1975 had a 44% probability of being cited within 1 year of their grant date, while applications in 1988 had a 53% probability of the same event. Notice that the probability of citation in the fifth year after grant is lower than the probability of citation in the first year (with one exceptional application year in 1977). The probability of citation in the tenth year after grant is lower still.

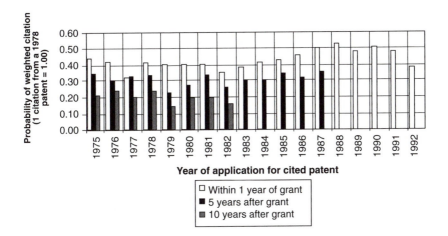

Fig. 11.23. Variations in average probability of citation at specified periods after grant, all granted US patents 1975–1992 by year of application.

While Fig. 11.23 shows no discernible trend over time in the citation of all patents (since they have all been corrected for citation inflation), biotechnology in Fig. 11.24 shows an increasing tendency towards being cited, even after correction for inflation. While they are still far less likely to be cited overall, with only 3% cited in their first year after grant, biotechnology patents are growing in their use as germplasm for future inventions.

Figures 11.25 and 11.26 summarize these results for all patents and for biotechnology patents. Using annual data on the probability of citations after each interval of time (as seen in the figures above), we present averages, maxima and minima over the entire dataset. Both series show the same

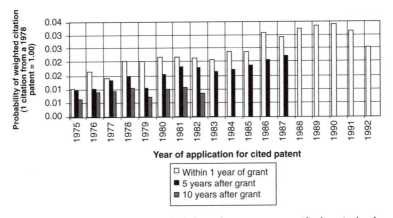

Fig. 11.24. Variations in average probability of citation at specified periods after grant, granted US biotechnology patents 1975–1992 by year of application.

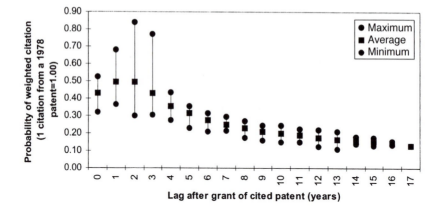

Fig. 11.25. Average probability of citation at specified periods after grant, all granted US patents 1975–1992.

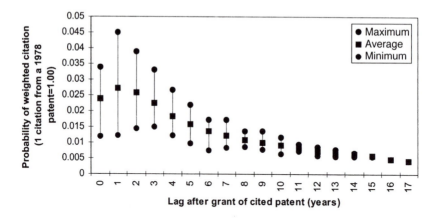

Fig. 11.26. Average probability of citation at specified periods after grant, granted biotechnology US patents 1975–1992.

pattern of highest citability 1–2 years after being granted, asymptoting to a low but still significant citability even 17 years after being granted.

We have shown that while biotechnology patents are infrequently cited compared to their peers in other fields of research, they have been increasing in importance as references by other patents, and show the same pattern of high citability early upon granting, with long tenure as citable material. Therefore biotechnology offers a small but growing spillover pool of germplasm to future inventors. An interesting question that this poses, and which will be addressed in future work, is the question of who uses (i.e. who references) biotechnology patents. Subsequent references can be sorted by product and industry for closer examination of the beneficiaries of biotechnological research.

Location of Applicants

To examine the location of applicants, we used the applicant's address for all granted biotechnology patents. Assignee addresses are also available but would presumably be biased towards states with large numbers of corporate headquarters facilities, instead of locations where research takes place. For this section, we had data not only on the 89,612 patents granted in the USA between 1975 and 1994, but also on 1613 patents granted by the EPO between 1980 and 1998.

In the USA, US applicants receive 63% of all biotechnology patents granted, while in Europe, US applicants receive only 34% of the total. The figures below discuss only non-US applicants, omitting US applications in order to show the distinctions between other nations.

Foreign applications in the USA are dominated by Germany, Japan, France and Britain which together comprise over 70% of all foreign applicants. The same nations are pre-eminent among EPO biotechnology patents, with Germany and France gaining in prominence slightly at the expense of Japan and Britain. So aside from the large difference in US involvement, the national composition of biotechnology is strikingly similar across the two important patent-granting offices.

Also of interest is a comparison between non-US applications and non-US references (see Fig. 11.27a and Figs 11.18 and 11.19). Japan is much more important as an applicant than as a cited source of knowledge. In contrast, Germany and Britain are more important as cited sources than as sources of new applications. This may be due to well-documented home-language biases in references which would under-represent Japanese-language patents in worldwide references.

Within the USA, the top four applicant states are consistently California, New York, New Jersey and Pennsylvania, as can be seen in Fig. 11.28. In fact, those states account for over 40% of all domestic biotechnology applications in the USA. The ranking (in number of applications) by state is quite stable over the entire 20-year period. In fact, the only states which move considerably in rank are Kansas, Louisiana and Idaho, all of which drop in rank in 1980 and then recover. Since all domestic biotechnology applications fell in 1980, this evidence suggests that states with fewer applications had more

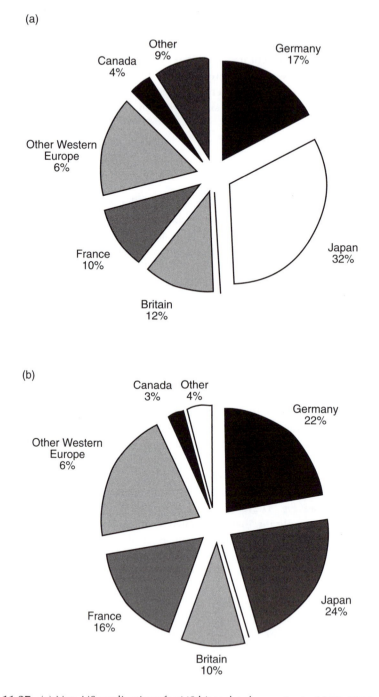

Fig. 11.27. (a) Non-US applications for US biotechnology patents, 1975–1994. (b) Non-US applications for EPO biotechnology patents, 1980–1998.

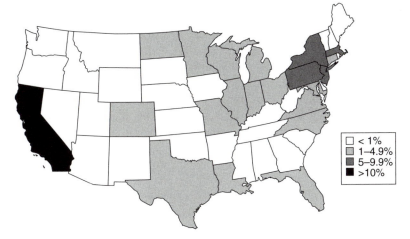

Fig. 11.28. Share of domestic biotechnology patents from applications, 1975–1994.

severe cuts in applications than leading states did. In other words, states with lower volumes of applications also had greater variability in the number of applications.

The evidence on applicant location suggests that biotechnology innovation is a highly clustered activity, and relies heavily on several key states and foreign nations for most patent applications. It is therefore clear that any change in biotechnology research or IPR will be borne by those regions most heavily.

Concluding Remarks

The use of patent data for the study of emerging technologies has limitations, but it also allows us to gather an enormous wealth of information about a research field, in order to point out key attributes of the technology in question. This chapter has explored several aspects of biotechnology, to direct future research in a number of new directions.

First, biotechnology patents face a longer lag between application and grant date, not only on average but across the entire distribution of patents. On average they take 150 days (or almost 20%) longer than other patents, and their secrecy would be heavily affected if legislation were to permit publication 18 months after application.

Second, they are (unsurprisingly) highly concentrated in industrial origin, coming almost entirely from the chemical, drug and instruments industries. They are used most heavily in the health sector, but have a wider spread in use than in origin. This result holds true in both European and US patents, and while individual assignment provides some detail about the health sector as an industry of origin, the results are virtually identical to those provided by mechanical means using the Yale Technology Concordance.

Third, while biotechnology patents started with fewer references than the average patent in the 1970s, they now have many more than average, with a special weight on academic or scientific literature and foreign patents. They cite newer patents, and cite primarily from a tightly concentrated group of research fields, half being from biotechnology fields themselves. A few foreign nations make up most of the references, and certain nations like Japan and Korea are more quickly cited than others.

Fourth, while biotechnology patents are not cited frequently on average, their rate of usage as germplasm is rising relative to the average, and they are cited more quickly than other patents (highest probabilities are 1–2 years after grant, compared with 2–3 years after grant for other patents).

Finally, applications for biotechnology patents are highly clustered geographically, both within the USA and in specific foreign nations applying for protection in the USA. The same clustering is evident in European patents, with the same nations applying for protection.

Future research should focus on the questions that have been uncovered. Why is there a longer lag for biotechnology patents? Is that lag valuable to inventors? Further research in progress already seeks to answer those questions. Do the tightly focused industrial origins, uses and spillovers of biotechnology present particular problems or incentives for economists to analyse? Are they recognized by researchers and firms in the field, or do they see their work as affecting a wider spectrum of sectors? What drives the speed of references between one generation of patents and the next? Are there issues relating to the flow of knowledge that explain all of these results, including geographic concentration of applicants and references? We look forward to pursuing these questions in continuing work.

Note

1. Most notably, see the *Economic Systems Research* Vol. 9, No. 2, 1997 which is devoted to a description, tests and applications of the Yale Technology Concordance.

References

Acharya, R. (1999) *The Emergence and Growth of Biotechnology*. Edward Elgar Publishers, Northampton, Massachusetts, USA.

Evenson, R.E. and Johnson, D. (1997) Introduction: invention input–output analysis. *Economic Systems Research* 9, 149–160.

Griliches, Z. (1990) *Patent Statistics as Indicators: A Survey Part I*. NBER Working Paper 3301.

Jaffe, A.B. (1986) Technological opportunity and spillovers of R&D: evidence from firms' patents, profits and market value. *American Economic Review* 79, 984–1001.

Jaffe, A.B. and Trajtenberg, M. (1995) *Flows of Knowledge From Universities and Federal Labs: Modeling the Flow of Patent Citations Over Time and Across Institutional and Geographic Boundaries.* NBER Working Paper 5712.

Johnson, D. and Evenson, R.E. (1997) Innovation and invention in Canada. *Economic Systems Research* 9, 177–192.

Johnson, D. (1999) *150 Years of American Invention: Methodology and a First Geographical Application.* Wellesley College Economics Department Working Paper 99-01.

Kortum, S. and Putnam, J. (1997) Assigning patents to industries: tests of the Yale Technology Concordance. *Economic Systems Research* 9, 161–176.

Lanjouw, J.O., Pakes, A. and Putnam, J. (1996) *How to Count Patents and Value Intellectual Property: Uses of Patent Renewal and Application Data.* NBER Working Paper 5741.

Office of Technology Assessment and Forecast (1998) *Patent Examining Technology Center Groups 1630–1650, Biotechnology.* US Patent and Trademark Office Technology Profile Report, July 1998.

Saviotti, P.P. (1998) Industrial structure and the dynamics of knowledge generation in biotechnology. In: Senker, J. (ed.) *Biotechnology and Competitive Advantage: Europe's Firms and the US Challenge.* Edward Elgar Publishers, Northampton, Massachusetts, USA.

Schankerman, M. and Pakes, A. (1986) Estimates of the value of patent rights in European countries during the post-1950 period. *Economic Journal* 96, 1052–1076.

Trajtenberg, M. (1990) A penny for your quotes: patent citations and the value of innovations. *Rand Journal of Economics* 21, 172–187.

Biotechnology Inventions: Patent Data Evidence

12

A. Zohrabyan and R.E. Evenson

Economic Growth Center, Department of Economics, Yale University, New Haven, Connecticut, USA

This chapter extends the analysis of patent data reported in the previous chapter in two dimensions. First, it defines biotechnology invention as proportions of international patent classes (IPCs) instead of as a specific set of biotechnology IPCs. Second, it provides tabulations or 'patent counts' for a number of developing and developed countries enabling an analysis of technological leadership (Johnson and Evenson, 1997).

Inventions based on the science and methodology of biotechnology are eligible for patent protection in all countries with functioning patent systems. The nature of this eligibility varies by country, however, as noted in earlier chapters in this volume. The patent system in the USA is the most expansive in terms of scope and coverage of biotechnology inventions (see D.D. Evenson, Chapter 1, this volume). The fact that patent systems do differ in terms of invention eligibility needs to be kept in mind as international data are interpreted.

In this chapter we report 'patent counts' for biotechnology inventions by year, country of patent grant, country of invention origin and sector of use (SOU). Several procedural steps are required for the development of these patent count indicators:

1. First, the proportion of biotechnology inventions in IPCs must be determined.
2. Second, patent counts for IPCs with biotechnology inventions must be obtained by period, country of patent grant and country of invention.
3. Third, the patent counts for each IPC must be assigned to sectors (some of which are industries) of use.

In the first three sections of this chapter, we discuss these three procedural steps. Then we discuss indexes of biotechnology invention in the USA during the 1990s. In the final section we discuss indexes of international biotechnology invention.

Identifying Biotechnology Inventions by IPC

The international patent classification system is not based on invention methods or on industrial relevance. It is based on technological characteristics (e.g. specific types of chemicals or properties of materials). The United States Patent and Trademark Office (USPTO) database has a search system based on 'keywords' appearing in the patent documents and in the abstracts. Most inventions based on biotechnology methods do note this in the document text and in abstracts.

After experimenting with alternative keywords, it was determined that the keyword 'biotechnology' best captured the meaning of biotechnology invention. Table 12.1 displays the computed biotechnology proportions for main IPCs. This procedure does show that some IPCs are predominantly biotechnology based. It also shows, however, that significant biotechnology inventions are made in IPCs which are not dominated by biotechnology inventions.

Developing Biotechnology Invention Counts by Year, Country of Grant and Country of Invention

The International Patent Documentation Center (INPADOC) (now administered by the European Patent Office; Bogsch, 1988; Yoshikawa and Kanri, 1992) database enables us to compute patent counts by period, country of patent grant and country of 'priority' (which is a good proxy for country of invention because this is where the first protection is obtained (see D.D. Evenson, Chapter 1, this volume)). By making the assumption that the US biotechnology proportions by IPC hold for all countries of grant and countries of priority, we can simply multiply patent counts by biotechnology proportions to obtain biotechnology patent counts. We do this, but we acknowledge that the difference between patent laws and administration in the USA and other countries may affect the biotechnology proportions. These proportions are probably higher in the USA than in other countries in most IPCs. This procedure produces data in biotechnology invention by IPC, by year, country of patent grant and country of priority.

Assigning Patented Inventions to Sectors of Use (SOUs)

The Yale Technology Concordance (YTC) allows us to 'distribute' on a probability basis, patents in an IPC both to four-digit industries of manufacture

Table 12.1. The computed biotechnology proportions for main IPCs.

International Patent Classification		Percentage of patents with 'biotech' in				Total number of patents with 'biotech' in 1998–1999	Total number of patents in 1998–1999
		1976–1999	1990–1999	1998–1999	1997–1999		
A01H	4	28.8	28.1	24.4	26.7	54	221
A01H	67	3.5	0.0	0.0	0.0	0	0
A01H	48	55.9	0.0	0.0	0.0	0	0
A23L	1	1.7	2.9	4.5	3.7	20	444
A23L	3	1.5	2.6	3.4	5.1	3	88
A61K	1	8.6	10.7	40.0	25.0	2	5
A61K	3	4.4	6.1	10.0	7.1	1	10
A61K	5	0.8	2.9	10.0	7.7	1	10
A61K	7	0.7	1.0	1.8	2.0	19	1061
A61K	9	5.2	6.7	12.4	10.8	142	1144
A61K	6	0.9	1.3	0.9	0.6	1	109
A61K	31	1.7	3.1	5.9	5.5	273	4654
A61K	35	6.5	12.0	21.6	20.5	82	379
A61K	33	1.6	2.9	4.0	3.4	7	176
A61K	37	9.0	14.5	25.0	21.1	19	76
A61K	39	21.7	31.4	41.6	39.9	432	1038
A61K	41	3.8	2.9	14.3	8.3	1	7
A61K	43	2.1	5.6	0.0	0.0	0	10
A61K	45	15.6	21.6	27.1	25.6	29	107
A61K	47	4.5	6.3	10.9	10.4	24	220
A61K	48	56.0	55.7	56.4	56.4	102	181
A61K	49	7.2	10.4	18.6	18.0	29	156
B01D	1	0.4	0.7	0.0	0.0	0	43
B01D	3	0.2	0.2	0.0	0.0	0	171
B01D	6	6.7	6.7	0.0	0.0	0	2
B01D	9	0.7	1.9	6.7	4.8	1	15
B01D	11	2.5	3.7	5.9	5.3	6	101
B01D	12	1.1	2.7	16.7	9.1	1	6
B01D	13	2.7	6.3	33.3	33.3	1	3
B01D	15	6.8	11.2	12.0	13.1	23	192
B01D	16	50.0	33.3	0.0	0.0	0	1
B01D	17	1.0	1.6	2.4	2.2	3	124
B01D	19	0.2	0.6	1.2	0.8	1	83
B01D	21	0.9	1.7	2.8	2.8	4	141
B01D	24	0.8	0.8	3.2	1.9	2	62
B01D	25	0.7	1.4	0.0	0.0	0	25
B01D	27	0.9	1.3	2.1	1.2	2	97
B01D	29	0.9	1.0	1.2	1.5	2	167
B01D	31	0.4	9.1	0.0	0.0	0	2
B01D	33	1.2	1.8	0.0	2.3	0	72
B01D	35	1.0	1.6	2.1	2.1	5	243
B01D	36	1.1	0.7	0.0	0.0	0	30
B01D	37	1.4	2.4	3.2	4.4	2	63
B01D	39	1.8	3.1	4.4	4.1	5	113
B01D	43	2.7	6.3	0.0	0.0	0	3
B01D	46	0.1	0.0	0.0	0.0	0	189
B01D	47	0.1	0.0	0.0	0.0	0	111
B01D	49	5.9	14.3	0.0	0.0	0	1
B01D	50	0.3	0.6	0.0	0.0	0	83
B01D	53	0.5	0.8	0.4	0.7	2	458
B01D	55	7.1	0.0	0.0	0.0	0	
B01D	57	10.4	15.6	0.0	0.0	0	3
B01D	59	1.0	1.0	2.8	1.9	2	71
B01D	61	6.7	6.7	10.8	7.5	17	157
B01D	63	9.4	9.4	9.0	9.1	6	67
B01D	64	100.0	100.0	0.0	100.0	0	0
B01D	65	8.8	8.4	8.3	8.7	1	12
B01D	67	6.2	6.2	0.0	0.0	0	3
B01D	69	5.2	5.3	15.0	7.5	3	20
B01D	70	0.0	0.0	0.0	0.0	0	0

Table 12.1 (*continued*).

International Patent Classification		Percentage of patents with 'biotech' in				Total number of patents with 'biotech' in 1998–1999	Total number of patents in 1998–1999
		1976–1999	1990–1999	1998–1999	1997–1999		
B01D	71	3.3	3.3	3.8	2.2	1	26
B01J	1	0.6	0.0	0.0	0.0	0	0
B01J	2	1.2	8.3	14.3	15.4	1	7
B01J	3	0.9	2.4	0.0	4.0	0	14
B01J	8	0.5	0.8	1.4	1.5	2	139
B01J	9	7.1	50.0	0.0	0.0	0	0
B01J	10	1.7	4.3	0.0	8.3	0	6
B01J	13	2.8	7.1	7.4	9.0	12	162
B01J	14	5.0	0.0	0.0	0.0	0	4
B01J	15	3.4	9.1	0.0	0.0	0	0
B01J	16	12.5	0.0	0.0	0.0	0	0
B01J	19	1.2	1.6	2.0	2.7	2	99
B01J	20	2.4	3.1	1.4	2.6	2	141
B01J	21	0.3	0.6	1.0	0.6	1	102
B01J	23	0.4	0.9	1.0	1.3	2	199
B01J	27	0.2	0.4	1.3	0.9	1	76
B01J	30	0.3	0.0	0.0	0.0	0	0
B01J	32	0.2	0.0	0.0	0.0	0	3
B01J	35	0.5	0.7	0.0	0.0	0	18
B01J	37	1.6	1.8	0.0	3.5	0	43
B01J	38	1.1	1.5	0.0	0.0	0	34
B01J	39	2.8	7.5	28.6	13.3	2	7
B01J	41	1.4	6.3	50.0	20.0	1	2
G01N	1	1.2	2.1	3.6	2.7	9	250
G01N	3	0.4	1.0	2.0	1.2	2	101
G01N	7	0.8	0.5	1.6	1.1	1	61
G01N	9	0.3	0.3	0.0	0.0	0	40
G01N	11	1.0	1.8	2.1	2.3	1	48
G01N	13	2.9	5.5	0.0	0.0	0	15
G01N	15	1.8	3.1	8.4	7.1	10	119
G01N	20	25.0	0.0	0.0	0.0	0	0
G01N	21	1.3	2.1	3.1	2.7	31	1005
G01N	23	0.5	0.9	1.7	1.9	2	120
G01N	24	4.3	5.4	17.6	11.5	3	17
G01N	25	0.7	1.1	2.0	1.4	2	98
G01N	26	16.7	16.7	0.0	0.0	0	0
G01N	27	3.3	5.8	10.1	8.8	62	611
G01N	29	0.0	0.0	0.0	0.0	0	192
G01N	30	4.8	5.3	5.4	6.2	4	74
G01N	31	1.1	2.4	5.7	5.5	7	122
G01N	33	11.0	17.2	25.6	24.3	461	1799
G01N	35	2.4	3.7	7.5	5.6	9	120
G01N	37	3.0	4.1	11.5	10.0	3	26
G01N	53	4.5	0.0	0.0	0.0	0	484
C02F	1	1.9	2.6	2.9	2.4	14	175
C02F	3	11.4	14.2	10.3	11.7	18	28
C02F	9	1.7	2.2	3.6	2.0	1	27
C02F	11	5.2	6.9	14.8	14.0	4	230
C07H	1	10.1	12.2	15.2	15.5	35	25
C07H	3	8.4	12.5	32.0	22.0	8	34
C07H	5	8.8	12.3	20.6	18.6	7	8
C07H	7	5.7	8.7	12.5	11.1	1	11
C07H	11	3.3	6.0	18.2	17.6	2	29
C07H	13	5.7	8.3	13.8	19.1	4	114
C07H	15	12.1	19.4	14.0	13.7	16	89
C07H	17	13.3	22.3	28.1	26.3	25	169
C07H	19	12.3	16.2	20.1	20.0	34	1860
C07H	21	45.5	47.1	52.2	50.1	970	5
C07H	23	10.5	13.6	40.0	18.2	2	432
C07K	1	32.1	34.0	44.9	40.3	194	12

Table 12.1 (*continued*).

International Patent Classification		Percentage of patents with 'biotech' in				Total number of patents with 'biotech' in 1998–1999	Total number of patents in 1998–1999
		1976–1999	1990–1999	1998–1999	1997–1999		
C07K	3	23.5	27.7	16.7	25.0	2	300
C07K	5	13.0	15.1	25.7	21.4	77	379
C07K	7	15.8	18.4	24.5	22.4	93	18
C07K	9	14.3	17.0	16.7	25.8	3	25
C07K	13	28.6	31.5	40.0	42.4	10	19
C07K	15	20.5	24.3	52.6	45.5	10	641
C07K	16	37.6	38.2	41.5	40.4	266	125
C07K	17	23.1	24.5	38.4	35.1	48	1
C07K	37	16.7	25.0	100.0	100.0	1	9
C08B	1	5.3	10.8	22.2	16.7	2	21
C08B	3	3.5	5.5	14.3	9.7	3	15
C08B	11	2.1	5.3	20.0	14.3	3	9
C08B	15	2.0	2.2	0.0	0.0	0	4
C08B	16	3.0	9.1	0.0	0.0	0	38
C08B	30	4.9	5.6	13.2	9.8	5	25
C08B	31	2.9	4.9	8.0	6.5	2	5
C08B	33	2.7	3.6	0.0	0.0	0	111
C08B	37	8.4	11.9	15.3	19.3	17	325
C11D	1	0.5	0.7	0.6	0.6	2	554
C11D	3	2.0	3.5	4.5	5.0	25	175
C11D	7	1.3	2.5	5.7	5.0	10	56
C11D	9	0.5	1.0	0.0	1.3	0	22
C11D	10	2.6	4.6	0.0	0.0	0	64
C11D	11	0.8	0.0	0.0	0.0	0	133
C11D	17	1.0	1.6	2.3	2.2	3	150
C12M	1	17.2	22.0	28.7	27.9	43	118
C12M	3	20.2	21.5	16.1	19.0	19	1027
C12N	1	35.0	42.7	56.1	54.3	576	5
C12N	3	3.8	5.9	0.0	16.7	0	1441
C12N	5	34.0	38.1	42.1	42.4	606	216
C12N	7	29.6	33.9	42.6	37.7	92	967
C12N	9	38.0	46.5	61.6	59.4	596	132
C12N	11	32.0	37.6	37.9	42.1	50	27
C12N	13	18.8	20.0	18.5	20.0	5	2791
C12N	15	45.8	50.5	57.8	56.7	1614	
C12P	1	26.9	37.5	54.2	51.1	32	59
C12P	3	32.7	43.8	60.0	60.0	6	10
C12P	5	19.2	25.0	50.0	33.3	1	2
C12P	7	38.0	44.4	50.7	51.2	75	148
C12P	9	25.0	29.4	40.0	28.6	2	5
C12P	11	47.7	53.8	41.7	46.2	5	12
C12P	13	24.5	32.6	48.3	46.7	42	87
C12P	17	19.5	25.7	38.1	33.3	24	63
C12P	19	36.5	43.3	48.9	48.4	410	838
C12P	21	38.9	47.1	57.0	55.0	505	886
C12P	23	59.3	68.0	66.7	68.8	6	9
C12P	25	14.3	16.7	0.0	0.0	0	0
C12P	29	16.7	0.0	0.0	0.0	0	1
C12P	33	17.2	25.0	30.0	27.3	3	10
C12P	35	46.0	59.1	87.5	64.3	7	8
C12P	37	48.6	73.7	100.0	87.5	7	7
C12P	39	33.3	40.8	33.3	50.0	2	6
C12P	41	34.0	35.6	44.0	41.0	11	25
C12Q	1	26.0	31.3	40.8	39.8	860	2107
C12Q	3	23.9	28.0	0.0	16.7	0	4
C12R	1	19.1	32.3	33.3	37.5	1	3
C12S	1	36.8	36.8	0.0	28.6	0	3
C12S	3	40.7	42.9	100.0	100.0	7	7
C12S	5	20.0	20.0	0.0	20.0	0	2
C12S	7	66.7	66.7	100.0	100.0	1	1
C12S	9	53.8	56.3	57.1	50.0	4	7
C12S	11	41.7	50.0	87.5	77.8	7	8
C12S	13	37.8	35.9	35.7	29.4	5	14

(IOM) and four-digit sectors of use (SOU). The YTC is based on industry and sector assignments made by the Canadian Patent Office. For approximately 300,000 patents granted in Canada from 1972 to 1998, examiners and classifiers assigned one or more four-digit IOM to each patent application and four-digit SOU to the same patent application (Evenson and Johnson, 1997; Kortum and Putnam, 1997). SOU include both manufacturing industries and non-manufacturing sectors such as agriculture and health. The YTC probability distributions are based on these assignments.

The YTC probability distributions are based on an international 'pool' of inventions from countries obtaining patent protection in Canada. Industries from the USA obtained the highest proportion of Canadian invention, but most European countries also obtain a significant number of patents in Canada.

Since patent assignments are made both on an IOM and SOU basis, it is possible to construct an IOM–SOU matrix for a given body of invention. Table 12.2 reports the IOM–SOU matrix for important manufacturing industries and sectors of use for 25,306 biotechnology inventions granted in the USA for the 1976–1998 period. It should be noted that the YTC considers only manufacturing industries to be IOMs. But IOMs are not necessarily the industry of invention. In fact, it is possible for a SOU to be the invention sector (Evenson and Johnson, 1998).

Biotechnology Invention by SOU in the USA

The procedures noted in the previous sections were applied to the USPTO database for all inventions for 1990 through to 1998–1999 (note the 1998–1999 column includes roughly 4 months for 1999). Tabulations are shown by SOU and year in Table 12.3.

First, consider total biotechnology invention. This has grown from 814 in 1990 to 4044 in 1997 and approximately 7000 in 1998. This high rate of growth is real in the sense that we know from many sources that biotechnology invention is growing rapidly. It is important to note that this growth has taken place in the IPCs identified as having high biotechnology proportions.

Table 12.2. IOM–SOU matrix of US biotechnology patents for 1976–1998.

Industry of manufacture	Sector of use					
	Agriculture	Chemicals	Drugs	Food	Health	Total
Agriculture	0.5%	0.0%	0.0%	0.0%	0.0%	0.6%
Chemicals	1.0%	3.8%	10.9%	1.2%	1.5%	20.2%
Drugs	1.4%	1.6%	22.7%	2.1%	35.7%	64.7%
Food	0.1%	0.0%	0.0%	1.1%	0.0%	1.2%
Total	3.3%	6.5%	34.3%	4.7%	40.4%	100.0%

Table 12.3. Biotechnology patents by sector of use in the USA, 1990–1999.

Sector of use	1990	1991	1992	1993	1994	1995	1996	1997	1998–1999
Agriculture – livestock	3.2	3.4	5.1	5.5	5.9	6.6	10.0	16.0	36.3
Agriculture – crops and combo farms	6.2	6.3	7.7	11.5	11.9	14.3	22.3	33.3	80.7
Agriculture – fruits and vegetables	0.6	0.6	0.8	1.1	1.2	1.4	2.2	3.3	8.0
Agriculture – horticulture	0.5	1.3	0.7	1.0	2.9	1.7	6.8	5.3	12.7
Agriculture – services to livestock	6.9	7.7	11.2	12.1	13.4	14.2	20.1	34.7	77.4
Agriculture – services to crops	3.2	3.3	3.8	6.1	6.4	7.8	12.5	19.0	45.5
Agriculture – other	1.5	3.4	3.8	3.3	6.8	4.4	15.5	13.3	31.0
Total agriculture	22.0	26.1	33.1	40.6	48.5	50.3	89.4	125.0	291.5
Food – meat, poultry and fish	1.4	1.6	1.8	1.9	2.2	2.7	4.1	5.0	11.5
Food – fruit and vegetables	1.1	1.2	1.3	1.6	1.8	2.2	3.5	4.8	11.1
Food – dairy products	3.6	3.7	4.6	6.5	6.9	8.2	13.1	19.6	46.7
Food – cereals and feed	2.8	4.9	4.9	4.4	7.5	14.3	19.0	15.4	50.7
Food – beverages	4.1	4.7	8.3	7.7	7.7	8.6	12.8	18.4	43.6
Food – tobacco	0.9	1.7	1.3	1.9	3.8	2.7	8.6	8.0	19.1
Food – other	24.1	25.4	34.5	41.0	41.5	49.5	75.6	109.2	259.9
Total food	37.9	43.2	56.7	64.9	71.4	88.1	136.8	180.3	442.6
Health	316.8	357.2	515.3	611.8	640.8	687.9	1055.9	1683.1	3884.6
Total number of patents used in all sectors	814	894	1311	1497	1589	1735	2662	4044	9505

It is not due to changing proportions as these have been held constant. We view this as evidence in support of the procedures employed here.

The allocation of biotechnology inventions over SOU is of interest. The proportion of biotechnology inventions used in agriculture is approximately 6% of total invention used in the agriculture, food industries and health sectors. (By 1999 this had risen to 6.3%.) Roughly 46–48% of all biotechnology inventions are used in manufacturing sectors, chiefly in the chemical and drug industries (see Table 12.2). The proportion of biotechnology inventions used in the food industries is roughly 10%. More than 80% of biotechnology inventions used in the agriculture, food and health sectors are used in the health sectors.

International Dimensions of Biotechnology Inventions

In Table 12.4 we report estimates of biotechnology inventions by agriculture, food and health SOUs (note that inventions used in the chemical and drug industries are included in the total grants line) for 1993 and 1995 (in some cases another year is reported where data are not available).

Data for 15 developed market economies, seven Eastern European and seven Developing countries are reported. Domestic, US and Japanese shares are reported (the residual share is the 'Other European' share).

We first note that biotechnology invention is dominated by developed market economies. The Eastern European economies account for only 1–3% of global biotechnology invention in 1995 and less than 1% of origin inventions. Developing countries granted 6% of total biotechnology inventions in 1995, and originated 3–4%. Within the Developed country group, the USA is clearly the dominant player. The USA grants roughly 12% of biotechnology patents but originated more than 45% of all biotechnology inventions in 1995 (and this share has probably increased after 1995 so it may be reasonable to attribute half of the world's biotechnology invention to US inventors). Japan is second in importance, granting 15% of biotechnology inventions but originating only 22% of biotechnology inventions. France and Germany are next in importance.

These data are characteristic of young invention fields. We observe that invention origins are highly concentrated with the USA and Japan accounting for more than two-thirds of biotechnology in 1995. We also observe relatively high ratios of diffusion of biotechnology invention particularly of US invention.

Table 12.4. Estimates of biotechnology inventions by agriculture, food and health.

	Australia 1993	Australia 1995	Belgium 1993	Belgium 1995	Canada 1993	Canada 1995	Switzerland 1993	Switzerland 1995	Germany 1993	Germany 1995	Denmark 1993	Denmark 1995	France 1993	France 1995	UK 1993	UK 1995	Greece 1993	Greece 1995
Agriculture – livestock	2.3	1.8	2.2	2.1	0.9	0.8	2.4	2.3	2.6	2.6	0.5	1.3	2.8	3.3	2.6	2.6	1.1	1.4
Agriculture – crops and combo farms	5.0	4.0	4.0	4.3	1.4	1.4	4.4	4.5	4.9	5.4	0.7	2.2	5.1	6.4	4.9	5.3	1.7	2.6
Agriculture – fruits and vegetables	0.5	0.4	0.4	0.4	0.	0.1	0.4	0.5	0.5	0.5	0.1	0.2	0.5	0.6	0.5	0.5	0.2	0.3
Agriculture – horticulture	0.2	0.2	0.2	0.2	0.1	0.1	0.2	0.2	0.2	0.3	0.0	0.1	0.3	0.3	0.2	0.3	0.1	0.1
Agriculture – services to livestock	6.1	4.5	5.6	5.4	2.4	2.2	6.1	5.9	6.7	6.5	1.6	3.7	7.3	8.5	6.7	6.6	3.1	3.8
Agriculture – services to crops	2.7	2.1	2.1	2.3	0.7	0.7	2.3	2.4	2.5	2.8	0.4	1.2	2.6	3.3	2.5	2.8	0.9	1.4
Agriculture – other	0.8	0.6	0.6	0.7	0.2	0.2	0.7	0.7	0.7	0.8	0.1	0.3	0.8	1.0	0.7	0.8	0.3	0.4
Total agriculture	17.6	13.6	15.2	15.5	5.8	5.5	16.4	16.3	18.1	19.0	3.4	9.1	19.4	23.3	18.2	18.9	7.3	10.0
Food – meat, poultry and fish	0.6	0.4	0.4	0.5	0.2	0.2	0.5	0.5	0.5	0.6	0.1	0.3	0.6	0.7	0.5	0.6	0.2	0.3
Food – fruit and vegetables	0.5	0.4	0.4	0.4	0.1	0.1	0.4	0.4	0.5	0.5	0.1	0.2	0.5	0.6	0.5	0.5	0.2	0.3
Food – dairy products-	2.6	2.1	2.1	2.3	0.7	0.7	2.2	2.3	2.5	2.8	0.4	1.1	2.6	3.3	2.5	2.8	0.9	1.4
Food – cereals and feed	3.2	2.1	1.3	1.2	0.8	2.9	1.7	1.6	1.6	1.6	0.3	0.7	2.0	1.9	1.6	1.6	0.6	0.7
Food – beverages	3.0	2.2	2.1	2.4	0.7	0.8	2.2	2.4	2.5	2.98	0.5	1.2	2.6	3.5	2.5	2.9	0.8	1.4
Food – tobacco	0.5	0.4	0.4	0.4	0.1	0.1	0.4	0.4	0.5	0.5	0.1	0.2	0.5	0.6	0.5	0.5	0.2	0.3
Food – other	13.1	10.2	11.7	12.1	4.3	5.0	12.6	12.7	14.7	15.8	2.7	6.8	15.5	18.9	14.7	15.5	5.1	7.0
Total food	23.4	17.8	18.3	19.3	7.0	9.7	20.1	20.4	22.7	24.9	4.0	10.6	24.3	29.5	22.7	24.4	7.9	11.3
Health	232.7	168.2	195.3	198.6	75.8	81.7	212.3	213.3	235.3	246.9	51.7	124.9	251.9	307.6	236.1	244.6	95.9	127.7
Total grants	543.8	399.7	457.0	479.1	178.5	185.6	484.9	495.2	562.6	610.9	121.6	281.8	604.2	739.9	562.9	602.3	207.2	288.4
Domestic share	4%	6%	na	na	7%	9%	2%	2%	15%	15%	5%	3%	13%	24%	12%	11%	na	na
US share	55%	53%	34%	42%	48%	54%	33%	41%	31%	38%	30%	32%	30%	32%	32%	39%	29%	38%
Japan share	7%	8%	13%	12%	12%	17%	15%	14%	20%	19%	13%	16%	19%	16%	20%	19%	10%	13%

Continued

Table 12.4 (continued).

	Ireland		Italy		Japan		Netherlands		New Zealand		USA		Bulgaria		Czechoslovakia		Slovenia	
	1993	1995	1993	1995	1990	1995	1993	1995	1993	1995	1990	1995	1988	1993	1991	1993	1993	1995
Agriculture – livestock	0.5	1.0	2.3	2.4	6.8	7.8	0.1	2.3	1.0	0.8	3.2	4.4	0.0	0.0	0.0	0.0	0.1	0.1
Agriculture – crops and combo farms	0.8	1.7	4.3	4.6	15.2	18.2	0.1	4.5	2.1	1.1	4.1	7.1	0.0	0.0	0.0	0.0	0.1	0.0
Agriculture – fruits and vegetables	0.1	0.2	0.4	0.5	1.5	1.8	0.0	0.5	0.2	0.1	0.4	0.7	0.0	0.0	0.0	0.0	0.0	0.0
Agriculture – horticulture	0.0	0.1	0.2	0.2	0.8	1.0	0.0	0.2	0.1	0.1	0.2	0.3	0.0	0.0	0.0	0.1	0.0	0.0
Agriculture – services to livestock	1.3	2.7	6.0	6.1	16.3	19.0	0.2	5.8	2.6	2.2	9.0	12.0	0.0	0.0	0.0	0.0	0.2	0.2
Agriculture – services to crops	0.4	0.9	2.2	2.4	7.7	9.4	0.0	2.4	1.1	0.6	2.1	3.7	0.0	0.0	0.0	0.0	0.0	0.0
Agriculture – other	0.1	0.3	0.6	0.7	2.2	2.7	0.0	0.7	0.3	0.2	0.6	1.1	0.0	0.0	0.0	0.0	0.0	0.0
Total agriculture	3.3	6.9	16.1	16.9	50.5	60.0	0.4	16.4	7.4	5.1	19.6	29.3	0.0	0.0	0.2	0.2	0.5	0.4
Food – meat, poultry and fish	0.1	0.2	0.5	0.5	1.6	2.0	0.0	0.5	0.2	0.1	0.5	0.8	0.0	0.0	0.0	0.0	0.0	0.0
Food – fruit and vegetables	0.1	0.2	0.4	0.5	1.5	1.8	0.0	0.5	0.2	0.1	0.4	0.7	0.0	0.0	0.0	0.0	0.0	0.0
Food – dairy products	0.4	0.9	2.2	2.4	7.6	9.3	0.0	2.4	1.1	0.6	2.1	3.6	0.0	0.0	0.0	0.0	0.0	0.0
Food – cereals and feed	0.3	0.5	1.3	1.4	6.4	8.5	0.0	1.3	0.8	0.3	1.8	6.6	0.0	0.0	0.0	0.0	0.0	0.0
Food – beverages	0.4	0.9	2.2	2.5	8.3	10.4	0.0	2.5	1.3	0.6	2.2	4.2	0.0	0.0	0.0	0.0	0.0	0.0
Food – tobacco	0.1	0.2	0.4	0.5	1.5	1.7	0.0	0.5	0.2	0.1	0.4	0.7	0.0	0.0	0.0	0.0	0.0	0.0
Food – other	2.5	4.7	12.4	13.5	47.1	52.0	0.3	13.0	5.6	3.0	15.1	24.4	0.1	0.1	0.2	0.1	0.1	0.2
Total food	3.9	7.6	19.4	21.2	73.9	85.7	0.4	20.6	9.4	5.0	22.5	41.1	0.1	0.1	0.3	0.2	0.3	0.3
Health	43.6	89.2	206.2	220.2	665.5	779.7	5.5	211.3	101.4	69.0	277.4	425.1	0.4	0.4	3.5	3.0	5.8	6.2
Total grants	92.6	193.3	486.9	530.0	1814.2	2155.6	14.0	512.2	227.6	140.9	619.7	958.9	1.2	7.3	10.3	5.4	10.1	11.4
Domestic share	na	3%	1%	3%	57%	32%	10%	2%	na	8%	72%	82%	na	na	10.3	73%	na	22%
US share	na	44%	na	41%	30%	28%	34%	41%	50%	45%	na	na	na	34%	na	na	30%	23%
Japan share	6%	4%	16%	15%	na	na	32%	14%	5%	5%	15%	8%	na	na	na	na	na	na

Agriculture – livestock	0.5	0.2	0.4	0.2	0.2	0.5	0.0	0.1	0.3	0.0	0.0	0.0	0.2	0.3	0.2	0.3	0.6	2.3
Agriculture – crops and combo farms	0.6	0.1	0.3	0.3	0.4	0.7	0.0	0.3	0.6	0.0	0.0	0.1	0.0	0.1	0.5	0.5	0.8	1.1
Agriculture – fruits and vegetables	0.1	0.0	0.0	0.0	0.0	0.1	0.0	0.0	0.1	0.0	0.0	0.0	0.0	0.0	0.0	0.1	0.1	0.2
Agriculture – horticulture	0.0	0.0	0.0	0.0	0.0	0.0	0.0	0.0	0.0	0.0	0.0	0.0	0.0	0.0	0.0	0.0	0.0	0.1
Agriculture – services to livestock	1.3	0.5	1.2	0.7	0.4	1.3	0.1	0.2	0.7	0.1	0.2	0.1	0.7	0.9	0.5	0.9	1.7	7.6
Agriculture – services to crops	0.3	0.0	0.2	0.2	0.2	0.4	0.0	0.1	0.3	0.0	0.0	0.0	0.0	0.1	0.3	0.3	0.4	0.7
Agriculture – other	0.1	0.0	0.1	0.0	0.1	0.1	0.0	0.0	0.1	0.0	0.0	0.0	0.0	0.0	0.1	0.1	0.1	0.2
Total agriculture	2.9	0.8	2.2	1.4	1.4	3.2	0.2	0.8	2.0	0.1	0.2	0.3	0.9	1.4	1.7	2.2	3.8	12.2
Food – meat, poultry and fish	0.1	0.0	0.0	0.0	0.1	0.1	0.0	0.0	0.1	0.0	0.0	0.0	0.0	0.0	0.1	0.1	0.1	0.2
Food – fruit and vegetables	0.1	0.0	0.0	0.0	0.0	0.1	0.0	0.0	0.1	0.0	0.0	0.0	0.0	0.0	0.1	0.1	0.1	0.1
Food – dairy products	0.3	0.0	0.2	0.1	0.2	0.4	0.0	0.1	0.3	0.0	0.0	0.0	0.1	0.1	0.3	0.3	0.4	0.6
Food – cereals and feed	0.2	0.2	0.1	0.1	0.1	0.2	0.0	0.1	0.2	0.0	0.0	0.0	0.1	0.1	0.2	0.2	0.4	1.7
Food – beverages	0.3	0.0	0.1	0.2	0.2	0.4	0.0	0.1	0.3	0.0	0.0	0.0	0.1	0.1	0.2	0.2	0.4	0.6
Food – tobacco	0.1	0.0	0.0	0.0	0.0	0.1	0.0	0.0	0.1	0.0	0.0	0.0	0.0	0.0	0.1	0.0	0.1	0.1
Food – other	2.0	1.0	0.9	1.0	1.4	2.0	0.2	0.8	1.7	0.0	0.0	0.3	0.1	0.5	1.9	1.9	3.4	4.6
Total food	3.1	1.3	1.4	1.5	2.1	3.2	0.3	1.2	2.6	0.1	0.1	0.5	0.2	0.7	2.8	2.7	4.8	7.9
Health	39.2	15.0	28.8	19.4	15.0	39.0	3.2	9.0	25.2	2.0	3.3	3.9	14.5	21.6	21.1	27.8	51.6	181.2
Total grants	84.7	28.5	51.2	39.5	49.9	90.4	6.2	29.4	62.9	3.4	5.0	12.4	21.6	34.6	55.0	75.0	136.8	318.5
Domestic share	17%	5%	20%	51%	44%	21%	9%	22%	9%	na	26%	49%	14%	9%	45%	33%	39%	62%
US share	25%	10%	30%	32%	29%	33%	56%	38%	45%	70%	47%	43%	49%	39%	25%	16%	30%	9%
Japan share	2%	4%	6%	6%	3%	3%	na	8%	4%	na	na	na	7%	4%	17%	26%	11%	10%

na, data not available.

References

Bogsch, A. (1988) INPADOC: an idea has become reality. *World Patent Information* 10(3).

Evenson, R.E. and Johnson, D.K.N. (1997) Introduction: invention input–output analysis. *Economic Systems Research* 9, 149–160.

Evenson, R.E and Johnson, D.K.N. (1998) *R&D Spillovers to Agriculture: Measurement and Application.* Wellesley College Working Paper 98–01.

Gonsen, R. (1998) *Technological Capabilities in Developing Countries: Industrial Biotechnology in Mexico.*

Johnson, D.K.N. and Evenson, R.E. (1997) Innovation and invention in Canada. *Economic Systems Research* 9, 177–192.

Kortum, S. and Putnam, J. (1997) Assigning patents to industries: tests of the Yale Technology Concordance. *Economic Systems Research* 9, 161–175.

Yoshikawa, I. and Kanri, J. (1992). *The Outline of Patent Databases in STN-INPADOC, INPAMONITOR.*

IN. America

Property Rights and Regulations for Transgenic Crops in North America[*]

13

Gerald Carlson and Michele Marra

Department of Agricultural and Resource Economics, North Carolina State University, Raleigh, North Carolina, USA

Crop biotechnology news is filled with stories of patent-infringement lawsuits, rapid increases in the prices of stocks of publicly traded companies, and glowing statements of the near-term benefits of the technologies by leading scientists and research directors. Corn with higher oil content and crops with genes giving both tolerance to herbicides and insect control are already on the market and used by many farmers in the USA and elsewhere. It is clear that there will be huge returns to transgenic crop research. However, little public attention is being given in North America to conflicts among various interest groups about the deployment of these new seeds. The battle lines seem to be drawn in Europe.

The potential external costs of herbicide tolerance (HT) moving into 'weedy relatives' from field test plots of herbicide-tolerant crops remains a concern, but is now better understood and does not seem to hinder decisions on the part of USDA to let testing go forward. The major external effect, which is influencing deployment of the new biotechnology crops, is the potential of insects resistant to crop Bt, *Bacillus thuringiensis*, spilling over to other crops where sprayable Bt is used. Both for farmers not adopting the crop Bt and for users of the sprayable Bt the claim is made that they will lose one of their best and safest pest management tools because of the potential development of insects resistant to the crop Bt.

The EPA is requiring as a condition for obtaining registration and the right to sell the crop seeds that all companies must have a resistance management plan. The crops containing Bt are regulated as 'plant pesticides' under

[*]Presented at the Agricultural Biotechnology Conference, held 1–2 June, 1998 at Università degli Studi di Roma 'Tor Vergata', Rome, Italy.

the standard pesticide law (FIFRA) as are the herbicides that can be used on the herbicide-tolerant crop cultivars. In the case of the HT crops, the force of these property rights restrictions (for health concerns) is illustrated by a recent cancellation of a HT crop herbicide after many years of research and 3 years of commercial sales.

There are also changes in producers' property rights as they buy the transgenic crops. Companies selling seed are using 'technology fees' and requiring growers to sign contracts limiting use of pesticides, prohibiting saving seed of the crops, and requiring that 'refugia' of conventional crop varieties are planted. Grower contracts and lengthy new contracts between local seed companies and the patent holder companies are changing the seed industry in the USA. One of the main motivations of the contracts is the prevention of dilution of the real and perceived quality (private spillovers) of the new products.

This chapter focuses on regulations affecting marketing rights for transgenic crops. Both Canada and the USA restrict field trials and selling of transgenic crops (Figs 13.1–13.5). We will try to explain the property rights situation for conventional pesticides in the USA so one might see how rights could evolve for the 'plant pesticide' products. Some observations on the private contracts are given as they relate to the seed-saving issue. We do not deal with the important potential external effects related to food residues, trade and the labelling of genetically altered food coming from biotechnology crops.

Theoretical and Historical Perspectives

Clearly the Demsetz (1967) view of evolving property rights fits for seed traits. As resources like seeds are developed which can carry stronger crop protection and other valuable characteristics, there will be higher derived demand for institutions to protect these characteristics. Therefore, we see the evolving legislative, legal and market institutions to protect rights to plants, genes and gene manipulation processes.

Table 13.1 shows some key dates and events in the evolution of property rights for North American crops. This set of events is familiar to us, and illustrates the role of court decisions, Patent Office actions and legislation on property rights. Later, we will return to the resale restrictions as they relate to HT crops.

Much of our later discussion of property rights changes has to do with the Environmental Protection Agency (EPA). For Canada, the regulation of seed testing and approval of varieties falls on the Plant Biotechnology Office (Agriculture Canada, website). These agencies are responsible for pesticide safety and efficacy. Vernon Ruttan uses the EPA to illustrate his application of the induced innovation notion to the evolution of institutions. Perhaps it is not surprising that EPA policies and not court rulings, patents or private contracts is the institutional change that is critical to the deployment of seeds

Table 13.1. Evolution of property rights for North American crops.

1970	Plant Variety Protection (PVP) Act passed
1971	First PVP Certificates issued
1980	Supreme Court upholds utility patents for microorganisms
1985	US Patent Office begins utility patents for plants
1988	Agriculture Canada begins regulating plants with novel traits
1994	Amendments to US PVP Act
	• Restricts farmers' rights to sell seed
	• Extends patent life from 17 to 20 years
1995	Court upholds resell restrictions
1998	Court rules in favour of inventor over first patent holder of Bt

effective against crop pests. However, it is quite likely that seed company executives did not anticipate the force of this agency in the modern, seed/pesticide industry.

Table 13.2 gives some recent events critical to crop biotechnology related to pest control. When you see the terms 'approval', 'registered' or 'cancelled', the EPA is the key decision-maker on these market deployment actions. The USDA entries refer to the approval process for conducting field tests. This step in the development process has become more streamlined, and it also provides information on likely new products by crop, company and technology type (Carlson *et al.*, 1997).

This audience does not need to be reminded of the high rates of return to agricultural research. Many of you have contributed to this research,

Table 13.2. Recent history of crop protection biotechnology in North America.

1987	First successful insertion of Bt toxin gene into plant
1990	First introduction of Bt into corn plant
1992	First field trials of Bt corn under USDA permit; Flavor Saver tomato approved
1993	USDA simplifies field test approval
1994	BXN (bromoxynil) cotton approved, first herbicide-tolerant crop
1994	First trials with plant pharmaceutical objectives begin in Canada
1995	Agriculture Canada approves herbicide-tolerant canola and soybeans
3/95	Ciba Seeds receives limited registration for planting Bt corn
8/95	First full registration of Bt corn by EPA
10/95	First Bt cotton and potatoes approved for planting in USA
1/96	Roundup-tolerant soybeans first marketed in USA
1/97	First 'stacked' gene product (Bt and RR cotton) approved
7/97	Roundup-tolerant corn seed approved for 1998 crop year
9/97	Petition charges EPA with 'gross negligence' in regulating genetically engineered plants
11/97	First cancellation of herbicide-tolerant crop herbicide
4/98	USEPA reverses cancellation of herbicide for herbicide-tolerant cotton

especially as it relates to breeding research and new crop varieties. One connection of our research on the returns to Bt cotton is the importance of including external costs and benefits to obtain a complete measure of net benefits. Capalbo and Antle (1989) and others have recognized this point in the literature, but it is often not measured. Both positive and negative external effects are possible, and especially critical when we are dealing with crop traits directed at mobile pests and pesticides.

One of the primary economic justifications for involvement of government agencies in markets is to correct for external effects (Baumol and Oates, 1988). With the attention given to 'government failure' in the Public Choice literature, it is important to remember that economic theory with transaction costs requires that the corrective action of government should not cost more than the social gains from reducing the external costs. In the pesticide area we usually associate EPA with actions related to food safety. But in decisions on deployment of crop biotechnology, EPA is very active in dealing with producer-to-producer external effects as well as worker and consumer safety.

Field trials of genetically transformed crops can indicate future commercially viable crop varieties. Figures 13.1–13.3 show the numbers of field trials (releases) of genetically engineered crops in the USA for the 1989–1997 period. These are only for crop protection attributes, primarily herbicide tolerance and insect-resistant varieties, but with more interest in disease protection in later years. Corn is clearly the most commonly tested crop. Releases of varieties with multiple or stacked traits begin to increase beginning in 1995. Figure 13.4 gives the number of separate submissions for field trials in Canada for 1988–1997. Canola is the most commonly tested crop with over 500 trials in 1997. Figure 13.5 shows the number of trials in Canada for the three crop protection groupings. Note the rapid increase in trials for insect, virus and fungus protection.

Pesticide Law and Changes in Property Rights

The federal pesticide law in the USA is FIFRA with amendments. The *Seed Regulations* give the primary regulations specific to plant biotechnology in Canada. The insecticides expressed in insect-resistant crops developed by biotechnology are being regulated as 'plant pesticides'. To better understand what could happen with both insect-resistant crops and herbicide-tolerant crops we might look at the major provisions of FIFRA. This 1947 law required that all pesticides must be registered with USDA before they begin market sales. This responsibility was turned over to the EPA in 1970, but the Federal Drug Agency retains responsibility for setting the acceptable pesticide residue tolerances. The tolerance-setting process has been revised by the 1996 Food Quality Protection Act.

New pesticides usually receive conditional registrations until all safety, efficacy and other conditions are met. For example, a herbicide registered in

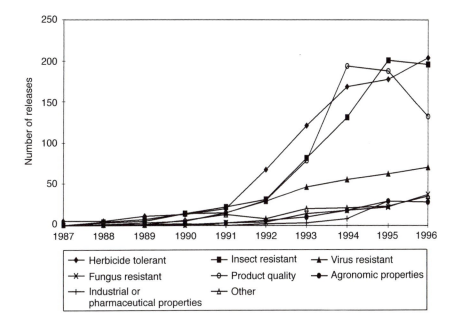

Fig. 13.1. Trends in US field releases by transgene category.

1990 was given a conditional registration, and the full registration depended upon reduced uses of other herbicides thought to be environmentally hazardous.

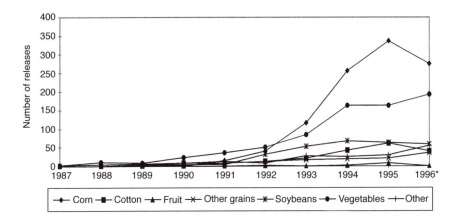

Fig. 13.2. Trends in US field releases by crop category.

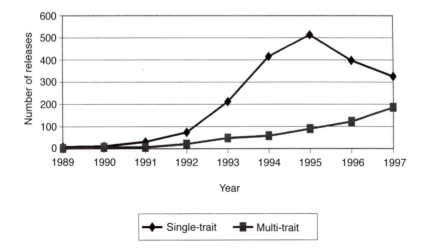

Fig. 13.3. US releases of genetically engineered plants.

Given the urgency to get approval to begin commercial marketing, manufacturers are willing to respond to agency demands for monitoring, label restrictions and other requests. Of course, delayed entry into a market will reduce income, help competitors and reduce benefits to final users. The primary objection of FIFRA actions is to avoid 'unacceptable adverse effects on the environment'.

Since 1972, the registration of new pesticides requires that the manufacturers provide test data on safety and efficacy. Later amendments clarify that re-registration and evaluation are required for all active ingredients. Also if there are any changes in information on either safety or efficacy of the pesticide, it is the responsibility of the manufacturer to make this information available to the agency. It seems as if it is a combination of the 'report changes in efficacy' and 'adverse effects on the environment' clauses which has led the EPA to assume the major responsibility for requiring Resistance Management Plans in order for sellers to receive conditional registrations for marketing. There is a formal legal petition charging EPA with 'illegal and gross negligence in failure to adequately regulate genetically engineered plants'. This mainly centres on making the refugia voluntary, but includes failure to file an environmental impact statement. It is interesting to note that resistance management plans have not been required for registration or re-registration of conventional insecticides.

Label restrictions are another way EPA limits the property rights of patent holders and users of pesticides. Label restrictions can specify where a chemical can be used (crops, counties), maximum amounts per application and per season, method of application, applicator equipment and exposure, and when the application can be made (crop stage, preharvest intervals). Again registrants are usually willing to accept label limitations to obtain registration.

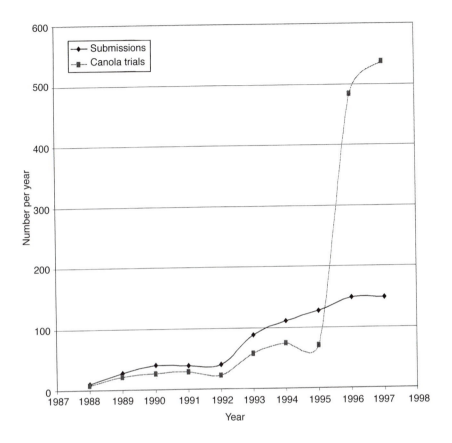

Fig. 13.4. Submissions and field trials, genetically engineered plant material, Agriculture Canada.

Finally, FIFRA provides for cancellation and suspension of registrations. Usually this process involves a consideration of benefits and costs, but the provisions of the 1996 Food Quality Protection Act limit when benefits of pesticides can be considered in the cancellation and registration decisions to times when there might be a 'significant disruption' of the food supply.

FIFRA and Changes in Crop Seed Property Rights

Clearly, USDA has limited choices of where and how biotechnology crops can be field-tested. Yet, since 1993 this process has been streamlined for the four or five major crops which do not have weedy relatives, and has not seemed to be a major limitation in the last few years. Canadian field testing

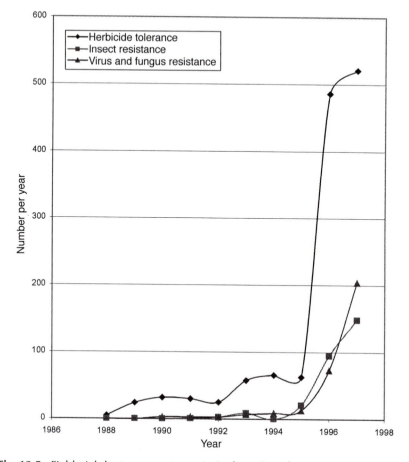

Fig. 13.5. Field trials by transgene type, Agriculture Canada.

for various crop protection and industrial product objectives is advancing quickly (see Figs 13.4 and 13.5).

EPA has, in some cases, limited the amounts of Bt crops that can be sold and where they can be sold. In 1995, Bt corn seed sales were limited to 9700 acres, and to about 500,000 acres in 1996. In 1997, when there were four different Bt genetic types or events for corn seed on the market, EPA limited the amount of Bt corn seed sold only in 'cotton counties' (counties with >100,000 acres of cotton) as part of the resistance management effort.

The resistance management restrictions have taken the form of no-planting zones or refugia on which Bt corn or cotton will not be planted on each farm. These conventional corn and cotton fields are intended to provide a place where insects susceptible to Bt can be produced and, thus, limit resistance build-up over time.

The extension of the regulation of chemical pesticides to 'plant pesticides' under FIFRA remains in a state of flux. The rule-making was first proposed in 1994, extended through 1996 for comments, and then in 1996 there was a consolidated report of 11 professional, scientific societies. Their report concluded, 'This policy, if adopted, will discourage the development of new pest-resistant crops, thereby, prolonging the reliance solely on synthetic chemical pesticides' (Ag Biotech Online, 1998). In the meantime, regulation of the seed/pesticide industry continues.

Evaluation of Refugia

Refugia were required in the first year of marketing Bt cotton and they began in 1997 for Bt corn sold by Monsanto. Generally they have been set as 5% of all corn or cotton on a farm if no insecticides are used in the refuge, and 20% if insecticides are applied. Scientists supporting the Union of Concerned Scientists are calling for 50% refugia.

The main objective of refugia is to prevent future resistance development of target insect species (European corn borer for corn; bollworm, budworm and pink bollworm for cotton). Bollworm is a pest of many crops including some fruits and vegetables, and a minor pest to corn, soybeans and sorghum. Classic external costs would be when bollworms develop resistance to users of sprayable Bt, closely related to the Bt in corn and cotton. The farmers who use sprayable Bt would suffer crop losses or have higher insecticide bills or both. Also farmers who would choose to use Bt crops in the future would find this technology ineffective. This could be a loss to these growers or to other sellers of Bt products.

A formal legal petition was filed against EPA's handling of the potential spillovers from Bt use. The filers were a coalition of 31 groups including the International Federation of Organic Agriculture Movement. This petition gives the EPA an additional reason to call for Resistant Management Plans from sellers of Bt cotton and corn. The plans were not mandatory for all sellers of Bt, but Monsanto and some companies have made all growers sign contracts saying they will comply with the overall plan.

The main economic benefit of the refugia is the delay or prevention of resistance development, which will maintain the efficacy of sprayable Bt on cotton and other crops. Clearly, the benefits to farmers of other crops are an external effect that is not considered by sellers of Bt corn or cotton. Gains to future adopters of the technology are external to current users of the technology, but internal for the sellers of the technologies. The patent holders have incentives to delay resistance onset so that they might sell larger quantities (Miranowski and Carlson, 1979). Biologists who study resistant insect development know that the outbreaks are localized. There do not seem to be any studies of the long-range movement of resistant insects to other crops. However, there is a study going on in North Carolina in an area where corn, cotton and potatoes are grown in close proximity.

Importantly, there are costs of operating the refugia, and economic benefits of planting the Bt crops. Refugia have costs in terms of direct monitoring costs, lost yields and higher insecticide bills in the short run. Our estimates from a farmer survey are that the Bt varieties of cotton yield 11% higher, and result in 72% less use of insecticides than conventional varieties (Carlson et al., 1998). There are also important external benefits of planting Bt cotton including preventing resistance development to current cotton insecticides and the reduced spillovers from the lower insecticide use on the Bt cotton. Since only about 4% of the corn acres are routinely treated for corn borers, there are not these same external benefits. The primary external benefit of Bt corn would be that associated with the use of about 8% less land to obtain the same output with Bt corn as with conventional corn.

An analysis of the refuge policy must consider the correct size of refugia to preserve Bt-susceptible insects and slow resistance development. The faster that resistance will develop to Bt and spread from the outbreak loci, the larger the non-Bt refugia should be. For cotton, there is resistance to the major substitute insecticide class, pyrethroids, in several states at the present time. Resistance to Bt will not occur for several years (several estimates say 4–10 years for the first occurrence), and its location and time of development is highly uncertain. So the tradeoff is between current income to users of Bt together with resistance prevention for the pyrethroids, against future, and uncertain, costs to Bt cotton users and sprayable Bt users. All of the above can be modelled as an optimal control problem with resistance level to Bt and pyrethroids as state variables, and refuge size as the control variable. Studies using this modelling approach are under way at Iowa State and North Carolina State Universities.

A further important factor in optimal use of the Bt resource is that the development of resistance to Bt gives increased incentives to find and market new Bt strains in crops. There is second generation Bt cotton already in the testing phase of development. Two new companies have been formed in the last 6 months to develop and market Bt cotton. In the corn market, there were four different Bt events being sold in 1997, but one did not perform as well against second generation corn borers and will be phased out.

Private Contracts

Sellers of herbicide-tolerant soybeans and cotton have implemented grower contracts as an instrument to maintain property rights to germplasm. The three provisions in these contracts have been to:

- Prevent seed-saving by buyers of glyphosate-tolerant (Roundup Ready, RR) cotton and soybeans.
- Restrict the use of glyphosate-tolerant products to the patent-holder's brand.
- Ask growers to sign Resistance Management Plans.

Table 13.3 gives some details on the incentives to prevent seed-saving. Cotton has a relatively lower seed cost relative to crop revenue when compared with corn, soybeans and potatoes. However, when the technology fee is included cotton has the highest seed cost premium for the transgenic seed relative to conventional seed. Saved seed is lower cost, but there may be some yield and quality sacrifices. In 1996, Monsanto asked all RR soybean users to sign contracts. There were some farmer objections, so in 1997 there was no separate contract, only provisions listed on the purchase invoice.

In March of this year, Delta and Pineland (company with 75% of the US cotton seed market), together with USDA applied for a patent on a gene that will stop germination of seeds from a transgenic crop when it is treated with a 'trigger' compound. This technology has been extended to other crops besides cotton, and has the potential to eliminate illegal use of seeds. This technology may be particularly important for enabling seed companies to extend the sale of genetically modified crops in developing countries, while protecting their property rights.

Herbicide-tolerant crops represent a tie-in sale if the same company owns the seed rights and the herbicide. This is the case for RR soybeans, cotton and corn, but not for BXN (bromoxynil-tolerant) cotton, and glufosinate (Liberty) corn. For the latter cases there are single sellers of the herbicides, and there was no attempt to sign contracts. However, Monsanto, not the only seller of glyphosate, wanted to ensure that its own brand of glyphosate is used, so they included this provision in their grower contracts. The penalty used for enforcement usually involves forfeiture of rights to use the transgenic crops in the future. However, there was at least one case where the farmer was prevented from selling his RR soybeans to the only RR soybean processor in the area.

Cancellation

The USEPA can cancel marketing rights for a pesticide. They have done this for the first herbicide-tolerant cotton variety, BXN cotton. This came as a

Table 13.3. Seed incentives for selected crops

	Seed cost as % of crop revenue	Percentage of 1996 seed purchased	Seed cost as % of conventional seed cost
Corn	8	100	40[a]
Soybean	7	76	46[b]
Cotton	2	66	300[a]
Potatoes	8	73	15[a]

[a]Bt; [b]RR.

Note: Seed cost includes technology fee.

complete surprise to the registrant, Rhône-Poulenc Ag, who had sold BXN cotton in cooperation with a cotton seed company for 3 years. A pesticide is not assured of moving from a conditional to a full registration. Bromoxynil is widely used on corn and small grains, but was first introduced to cotton as the first registered herbicide-tolerant crop. Under the cancellation, the genetically altered cotton variety could be sold, but bromoxynil could not be applied to cotton. This cancellation shows that there is a different set of property rights limitations on herbicide-tolerant crops versus insect-resistant crops. Four months following the cancellation announcement, EPA has examined additional safety data and reversed their decision. They will allow the continued sale of bromoxynil on herbicide-tolerant cotton.

Research Implications

One of the general themes of this chapter is that external benefits and costs should be considered in assessing the returns to transgenic crop research. This is difficult to do because off-site effects are usually not easily revealed in market transactions. Perhaps, there is some part of the technology fees charged to growers for use of a transgenic crop which is related to these spillovers, but most pesticide and seed companies are only beginning to understand these costs. The actions of EPA to cancel products, to require Resistance Management Plans, and limit crop sales will reduce short-term profits to these industries and to the final users. The effect of EPA actions should be assessed in some broad-scale returns to transgenic research studies. Care is needed to evaluate both positive and negative spillovers. For example, we have not considered the information and other spillovers of transgenic research on other crops and countries.

The major new instrument that EPA has introduced, partially because of pressure from environmental and organic farming groups, is the no-planting zone or refuge. For the case of corn, the economic tradeoff for Bt corn users is between higher near-term profits from using more Bt (no or small refugia) versus longer-term benefits from prevention of resistance development. Spillovers in the form of resistant bollworms moving into organic farms and other crops is the main justification for a limitation on property rights to sell and plant Bt corn. Future damage to corn growers from resistant corn borers can be offset by new types of Bt corn – a backstop technology. Clearly research is needed that looks at the optimal type and size of resistance management tools for Bt corn.

Use of refugia in cotton is more complex than in corn because of the presence of current and future resistance development to other insecticides. The near-term suppression of insects resistant to pyrethroids can be a significant gain to Bt cotton use. Reducing yield losses and income uncertainty associated with pyrethroids is a current gain to weigh against distant future, and uncertain, losses from development of Bt-resistant insects which attack cotton and other crops. As with Bt corn, there are replacement Bt cottons in the testing phase of development. Each of these components, along with other external effects, needs serious evaluation.

There are many active players in the transgenic crop markets, and the stakes are high. Previously, my co-authors and I (Carlson *et al.*, 1997) have tried to describe the many different marketing and structural changes going on in the seed and pesticide industry. This is a ripe field for examining changes in property rights by court decisions, contracts, exclusive and non-exclusive agreements, mergers and other instruments. Imperfect competition models, game theory and rent-seeking studies are needed.

We are just beginning to find out how profitable the new crops are in the field. Data from a survey of cotton growers adopting Bt cotton show adopting farmers increased yields an average of 11%, reduced insecticide use 72% and increased profits. Even paying the higher seed and technology fees, the adopting farmers increased profits $142 per hectare or a 155% return on the additional seed investment (Carlson *et al.*, 1998). Even with these high returns there is discounting of technology fees in some cotton-growing areas where the returns are not as high. This should continue as competing seed companies enter the Bt cotton market. Because of the competition in the Bt corn market, there is discounting of seed prices for the 1998 crop year.

We have found that the 'technology fees' which various firms charge in addition to direct seed costs are useful in examining farmers' willingness to pay for particular genetic traits. We asked a sample of farmers about their willingness to adopt Bt cotton at lower technology fees and found that they were quite responsive to lower fees (elasticities of -1.6 to -3.3) (Hubbell *et al.*, 1998).

There are many research opportunities in the pricing and organization of the delivery of the new crop seeds. The increased value of the traits and the technologies themselves will encourage and enable changes in property rights. The large increase in stock market prices of seed companies indicates the economic importance of these technical and market opportunities.

References

Ag Biotech Online (1998) Plant pesticides under FIFRA, at: http://nbiap.biochem.vt.edu/epasrc/proposed/fifra.

Agriculture Canada, Plant Biotechnology Office, at: http://www.cfia-acia.agr.ca/english/food/pbo/trial.html.

Baumol, W.S. and Oates, W.E. (1988) *The Theory of Environmental Policy*. Cambridge University Press, New York.

Capalbo, S. and Antle, J. (1989) Incorporating social costs in the returns to research. *American Journal of Agricultural Economics* 71, 458–463.

Carlson, G.A., Marra, M.C. and Hubbell, B.J. (1997) Transgenic technology for crop protection: the new super seeds. *Choices* 1997(3), 31–36.

Carlson, G.A., Marra, M.C. and Hubbell, B.J. (1998) Yield, insecticide use, and profit changes from adoption of Bt cotton in the southeast. *Proceedings of the Beltwide Cotton Conference*. San Diego, California, 2, 973–974.

Demsetz, H. (1967) Toward a theory of property rights. *American Economics Review* 57, 347–359.

Hubbell, B.J., Marra, M.C. and Carlson, G.A. (1998) *Using Stated and Revealed Preferences to Estimate the Demand for a New Technology: The Case of Bt Cotton.* Working Paper, Department of Agricultural and Resource Economics, North Carolina State University, Raleigh, North Carolina.

Miranowski, J.A. and Carlson, G.A. (1979) Economic issues in public and private approaches to preserving pest susceptibility. In: *Pesticide Resistance: Strategies and Tactics for Management*. National Academy Press, Washington, DC, pp. 436–48.

Ruttan, V.W. (1982) *Agricultural Research Policy*. University of Minnesota Press, St Paul.

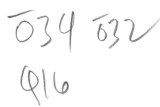

14

Intellectual Property Rights, Canola and Public Research in Canada

Peter W.B. Phillips

University of Saskatchewan, Saskatoon, Canada

Agriculture has been one sector where the state has historically contributed a significant share of research resources and undertaken a large share of the research effort. Except for those products with effective hybrids (e.g. maize corn), most of the effort has been undertaken by governments, publicly funded universities or by private companies funded by public grants.

That relationship held true in the canola sector, in Canada and globally, until the early 1980s. Since then, however, new, proprietary technologies have been developed and most of the resulting crop innovations have been commercialized by private companies. The transformation from a largely public industry to an increasingly private one has been precipitated by new, more cost-effective technologies, by significant industrial restructuring facilitated by large financial investments and by the introduction of legally sanctioned intellectual property rights (IPR) for biotechnological processes, genetic discoveries/constructs and commercial varieties.

As the germplasm, technologies, genes and seeds industry have been privatized, the public sector has been forced from its historical role as lead innovator and is seeking a new way to contribute to continued agri-food development. In the past the public sector financed, undertook and commercialized the innovations for canola; now public institutions are testing a variety of new roles, ranging from regulator to partner.

The optimal role for the public sector in coming years will be determined by the characteristics of innovation in the sector, the corresponding industrial structure and the effective IPR regime.

Background

To get a full appreciation for the extent of innovation since 1980, it is instructive to look at the endpoints in the process. As recently as 1982, there were only six canola cultivars actively grown in the world, all bred by public sector institutions in Canada: the Agriculture and Agri-food Canada (AAFC) research stations in Saskatoon, Alberta and Ottawa, the National Research Council (NRC) in Ottawa and Saskatoon and the Universities of Manitoba, Alberta, Saskatchewan and Guelph. They used largely non-proprietary technologies developed by those institutions: the half-seed breeding technique and special applications of a gas–liquid spectrometer (Kneen, 1992). All of the seeds produced and sold in Canada until then were in the public domain. The rate of development of new varieties was also relatively slow, with an average of one new variety every 2 years, and the average lifespan of a cultivar was about 10 years.

About 1985 there was a sharp acceleration of private sector research and investment in canola development. Four key factors led to the infusion of private money. First, health research and market development efforts throughout the 1980s opened the market for expanded production, which made further investment in seed varieties more commercially viable. In 1984, for the first time, it was shown in health studies that the consumption of mono-unsaturated fatty acids such as canola is preferable to poly-unsaturated fatty acids, because mono-unsaturated fatty acids lower LDL (harmful) cholesterol levels without affecting HDL (beneficial) cholesterol levels (Malla, 1996, pp. 16–17). Then, in 1985, the USA affirmed low erucic acid rapeseed oil as a food substance 'Generally Regarded as Safe' (GRAS) and in 1988 the use of the name 'canola' on food labels in the USA was approved. Second, breakthroughs in breeding methodologies improved the economics of private sector breeding. The general practice of shuttling seeds between northern and southern climates (e.g. between Canada and Chile) and the application of computers as aids in the laboratories shortened the traditional breeding period significantly. This was also the period when new biotechnology processes (i.e. cell fusion, genetic recombination, polymerase chain reaction and genome maps) shortened the development process, from an average of 12 years to as short as 3 years for in-fill varieties. Third, financial deregulation in the early 1980s in North America led to a large pool of capital seeking new investment opportunities, which coincided with the budget crunch in universities and public institutes and new pressures to commercialize new technologies for profit. As a result, the biotechnology industry became a focal point for private investment. The fourth and perhaps most crucial factor was the introduction of IPR for biological inventions. In 1980, a US Supreme Court decision (Chakrabarty v. Diamond) explicitly allowed patents for living organisms, and in 1985 US plant patents were explicitly allowed (Lesser, 1998). In 1990, after a 10-year domestic debate, Canada assigned IPR to private developers (via the Plant Breeders' Protection Act).

These changes, combined more recently with successful development of hybrid technologies for canola, helped private firms to capture the profits of innovation, setting the stage for intensive innovative activity in the sector in the 1990s. Between 1982 and 1997, a number of new proprietary technologies replaced the publicly developed breeding methods and more than 125 new varieties were introduced (Table 14.1). More than 75% of the new varieties were developed by private companies, so that by 1996 only about one-quarter of the seed sold in Canada had been developed by public institutions (this may understate the role of the public sector somewhat because many of the privately registered varieties were either developed using AAFC germplasm or were developed in collaboration with AAFC or NRC). The average active lifespan of a cultivar declined to about 3 years by 1997.

The public research institutions – the universities and public laboratories – have been seeking a continuing role, now that the technologies and the marketplace have been effectively privatized. The optimal role for the public sector in coming years will be determined by the characteristics of innovation in the sector and the effective IPR regime.

The Rationale for Public Investment in Agri-food Research

Public involvement in agri-food research has historically been justified based on a number of factors.

First, governments argued that private firms were not doing the optimal amount of research to develop new varieties for farmers. Numerous studies show that research in agriculture provides high returns; Nagy and Furtan (1978) estimated that public canola research up to 1979 yielded a 101% internal rate of return. This high rate of return can be explained by two factors. First, without any means for private investors to capture the gains from their research (e.g. IPR), they under-invest, causing higher marginal returns to research. This has been borne out by studies that show that private returns average less than half of total benefits of research (Ulrich *et al.*, 1986). Less often stated but perhaps as important, most studies show that farmers tended to bid away the gains from agronomic, yield-enhancing innovations, so that consumers ultimately gain (Akino and Hayami, 1975; Hayami and Herdt, 1975; Scobie and Posada, 1978; Nagy and Furtan, 1978; Mullen *et al.*, 1988; Lemieux and Wohlgenant, 1989). Hence, public investment was one means of supporting consumers.

Second, concerns about economic development and diversification have driven government efforts to develop new varieties. The Canadian government had from the beginning of its canola research effort a goal to establish a new crop and income option for Western Canadian farmers (NRC, 1992, p. 2). Canola has successfully provided a diversified option to traditional wheat, durum, barley and oats crops, now using on average 11 million acres annually and producing a crop worth on average more than C$2.5 billion

Table 14.1. Canola varieties developed by institution and by year.

Years	1940–1959	1960–1969	1970–1979	1980–1984	1985–1989	1990–1994	1995	1996
Number of Argentine varieties developed								
Public institutions	2	4	5	5	10	9	2	2
Private companies	0	0	0	0	7	24	16	23
Total all institutions	2	4	5	5	17	33	18	25
Number of Polish varieties developed								
Public institutions	2	2	3	1	0	3	0	2
Private companies	0	0	0	0	2	8	2	5
Total all institutions	2	2	3	1	2	11	2	7
Market share by institution[a]								
Public institutions	100%	100%	99.8%	99%	98%	49%	27%	26%
Private companies	0%	0%	0.2%	0.7%	0.4%	43%	57%	61%

Source: Canola Council of Canada, Canola Growers Manual (http://www.canola-council.org/manual/canolafr.htm); market share estimates by Nagy and Furtan (1940–1978), Three Prairie Pools Varieties Survey (1978–1991) and author (1991–1996).
[a]Market shares do not add to 100% due to some acreage not being reported to specific varieties.

annually, which at times vies for wheat as the most valuable crop in Western Canada.

Third, governments have always been concerned about equity issues, specifically how the gains to research are shared among producers, private companies and consumers. Recent economic research shows that imperfect competition in the input sectors – the four-company concentration ratio is 67% in the canola seed industry (Phillips, 1998) and 65% in the chemicals industry (Just and Hueth, 1993) – and the monopsonistic nature of the food-processing industry reduces the returns to farmers and possibly to consumers. The presence of a public sector seed developer that gives away its intellectual property effectively reduces the market power of oligopolies and potentially increases the returns to farmers and consumers.

Fourth, some governments have viewed public research, especially in the 1990s, as a factor in competitiveness. If knowledge spillovers are limited to a specific location, then that creates the possibility that 'comparative advantage is endogenously generated' because as 'countries engage in technological competition, comparative advantage evolves over time' (Grossman and Helpman, 1991, p. 338). Thus, if the final product is tradable but the innovation-based knowledge is a non-transferable intermediate factor of production, then the fact that innovation begins or is supported in one juris-diction could indefinitely put that site on a higher trajectory of R&D and new product development (Grossman and Helpman, 1991, pp. 220–221). As a result, the high-technology share of GDP and of exports will be higher than otherwise, and farmers could realize higher incomes as they earned a premium for being early adopters.

The author's purpose in this chapter is not to examine whether these reasons for public investment were appropriate in the past but to determine whether any of them hold now that IPRs exist and new biotechnologies have been developed.

The Characteristics of Innovation

Innovation yields knowledge that exhibits a number of different traits in terms of how it can be used, who can use it and how widely or narrowly it can be applied. An examination of the innovation process provides some insight into which types of knowledge the private sector may adequately provide while identifying those areas where public effort may be required.

The innovation process has historically been viewed as a linear process, starting with research and leading through development, production and marketing phases (Fig. 14.1). Although this may have made some sense in earlier times when many innovations were simply the product of inventors' ingenuity, it is clear that a new model is needed that incorporates the non-linear nature of innovation and the increasingly important role for market knowledge in the process.

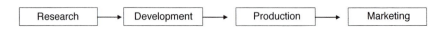

Fig. 14.1. The linear model of innovation. Source: Klein and Rosenberg (1966).

Klein and Rosenberg (1986) provide an approach that explicitly identifies the role of both market and research knowledge. Their 'chain-link model of innovation' (Fig. 14.2) involves a basically linear process moving from potential market to invention, design, adaptation and adoption, with feedback loops from each stage to previous stages. This model also provides the potential for the innovator to seek out existing knowledge or to undertake or commission research to solve problems in the innovation process. This dynamic model raises a number of questions about the types and roles of knowledge in the process.

Malecki (1997) provides part of the answer, with the categorization of four types of knowledge: know-why, know-what, know-how and know-who (Table 14.2).

Each of the four types of knowledge has specific features.

- *Know-why* refers to scientific knowledge of the principles and laws of nature, which in the case of plant breeding relates to the science of plant physiology, plant molecular biology, theoretical and applied genetics, genomics and biochemistry. Most of this work is undertaken in publicly funded universities and a few research institutes and is subsequently published in academic or professional journals. This knowledge would be in the knowledge block in the chain-link model, having been created almost exclusively in the research block.
- *Know-what* refers to knowledge about facts: in the case of plant breeding, this would include the specific steps involved in key transformation processes. This type of knowledge can often be codified and thereby acquire the properties of a commodity. In the case of canola, much of this knowledge is produced in private companies and public laboratories

Table 14.2. Types of knowledge based on who produces it, how codifiable it is and how accessible it is.

Degree of codification	Produced by private sector	Produced by public sector	Extent of disclosure
Completely codified	Know-what protected by patents	Know-why published in scientific papers	Fully disclosed
Completely tacit	Know-how and know-who produced within community		Restricted access

Source: Adapted by author from Malecki (1997, p. 58).

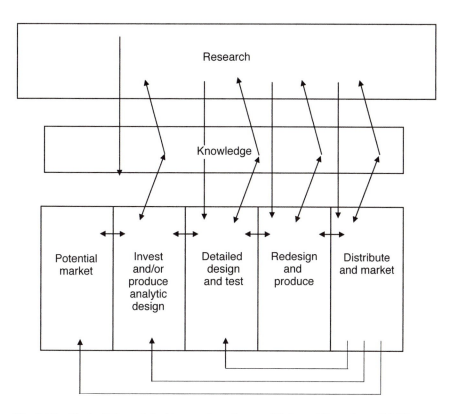

Fig. 14.2. Chain-link model of innovation. Source: Klein and Rosenberg (1966).

and is protected by patents. The stock of know-what would be in the knowledge block in the chain-link model, having been created in the research, invention, design and adoption blocks.

- *Know-how* refers to the skills or capacity to do something: in the canola case this involves the ability of scientists to combine the know-why and know-what to develop new varieties. This capacity is often learned by doing, which makes it more difficult to codify and to transfer to others. Know-how would be represented in the research block and also in the invention, design and adaptation stages.

- *Know-who* 'involves information about who knows what and who knows how to do what' (OECD, 1996, p. 12). It is becoming increasingly important in the biotechnology-based agri-food industry because, as the breadth of knowledge required to transform plants expands, it is necessary to collaborate to develop new products. Know-who knowledge is seldom codified but accumulates often within an organization or, at times, in communities where there is a cluster of public and private entities, all engaged in the same type of research and development, and all of which exchange technologies, germplasm and staff. This type of knowledge would be represented by the arrows in the chain-link model, as know-who is the basis for those flows.

The new growth theory (Lucas, 1988; Romer, 1990; Grossman and Helpman, 1991) adds a further element by distinguishing innovations by two additional characteristics: rivalry and excludability. Rivalry measures whether the innovation results in a good or service that can only be used by one person at one time (such as a product or personal service) or in an output (usually knowledge) that for little relative expense, or in some cases no cost, can be disseminated to and used by every producer in a country or the world, and one's use is not limited by another's use. Excludability measures whether the innovation is protected from widespread use by legal means (e.g. patent) or whether its adoption is limited by industrial organization requirements or climate. If it is excludable, then the innovator can appropriate all the benefits from the innovation.

Table 14.3 identifies how rivalry and excludability influence growth. With rival innovation and excludability – e.g. hybrid corn varieties or, more recently, canola varieties protected by Plant Breeders' Rights (PBR) – there should be little need for public investment as private investment is likely to be forthcoming. With rival innovations (e.g. new varieties) but no excludability – the traditional case presented for public investments in agricultural and canola research – there would be no basis for private innovation and hence there is a role for public investment. Increasingly, however, the research effort is targeted less on rival varieties (which simply could be encouraged through PBR, hybrids or contracts) but more on new non-rival innovations – either blueprints or applied science – which have the potential to provide a competitive advantage to a firm, while at the same time exhibit increasing returns to scale which, if realised, have the potential to raise and sustain global growth rates. That is clearly of great interest to the public sector.

If non-rival innovations are fully excludable, then they would exhibit decreasing returns. As Grossman and Helpman (1991, p. 53) observe, there is limited demand, so that as the number of innovations rises (e.g. different transformation technologies or different herbicide-tolerant genes), the average sales per innovation will fall. Eventually profit per innovation will stabilize and innovation will converge to a stable path.

The key factor is the non-appropriability of some of the results of innovation, which theory suggests would lead to under-investment in this type of research. Although economists have modelled differently the effect of general or applied science innovations, the results converge on a common view – some parts of the non-rival knowledge accumulated (largely know-why and parts of know-how and know-who) are not excludable. With technological change – Romer (1990, s72) defines this as 'improvement in the instructions for mixing together raw materials' – non-excludable knowledge spills over into the economy as a whole and raises the marginal value of new innovations.

Table 14.3. Categories of innovation and their outcomes.

	Excludable	Not excludable
Rival	Good or product protected by patent or copyright; decreasing returns to scale; e.g. hybrid corn	Good or product is fully transferable; perfectly competitive example; no basis for innovation; e.g. common case for public investment in agricultural research
Non-rival	Knowledge/blueprints that are protected by patent or copyright or are non-transferable due to climate/industrial organization – if knowledge is perfectly excludable, the innovation would exhibit decreasing returns to scale because of declining average sales per process	Know-why knowledge; within firms the innovation exhibits decreasing returns to scale but externalities due to full transfer of knowledge lead to increasing returns to scale in economy; e.g. endogenous growth case

Hence, the positive externality associated with private investment leads to a sectoral or national production function with increasing returns to scale.

Intellectual Property Rights Regimes

The key to private research activity, then, is the appropriability of the resulting gains. There are a wide range of means to ensure excludability of the results of the research, ranging from climatic or locational factors that restrict the transfer of technologies geographically, to measures that firms can undertake on their own – such as vertical integration between researchers and the unit doing the marketing, contracts and trade secrets – to legally sanctioned protection for intellectual property, as provided by patents and Plant Breeders' Rights (see Table 14.4).

There are a number of non-legislative approaches to ensuring excludability and capture of the rents on canola research.

Selective choice of research priorities has helped to make the research results more excludable (Rosenberg *et al.*, 1992, p. 179). Given that know-who and know-how tend to be found within firms or larger geographic clusters of research, there is a strong tendency for research communities to produce competitive, like-types of innovation which relate to the specific climate, soil characteristics, microbiology and industrial structure. In the canola sector, for instance, some of the varieties can only produce in the Canadian climate (certain pests or microbes limit or curtail production in other areas) and many of the new genetically altered varieties require a certain scale of production (e.g. total acreage or average field size) or complementary investments (e.g. mechanized seeding, spraying and harvest equipment). As a result,

Table 14.4. IPR regimes for 96 canola varieties developed during 1990–1996.

	Number of varieties	Percentage of varieties	Percentage of market share in 1997
Production input contracts involving proprietary complementary technologies (e.g. HT varieties)	4	4	35
Identity preserving production contracts for novel traits	10	10	<5
Hybrids/synthetics	17	18	15
Plant Breeders' Rights[a]	36	>37[a]	70

Source: Canola Council of Canada webpage (see Table 14.1) and author's calculations.

[a]186 applications had been received by CFIA as of March 1998, many of which were pending (CFIA, 1998).

some of the Canadian innovation into canola cannot be transferred elsewhere, setting the base for excludability between jurisdictions.

Industrial restructuring has been at least partly driven by efforts to capture the returns to intellectual property. Perhaps most dramatic was the industrial restructuring that occurred in the chemical sector itself. As Just and Heuth (1993) point out, chemical firms had an incentive to invest in genetics to protect the value of their IPR in patented herbicides. As a result, all of the large chemical companies moved to partner their agrochemical divisions with genetics and seeds units. AgrEvo in 1996 purchased 75% of Plant Genetics Systems of Belgium, an early leader in transgenics in canola and the owner of the InVigor™ hybrid technology. DowElanco owns Mycogen (the owner of the Bt gene and a variety of transformation technologies). In 1996 Monsanto purchased Calgene (the owner of the patented agrobacterium transformation technology for canola) and has since acquired significant interests in DeKalb and Limagrain Canada. Zeneca bought Mogen while DuPont in 1997 invested $1.7 billion for a 20% stake in Pioneer Hi-Bred. As a result, the private genetics and seeds business has become almost fully vertically integrated. This integration has allowed the major agrochemical companies to acquire or to develop proprietary technologies that support their core agrochemical businesses.

Production input contracts (Rosenberg *et al.*, 1992, p. 183) have been used by most of the companies that have developed herbicide-tolerant varieties of canola. AgrEvo's Liberty Link™ system, for example, includes a package sold to farmers of a glufosinate-tolerant variety protected by PBR and the patented Liberty glufosinate herbicide. Given that Liberty™ is only licensed in Canada for use on AgrEvo's varieties, it is difficult for farmers to use bin-run seed for replanting in future years as they would be unable to purchase the herbicide. Monsanto, the producer of Round-Up™ herbicide, has significant competition in the herbicide market (given that its primary patent has expired) and so has adopted another approach to marketing its herbicide-tolerant varieties. It has developed and patented a Round-Up™ Ready (RR) gene, which it licenses to any other breeder (by 1998 to Alberta Wheat Pool, Pioneer Hi-Bred, AAFC, Svalof Weibull and Limagrain). In order to acquire these new seeds, farmers are required to attend a sign-up meeting, to agree to a Technology Use Agreement (which prohibits bin-run seeding and grants Monsanto rights to inspect fields for their seed), to pay a $15/acre technology fee and to buy a package of seed and Round-Up™ herbicide. Monsanto is actively enforcing its production input contracts – it has hired field investigators in Western Canada and expended more than C$100,000 by 1998 to search for infractions.

Identity-preserved production contracts are used increasingly to capture some of the added-value resulting from canolas with novel traits. Canola has already been modified to produce a wide variety of engineered fat chains, industrial oils (e.g. laurate) and proteins, including low-value, end-of-the-scale proteins for improved nutritional value of the seeds, intermediate-value, bulk proteins such as industrial and food enzymes, and high-value proteins, mainly of interest to the pharmaceutical industry. End-users, such as Procter & Gamble, Nabisco, Frito Lay, Lubrizoil, Mobil Oil, Shell Oil and Ciba Geigy, are showing significant interest. Between 1994 and 1997 in Canada there were 184 field trials of transgenic varieties of canola that were manipulated to modify the oil composition, change the nutritional balance of the seed or to produce nutra- or pharmaceutical products (CFIA, 1997). Each of these products is produced with an intellectual property protection production contract in order to capture from the marketplace the value inherent in the new end-use attributes.

The development of effective *hybrid technologies* for canola has provided another technical mechanism for protecting intellectual property. It is uneconomic for farmers to replant seed from a hybrid or synthetic crop as they will lose half of the specific genetic traits with each successive planting and the resulting crops exhibit uneven growth. Firms that sell hybrid varieties are almost certainly assured that farmers will return each year to purchase new seed. The first canola hybrids were developed in the late 1980s and between 1990 and 1996 there were 17 hybrid/synthetic varieties developed and introduced, accounting for about 18% of all the new varieties over the period. Only a few firms are actively breeding hybrids – Zeneca has about half of the varieties while AgrEvo, with its purchase of Plant Genetic Systems and its In-Vigor™ technology, is expanding its use of hybrids.

Companies also rely on *trade secrets* to protect their proprietary investments in oil-modification technologies and germplasm. Historically, germplasm was public. Now, apart from the deposits of germplasm for PBR protected varieties, private breeders withhold access to all breeding lines and use them as bargaining chips in negotiating collaborations with other private companies.

No commercial firm relies exclusively on non-legal means to control the use of its intellectual property. All use one or more of the formal mechanisms, including patents, PBR or trademarks. An examination of the canola breeding system shows the dominance of private companies in key stages of the process. Virtually every step of the research process is patented or otherwise protected, mostly by entrepreneurial start-ups which are now part of the larger agrochemical seed industry. The public sector, both in Canada and elsewhere, has been largely absent from the key areas of the know-what knowledge required to transform canola.

Both original *patents* (i.e. mechanical or electrical inventions) and the new extended patents (for genes or gene processes) have been actively used by the research community (Evenson, 1998). Given that Canada was slower to introduce extended patents, most of the early patenting for canola was done in the USA (only 19 patents for canola-related work have been provided by the Canadian Intellectual Property Office (CIPO) between October 1989 and March 1998, compared with about 120 patents issued by the US Patent Office over the same period). Before 1982 all of the processes used to develop new canola varieties were in the public domain. Since then, there has been a rapid expansion of effort globally, with the result that most of the processes now are owned by others. The US patent database shows that of the 154 patents issued for canola inventions since 1981, about 40% were issued for process inventions and 60% for products (Table 14.5). As one might expect, the public sector (universities and governments) has done significantly less patenting (12% of total patents) and almost all of their patents have been for processes (CIPO data show that four of the 19 or about 21% of canola-related patents applications in Canada between 1989 and 1998 were by the public sector). In contrast, the patent data for private companies suggest that about one-third of their work is focused on processes and two-thirds on product development. The CIPO data, which goes up to 1997, shows an increase in transformation process patents that have not been filed in the USA. Almost 60% (11 of 19) of the patents were for transformation processes (e.g. promoter genes, hybrid technologies).

Looking at the data by firm, we see that among those companies patenting more frequently, the bulk of the patents have been issued to end users of canola (e.g. the big food processors such as Nabisco and Procter & Gamble), with a little interest from industrial users (e.g. Shell Oil) and the

Table 14.5. Canola-related patents, by type and patent holder.

	Company		School/government		
	Product	Process	Product	Process	Total
1981–1989	14	12	0	9	35
1990–1996	75	35	2	7	119
Total	89	47	2	16	154

Source: IBM Internet US Patent Database.

rest produced by the plant breeding and chemical companies (e.g. Pioneer Hi-Bred, Calgene and Monsanto) (Table 14.6). The Canadian data show a much greater bias to the plant breeding ventures, with almost half of the canola patents since 1989 issued to breeding companies.

One interesting feature is that some of the technologies have been patented only in the USA. For example, Calgene's two patents on agrobacterium transformation for canola are only in the USA. Although that would suggest that those technologies are unprotected in Canada, the fact that resulting transformed canola may be exported to the USA constrains Canadian breeders and effectively forces them to get licences for the use of these technologies.

Trademarks have also been used by parts of the industry to distinguish 'canola' grade rapeseed from other varieties. In 1978, the Rapeseed Association (now the Canola Council of Canada), trademarked the new low erucic acid, low glucosinolate rapeseed as 'canola'.[1] Since then there have been seven attempts by private firms (mostly breeders or food processors) to trademark either new varieties or to trademark specific canola oil food preparations (CIPO). In addition, all agricultural chemicals are trademarked and a number of the breeding companies have trademarked their industrial processes (e.g. Plant Genetic System's In-Vigor™ hybrid process). In almost every case, adoption of trademarks has been designed to supplement other intellectual property protection and to differentiate for marketing purposes the specific products.

Plant Breeders' Rights, finally introduced in Canada in 1990 (in place in the USA in the 1930s), provide somewhat weaker protection than patents for new varieties. Although the period of protection is almost as long as patents (18 years from the date of registration) and the holder of the PBR is required to deposit and make available for research purposes a propagating sample (usually deposited in the National Seed Collection in Saskatoon), farmers have the right to retain seed for their own use. Since PBRs were introduced in 1990, breeders have automatically applied for PBR on virtually all new open-pollinated varieties (186 applications by March 1998) but only 36 of the varieties were awarded a certificate by March 1998. As noted above, some companies seek to go beyond the protection granted by PBRs, requiring farmers to sign away their farmer's exemption in order to gain access to the seed. An additional concern raised recently by breeders is that

Table 14.6. Patents for canola processes or products, by firm.

	Nabisco	Proctor & Gamble	Pioneer Hi-Bred	Calgene	Shell Oil	Monsanto
1982–1988	1	4	0	0	4	0
1989–1995	25	18	8	10	1	3
Total	26	22	8	10	5	3

Source: IBM Internet US Patent Database.

the interaction of PBRs and patents may diminish the research exemption provided under PBR legislation. US patent law does not readily allow breeders to use patented materials (e.g. varieties with patented genes) to develop new varieties. Thus, although PBRs allow breeders to access the germplasm, companies holding patents on elements embedded in the germplasm may effectively block commercialization of any varieties that use some of that germplasm, even if the element used is not explicitly patented (confidential discussion regarding FIS report).

Academics, public research institutions and some private companies choose not to exercise their IPR for immediate monetary gain and instead *publish the results of their research in academic journals* – mostly know-why knowledge that is vital to future research but often has little commercial application. This includes the *Arabidopsis* genome project which is being developed and so far has been put into the public domain through academic publication.

The genomic information, however, has significant potential to be codified and thereby become a commodity that is rationed based on price.[2] Prior publication, except in limited cases within a year of patent application in Canada, effectively precludes future efforts to protect the resulting intellectual property through patent or PBR. As such, publication effectively grants the author rights to citation by subsequent researchers (a key currency of academics) but allows the economic benefits of the innovation to become public property (i.e. non-rival, non-excluded knowledge).

Taken together, the informal mechanisms and legal rights have effectively protected the vast majority of the technologies being used and the products flowing from the canola research community. The public role has been thereby changed.

An Evolving Role for the Public Sector

The public sector no longer plans and invests as if it is the only actor in the canola development industry. The significant presence of the private sector in the research of know-what knowledge and in the product commercialization stages means that the public objectives may in many cases already be realized without public involvement beyond setting the environment for private efforts.

It is instructive to look at the role of the state in the four elements of knowledge development and more generally in the product development process, as characterized by the chain-link innovation model.

Product Development

All of the early work on canola was done by the public sector based primarily on a linear model of innovation (Fig. 14.1). Although researchers from Canada Packers were involved in and funded some of the work in a search for a Canadian-sourced edible oil, the bulk of the product development effort was done by scientists in AAFC, the NRC and four Canadian universities. Until 1985, all of the varieties were developed and registered by one of those institutions. Since the mid-1980s, however, a rapid expansion of private investment in canola research has supplemented and almost overwhelmed the public effort.

This research effort conforms more to the chain-link model of innovation than the linear model. AgrEvo, for example, identified the market opportunity for herbicide-tolerant canola, undertook much of the basic gene isolation work in Frankfurt and then partnered with AAFC to get access to a base of canola varieties and to tap into its know-how and know-who to ultimately develop its Liberty-link canola. It then partnered with the Wheat Pools in Western Canada to prove up the product and market it. Since 1985, more than 75% of the new varieties have been privately developed along these lines (often developed directly by public institutions using private funds) and the seeds market has shifted heavily towards private seed sales, accounting for an estimated 60% in 1996, up from only trace amounts in the mid-1980s (Table 14.1).

Using the four public objectives as criteria, it is not clear that the state has any continuing justification for investing public funds in varietal development. Recent rates of investment indicate that instead of under-investing in variety development, private industry may in fact be over-investing in research and development for canola varieties. Industry participants suggest each new agronomic variety requires demand for seed for about 250,000 acres per year for 3 years to yield the targeted rate of return for biotechnology investments. Given an average of about 11 million acres planted in Canada, that would suggest only about 45 varieties could be sustained over the long term. As of 1996, more than 100 varieties were registered for sale. Furthermore, with an average life of 3 years, the optimal annual replenishment rate of new varieties should be about 15, not the current 30 per year. The potential to capture new market share for farm chemicals (upstream value added) or in the specialty oils market (downstream value added) may justify this rate of investment from a firm perspective, but this accelerated 'creative destruction' may be socially wasteful. Economic development and diversification also seem to be progressing apace, with new agronomic traits being bred into commercial varieties. The dispersion of canola into new growing areas has actually accelerated since 1985, at least partly due to the profit incentive of the seed merchants to develop and market new varieties for new growing areas. The total area seeded to canola in Western Canada rose to a record 14 million acres in 1994, equal to about 15% of Canada's total crops acreage. All indications are that more new private varieties suited to new areas are imminent. Between 1994 and 1997, there were 97 field trials for transgenic varieties that involved introducing stress, insect, viral and fungal resistance into canola (CFIA, 1997). Equity continues to be a key concern of the public sector. But recent economic research suggests that rapid innovation rates observed in the industry may effectively reduce the market power resulting from imperfect competition in the input sectors and the monopsonistic nature of the end-users. Extending Green's (1997) analysis, one could argue that the shorter breeding cycle and the resulting short lifespan of each new variety (approximately 3 years) may effectively limit the market power. Competitiveness in the research and seeds business is more a local than a global concern, but it has driven and is continuing to influence Canadian public research policy. Given the recent consolidations of the seeds industry (both horizontally and vertically), however, it is hard to see how public marketing of seeds helps Canada remain competitive in the industry. It is possible that public varieties instead reduce the potential market for private breeders, which reduces their incentive to locate locally.

Based on the above, the decision by AAFC in the late 1980s to reduce its efforts on direct varietal development and sale appears to have been wise. Rather than re-enter the business, the government may want to review its remaining support for breeding public commercial varieties. This is especially true as access to the seeds market is getting more difficult.

Know-why Knowledge

After knowledge of the marketplace, basic scientific knowledge is the second most critical factor in developing and sustaining a knowledge-based industry or economy.

As one might expect, few private companies undertake know-why research. Clearly, without a financial incentive, there is little reason for this activity. A search of the ISI special database of canola-related research, published in academic or scientific journals between 1981 and 1996, shows that staff from about 130 private companies published at least one journal article in that period, in total accounting for about 6% of published articles (Table 14.7). More than half of the companies had only one article credited to one of their staff. Only three companies – Allelix Crop Technologies (now merged with Pioneer Hi-Bred), Calgene and Unilever – published an average of more than one journal article per year. The vast majority of know-why work, as one might expect, is done by the public sector, 58% in universities and 36% in publicly funded research agencies.

The private sector simply has not and, based on theory, likely will not do an adequate amount of research to add to the stock of know-why knowledge. This would appear to be a critical, long-term role for the public sector.

Two recent trends in the public sector, however, may jeopardize the development of new know-why knowledge. First, the recent efforts by public institutions – both universities and research institutes – to enter the know-what business by patenting their knowledge has directed much public

Table 14.7. Sources of canola-related know-why knowledge.

	Number of entities	Number of articles	Citation rate
Private companies	130	358	7.9
Universities	660	3616	6.0
Public institutes and agencies	670	2305	3.4
Total institutions	1460	6279	5.9

Source: Author's calculations using ISI special tabulation of academic publications related to canola.

academic and research effort toward patent counts and commercially valuable research. All of the universities, AAFC and the NRC have actively moved their organizations to protect and exploit their intellectual property, first by setting up intellectual property offices and then by patenting and licensing their 'know-what' innovations. To support that drive, faculty and research scientists are now rewarded for their commercial innovations, both with a share of the financial returns and with patents providing credit toward merit increases and promotion. Second, the public institutions have begun to sell their services either on a straight fee-for-service basis or through 'collaborations'. Many of the faculty and research scientists at all of the universities working on canola have entered contractual or collaborative relationships with the private companies (Alberta with Alberta Wheat Pool, Calgary with DowAgrosciences, Manitoba with Rhône-Poulenc, UGG and Saskatchewan Wheat Pool and Saskatchewan with Saskatchewan Wheat Pool) while AAFC has undertaken extensive fee-for-service varietal development work. The NRC, in contrast, has engaged in less fee-for-service work and instead has favoured extensive collaborations on more basic research where both cash and intellectual capital are exchanged.

The evidence suggests that these shifts have diminished the output of know-why research from the public institutions. After engaging in commercial arrangements, AAFC, and the five Canadian universities lost market share while only the NRC gained market share (Table 14.8). It is perhaps more disconcerting that the quality of the work being published publicly (based on the number of citations) in most Canadian institutions has dropped relative to the rest of the institutions doing research (Table 14.9). The research being published by AAFC and the four traditional canola research universities has a lower citation rate than the average in the period after they began to work in collaboration with industry.

The fact that the quantity and quality of the NRC output has risen both absolutely and relatively to the total while AAFC output has fallen relatively over the past 5 years suggests that the two institutions may be pursuing different strategies. The NRC since 1989 has done significant work with others, 90% of which has been via joint-venture collaborations with groups of private companies, that involve the pooling of money, staff and

Table 14.8. Output of the top Canadian research centres relative to the canola research undertaken globally.

	Percentage of total papers per period		
	1981–1985	1986–1990	1991–1996
AAFC	9.9	6.2	7.8
NRC/PBI	0.7	0.7	1.2
University of Guelph	5.5	6.4	2.6
University of Saskatchewan	5.0	4.9	3.2
University of Alberta	3.6	3.9	2.3
University of Manitoba	2.5	5.1	3.8
University of Calgary	0.0	1.0	1.3
Total seven institutions	27.2	29.5	23.6

Source: Author's calculations using ISI special tabulation of publications related to canola.

intellectual property. In contrast, AAFC has tended to do a significantly larger share of its work with single companies via 'fee-for-service' work, which has not led to any other contribution than money. In the NRC case, the greater exchange of non-financial information appears to support the development of know-why knowledge. This difference of operation may help to explain why the NRC has seen a significant rise in its volume and quality of know-why work, while AAFC has seen a fall in both.

Some argue that information in patents becomes public so, even if effort is diverted to know-what research, the results become known. Practically, about 70% of the information contained in patents does not appear in any trade journal for at least 5 years after the patent has been granted and at least 50% of this information is never published in mainstream technical journals (Industry Canada, 1988). Given that in North America the information included in a patent application is kept confidential until the patent is

Table 14.9. Relative citation rate for pure agricultural research papers produced by the top Canadian research centres for canola (average for all canola papers in period = 1.0).

	1981–1985	1986–1990	1991–1996
AAFC	0.84	1.23	1.00
NRC/PBI	1.80	1.94	2.30
University of Guelph	1.05	1.13	1.22
University of Saskatchewan	1.53	0.67	0.87
University of Alberta	0.98	0.78	0.91
University of Manitoba	0.94	0.86	0.94
University of Calgary	—	3.19	1.67

Source: Author's calculations using ISI special tabulation of publications related to canola.

issued (up to 2 years), this diversion of output to the proprietary route slows the dissemination of information, and the cost and difficulty of accessing full patent information at times may make the results of the research inaccessible to many academics.

Know-what Knowledge

All participants in the Canadian canola research community – both public and private researchers – are focused on attempts to protect and capitalize on new innovations. Although most of the patents issued are to private companies, there has been an increase in recent years of public patenting as public laboratories and universities have sought either to justify their existence or to have sought new sources of funding for on-going research.

As indicated in Table 14.10, private companies hold patents on most of the key technologies involved in the transformation of canola. Given the variety of technologies now available, it is unclear whether there is any shortage of supply. From a corporate perspective, the key issue is not how to get more resources for research but how to ensure international market access, because as noted above, the rate of innovation is a function of the market size. Hence biotechnology companies are extremely concerned about technical barriers to trade, such as differing sanitary and phytosanitary standards, incomplete IPR and trade-related investment measures, which impede international trade.

Public breeders (or scientists who recently moved from the public to private sector) appear to be the most concerned about the privatization of the technologies, partly because it is a radical change in the culture of the industry (which was open and collegial until recently) and partly because licence fees and Materials Transfer Agreements place strains on already tight budgets. One response of the public breeders has been to seek to protect and exploit any intellectual property they develop in order to keep in the game and have 'chips' for bargaining with the private companies (Lesser, 1998). NRC and AAFC both stipulate in their collaboration agreements that any resulting innovations will be the intellectual property of the public institution, and that the private collaborator has a right of first refusal on commercializing the technology. Although the public laboratories (and at times universities) have thereby begun to develop a 'portfolio' of intellectual property, so far all of the innovations have been useful but relatively minor and the revenues from the licensing of the technologies has not repaid the cost of patenting them and running their respective intellectual property offices.

Furthermore, some private companies which collaborate with NRC or AAFC to develop new technologies (which the public agencies patent) are concerned that public IPRs reduce their ability to use the technologies. They say that potential private sector partners want clear ownership lines before

Table 14.10. IPRs related to canola breeding processes.

	Key technologies (and owner, if any)	IPR regime
Genomic information	• *Arabidopsis* genome project • Amplified fragment linkage polymorphing for gene mapping (patented) • Molecular markers	Data is in public domain but AFLP technology is patented
Germplasm	• Public gene banks in Canada, USA, Germany, Russia, India, Pakistan, Australia, Japan and others • Private gene collections	Restricted access only for private collections
rDNA strands/genes	• HT genes (Monsanto, AgrEvo, American Cyanamid and Rhône Poulenc) • Antifungal proteins (Zeneca) • Antishatter (Limagrain) • Fatty acids (Calgene) • Pharmaceutical compounds (Ciba Geigy)	100% private patents
Transformation technologies (general)	• Agrobacterium (Mogen, Plant Genetic Systems) • Whiskers (Zeneca) • Biolistics (Dupont) • Chemical mutagenesis (public domain)	100% private patents except mutagenesis
Transformation technologies (*Brassica*-specific)	• Agrobacterium methods for *Brassica* (Calgene has two patents that effectively control all transformation in the genus)	100% private patents
Selectable markers	• Large number of privately patented markers for selecting specific transformants (Monsanto, Plant Genetic Systems, others)	100% private patents
Growth promoters (constitutive)	• Constitutive promoters (e.g. for HT, disease, drought, salt resistance, to express genes in all cells in plants, including 35S (Monsanto)	100% private patents
Growth promoters (tissue specific)	Tissue specific promoters: • Pod/shatter control (Limagrain) • Floral morphology (AgrEvo and others; multiple) • Oil traits (AAFC and others)	100% public and private patents
Hybrid technologies	• In-Vigor™ (Plant Genetic Systems) • CMS System (Zeneca) • Ogura CMS Systems (INRA) • Lemke (NPZ) • Kosena system (Mitsubishi) • Polima (China; public domain)	All patented except Polima, which is in the public domain
Oil-processing technologies	• Oleosin partitioning technology for separating and purifying recombinant nutraceutical or pharmaceutical proteins (SemBioSys) • Other oil processing technologies	100% patents or trade secrets
Traditional breeding technologies	• Double haploid process • Backcrossing • Gas–liquid spectrometer analysis	All in public domain

Source: Personal communications with canola researchers and patent searches.

they will agree to use this new technology. Publicly held patents do not appear to provide this certainty.

Instead of volume of research, the issue appears to be access to the supply of technologies, or in the jargon of the industry 'freedom to operate'. Most companies provide access to their proprietary technologies at least partly because few if any of the companies are fully self-sufficient. Although a firm may control one or more patents, it usually will need to license or joint-venture with some other patent holder to get access to parts of the trans-formation process for which they do not have patents. This reciprocal dependence keeps at least some access. Nevertheless, there have been sugges-tions from within the industry that some firms have at times strategically withheld access to the best patented technologies in order to slow competitors while others appear to restrict access to technologies if the resulting product would compete with the patent holder's product line. At other times, the patents appear to be used by their holders to negotiate an equity stake in follow-on inventions. Most concern focuses on Calgene's two patents for the agrobacterium transformation of canola. The unusual feature is that Calgene has both a process patent and a patent that covers all *Brassica* transgenic constructs, whether developed using the agrobacterium method or not. Many fear that this gives Calgene absolute control over all transgenic canola work.

Rather than have the public sector invest to duplicate private research to ensure open access to technologies, the state would be wiser to use the powers vested in its IPR regime or competition laws to encourage greater dissemination of non-rival, patented innovations to generate more access and hence greater spillover effects. Canadian patent law and the Plant Breeders' Protection Act both provide for compulsory licences to remedy what is called 'abuse' of patent rights. If firms use their patents to 'hinder' trade and industry – i.e. not meeting demand in Canada, hindering trade or industry in Canada by refusal to grant a licence (if such a licence is in the public interest), attaching unreasonable conditions to such a licence, using a process patent to prejudice unfairly production of a non-patented product or allow the patent on such a product to prejudice unfairly its manufacture, use or sale – another company or the state can challenge them after only 3 years of the patent grant (CIPO, 1998). Meanwhile, the anti-combines provisions of the Competition Act allow the state to pursue anti-competitive behaviour through investigation and prosecution. Neither provision has yet been used in Canada in the area of biotechnology.

As far as *competitiveness* is concerned, it would appear that knowledge of basic transformation processes (the know-what patentable recipes) can flow relatively freely across borders or continents, given a basic level of prior learning (or 'know-why'). All the appropriate technologies are in use in Canada. Therefore, it is not clear that the transformation processes need to be developed within the local research community in order for the research centre to produce commercializable products that add greater value to the local economy. Rather, it may be adequate for the technologies to be available.

Looking at the chain link model of innovation, the key to success is to take these new ideas and ultimately place them in the market to earn a return. The question for a region worried about competitiveness, then, is how to assemble the various pieces in a way that the local economy and society benefit from the effort; this points directly to the know-how and know-who elements of knowledge generation.

Know-who and Know-how Knowledge

Potentially the most important public policy role and arguably the key to regional competitiveness in a knowledge-based sector is the generation and transmission of the non-codified knowledge that holds things together – the know-how and know-who. Most economies operate under the assumption that the human elements of a firm or industry operate in some black box, governed by either the 'invisible hand' or a Walrasian auctioneer. In reality, there is something that holds an economy together that goes beyond economic transactions; people develop skills and have relationships which together convert bits of information into operable knowledge. This tacit type of knowledge is learned almost exclusively through experience. Researchers learn how to do things and who to work with through trial and error. Most of the innovation literature assumes that this know-how and, perhaps more importantly, this know-who evolves within corporations or institutions. That may hold true in an industry or within firms that are largely self-sufficient but, as noted above, there are few firms that have the internal capacity to undertake all the research and development necessary to create a marketable variety. Some companies may have that capacity within their global operations (e.g. Monsanto/Calgene, AgrEvo/Plant Genetic Systems, Pioneer Hi-Bred) but in many cases working through the geographically dispersed multiple layers of these multinational enterprises is more complex and less cost-effective than buying-in from a more accessible and timely local source. Hence, although Monsanto and AgrEvo both have giant research 'universities' and laboratories at their headquarters in the USA and Germany, respectively, both have collaborated extensively in Saskatoon with both Agriculture Canada and the NRC. Furthermore, in knowledge-based industries training and upgrading are critical, making it essential for private researchers to interact with the broader research community. For all these reasons, most of the firms in the industry have developed an extensive 'community' of networks with both collaborators and competitors, involving other private companies, universities, AAFC and the NRC.

As with most communities, proximity matters. Formal and informal face-to-face meetings and working side-by-side on laboratory benches and in the greenhouses are critical elements of both developing the know-who and transmitting the know-how. It is highly unlikely that the community would have developed if there were only competitive firms in Saskatoon; the non-competitive environment offered by AAFC and NRC create the platform for these relationships. Table 14.11 outlines the depth of these arrangements at NRC.

Collaborations are the key to the public institutions. Both AAFC and NRC have extensive arrangements with each other, public universities and private companies. In 1995–1996 alone, NRC had more than 31 arrangements – ranging from research agreements to collaborative work agreements and licences – that brought more than 65 guest researchers from other institutions into the NRC laboratories (NRC, 1997). The NRC set a goal in 1996 to expand that effort by at least 15% by 1998–1999. The key feature of these arrangements would be that the core research team at NRC is able to learn from all of the collaborations, thereby adding further to the know-how knowledge and provide a visible, efficient point of entry for know-who knowledge.

The training and recruitment role played by the two key public institutions helps to solidify the sense of community. Both institutions have scale, with a significant number of full-time permanent scientists working within their operations and with a regular flow of young post-doctoral scientists who work in the public laboratories on the way to a permanent career. The NRC collaborations provide a handy recruitment and screening system for the companies. Once a collaboration is begun between the NRC and a private company, the NRC usually hires a recently graduated PhD scientist, most frequently on a 1–3-year contract, to undertake the work. The permanent staff at the NRC collaborate with the private sector scientists to manage the

Table 14.11. Relationships between NRC and other institutions, 1995–1996 (total number of guest researchers in laboratory).

	Location	NRC guest researchers
AAFC	Saskatoon	8
AgrEvo Canada Inc.	Saskatoon	17
CanAmera Foods Inc.	Saskatoon	2
Canola Council of Canada	Winnipeg	10
DowElanco Canada Inc.	Saskatoon	1
Limagrain Canada Inc.	Saskatoon	Alliance
MicrobioRizogen	Saskatoon	1
Monsanto Canada Inc.	Saskatoon	Collaborative agreement
New Leaf Biotechnology Inc.	Saskatoon	1
Plant Genetic Systems Canada Inc.	Saskatoon	2
Prairie Plant Systems	Saskatoon	5
Saskatchewan Wheat Pool	Saskatoon	9
University of Calgary	Calgary	Collaborative agreement
University of Manitoba	Winnipeg	1
University of Saskatchewan	Saskatoon	7
Zeneca Seeds	Winnipeg	2

Source: http://www.pbi.nrc.ca/96annrpt/bus.html.

work of the contract employee(s). At the end or, commonly, before the end of the collaboration, the contract research scientist may be offered a permanent appointment with the private sector collaborator. In essence, the collaboration provides a screening process for recruitment. If the contract scientist does not meet expectations, the private company is not obligated to hire the person. The process also has the benefit of being efficient – the NRC has at any one time on average 15–20 contract scientists on staff, which enables them to develop the special mentoring and assessment skills that both help the entering scientist and reduce the costs.

As far as competitiveness is concerned, one gets a sense of their importance in the system when one examines the list of NRC collaborators and their location (Table 14.11). Even firms not resident in Saskatoon have developed extensive links to gain access to the knowledge in those two institutions, which suggests that spillover benefits from the know-how and know-who located in Saskatoon may be significant and may not move far from Saskatoon. So far, the pull of externalities has not been strong enough to concentrate the entire industry in Saskatoon, as theory would suggest. Interviews with firms that have collaborations in Saskatoon but are not resident in Saskatoon revealed that undepreciated investments elsewhere, economies of scale within corporate 'discovery' laboratories and specific agronomic features (e.g. growing season) offset some of the pull.

Although one cannot state conclusively that an efficient knowledge of know-how and know-who would not be generated without public institutions, the evidence to date strongly supports the contention that public institutions have been and are critical to the creation of know-how and know-who knowledge that makes competitive canola development possible.

Conclusion

The combination of a transformation in the innovation process – away from a supply-driven linear model and towards a demand pull, chain-link system – and the introduction of a new IPR regime have both worked to shift the impetus in canola development towards private sector investment and away from public involvement. As a result, the public sector in Canada has been challenged to find a new role.

This analysis concludes that the public sector has little reason to undertake canola varietal development (and possibly strong reasons not to do so) or to undertake research to create new patentable processes. Instead, public funds would appear to be best used to undertake basic know-why research and to partner with the private sector through collaborations to develop a community platform for the creation and dissemination of tacit know-how and know-who knowledge. Public research efforts, however, are unlikely to be able to address satisfactorily concerns about equity and competition – those problems are more appropriately and likely more effectively dealt with through regulatory and competition policy.

Notes

1. This new type of rapeseed had 5% or less of erucic acid and less than 3 mg of glucosinolates per gram of air-dried meal. The quality standards for canola were tightened in 1996 to allow only 2% erucic acid and less than 30 μM of glucosinolates per gram of meal.
2. Other genome projects have been effectively privatized by firms that have taken and assembled the public information in a way to extract economic gain.

References

Akino, M. and Hayami, Y. (1975) Efficiency and equity in public research: rice breeding in Japan's economic development. *American Journal of Agricultural Economics* 59(1), 245–256.

Canadian Intellectual Property Office (1998) http://strategis.ic.gc.ca/sc_mrksv/cipo/prod_ ser/online/guides_e/pateng/III.html.

CFIA (Canadian Food Inspection Agency) (1997) *Summary of Experimental Releases.* Special Tabulations for Canola. CFIA, Ottawa, Canada.

CFIA (Canadian Food Inspection Agency) (1998) *Status of New Plant Varieties Applied for Protection under PBR: List of Varieties, by Crop Kind.* http://www.cfia-acia.agr.ca/english/plant/pbr/home_e.html.

Canola Council of Canada, *Canola connection* (http://www.canola-council.org/index.shtml).

Evenson, R. (1998) The economics of intellectual property rights for agricultural technology introduction. Paper presented to the NC-208 meeting at CIMMYT, 6 March.

Green, C. (1997) The industrial economics of biotechnology. http://strategis.ic.gc.ca/SSG/ca00913e.html.

Grossman, M. and Helpman, E. (1991) *Innovation and Growth in the Global Economy.* The MIT Press, London.

Hayami, Y. and Herdt, R. (1975) Market price effects of technological change on income distribution in semisubsistence agriculture. *American Journal of Agricultural Economics* 59(2), 245–256.

Just, R.E. and Hueth, D.L. (1993) Multimarket exploitation: the case of biotechnology and chemicals. *American Journal of Agricultural Economics* 75(4), 936–945.

Klein, S. and Rosenberg, N. (1986) An overview of innovation. In: Landau, R. and Rosenberg, N. (eds) *The Positive Sum Strategy: Harnessing Technology for Economic Growth.* National Academy Press, Washington, DC.

Kneen, B. (1992) *The Rape of Canola.* NC Press, Toronto.

Lemieux, C. and Wohlgenant, M. (1989) Ex ante evaluation of the economic impact of agricultural biotechnology: the case of porcine somatotropin. *American Journal of Agricultural Economics* 71(4), 903–914.

Lesser, W. (1998) Managing IPR and the agricultural research process: lessons from University Technology Transfer Offices. Paper presented to the NC-208 meeting at CIMMYT, 5 March.

Lucas, R. (1988) On the mechanics of economic development. *Journal of Monetary Economics* 22(1), 3–42.

Malecki, E. (1997) *Technology and Economic Development: The Dynamics of Local, Regional and National Competitiveness.* Longman, Toronto.

Malla, S. (1996) The distribution of economic and health benefits from canola research. Unpublished M.Sc. thesis, University of Saskatchewan.

Mullen, J., Wohlgenant, M. and Farris, D. (1988) Input substitution and distribution of surplus gains from lower US beef-processing costs. *American Journal of Agricultural Economics* 70(2), 245–254.

Nagy, J. and Furtan, W.H. (1978) Economic costs and returns from crop development research: the case of rapeseed breeding in Canada. *Canadian Journal of Agricultural Economics* 26(1), 1–14.

NRC (National Research Council) (1992) *From Rapeseed to Canola: the Billion Dollar Success Story.* NRC, Ottawa, p. 2.

NRC (National Research Council) (1997) *Bi-annual Report.* http://www.pbi.nrc.ca/96annrpt/bus.html.

OECD (1996) *The Knowledge Based Economy.* OECD, Paris. http://www.oecd.org/dsti/sti/s_t/inte/prod/kbe.html.

Phillips, P. (1998) Innovation and restructuring in Canada's canola industry. *Proceedings of the 3rd International Conference on Chain Management in Agribusiness and the Food Industry* May.

Romer, P. (1990) Endogenous technological change. *Journal of Political Economy* 98(2), s71–s102.

Rosenberg, N., Landau, R. and Mowery, D. (1992) *Technology and the Wealth of Nations.* Stanford University Press, Stanford, California, p. 183.

Scobie, G. and Posada, R. (1978) The impact of technical change on income distribution: the case of rice in Colombia. *American Journal of Agricultural Economics* 60(1), 85–91.

Ulrich, A., Furtan, H. and Schmitz, A. (1986) Public and private returns from joint venture research: an example from agriculture. *Quarterly Journal of Economics* 101(1), 103–129.

Index

Figures in **bold** indicate major references.
Figures in *italic* refer to diagrams, photographs and tables.